BECAUSE THIS LAND IS WHO WE ARE

BECAUSE THIS LAND IS WHO WE ARE

Indigenous Practices of Environmental Repossession

Chantelle Richmond, Brad Coombes,
Renee Pualani Louis

BLOOMSBURY ACADEMIC
NEW YORK • LONDON • OXFORD • NEW DELHI • SYDNEY

BLOOMSBURY ACADEMIC
Bloomsbury Publishing Plc
50 Bedford Square, London, WC1B 3DP, UK
1385 Broadway, New York, NY 10018, USA
29 Earlsfort Terrace, Dublin 2, Ireland

BLOOMSBURY, BLOOMSBURY ACADEMIC and the Diana logo are trademarks
of Bloomsbury Publishing Plc

First published in Great Britain 2024

Cover image: Protectors stand in unity committed to protect their sacred mountain,
Mauna Kea from desecration and destruction from the proposed construction of an
18 story Thirty Meter Telescope. Source: Kapulei Flores

A catalogue record for this book is available from the British Library.

A catalog record for this book is available from the Library of Congress.

ISBN: HB: 978-1-3502-4767-3
        PB: 978-1-3502-4766-6
        ePDF: 978-1-3502-4769-7
        eBook: 978-1-3502-4768-0

Typeset by Integra Software Services Pvt. Ltd.
Printed and bound in Great Britain

To find out more about our authors and books visit www.bloomsbury.com and sign
up for our newsletters.

CONTENTS

Chapter 4
CULTIVATING BOUNDARY CROSSERS: TRESPASS GARDENING
IN THE STONEFIELDS

Chapter 5
GATHERING FOR WELLNESS IN BIIGTIGONG NISHNAABEG

FIGURES

INTRODUCTION

From across the Seas, We Are All Connected

On March 5, 2021, three strong earthquakes occurred deep in the South Pacific Ocean, about 1,000 kilometers northeast of Aotearoa New Zealand. The strongest earthquake, measuring 8.1 on the Richter scale, occurred about 8:40 a.m., when families were readying children for school or commencing their workdays. New Zealand's *National Emergency Management Agency* issued tsunami warnings and people were urged to "walk, run or cycle" to higher ground to avoid the chance of being stuck in traffic. Sitting in her home office some 14,000 kilometers away in London—a city in Ontario, Canada—Chantelle was initiating a Zoom meeting to discuss with her colleagues their research project on Indigenous environmental repossession. Renee was calling in from the Big Island of Hawai'i, and Brad was connecting from Auckland in Aotearoa, where the tsunami order was now in effect. As the Zoom meeting opened, Chantelle and Renee were shocked to find Brad sitting calmly before his computer: "I have some time before I need to head to higher ground, so we may as well carry on until then." They discussed the research updates from their respective community studies. About forty-five minutes later, Brad's son interrupts the meeting; it is time to leave the house for higher ground. Renee stays on the line, estimating that she has about four hours before any tsunami-generated waves will reach Hawai'i.

In subsequent meetings, we returned to this moment as a reminder of our interconnectedness. We live continents apart and must rely on Zoom to connect us, but our adaptiveness within digital platforms is a tame microcosm of how Indigenous communities have adapted to settler society violence, environmental crises, and land loss. Indeed, the trials of research and writing under pandemic conditions required us to consider more deeply the forces which unite Indigenous peoples to pursue common causes. As will be shown in our conclusion (Chapter 6), we used Zoom to extend our analyses to retrospective and reflexive critique of what environmental repossession means and what social work it performs. In one moment of the group interview we conducted for the conclusion of this book, Brad discussed resistance of his research partners to the concept of repossession:

> **Brad**: One of the [youth participants in a discussion workshop …] asked, "Well, what does repossession mean?" In the discussion, another says, "Yeah, it's like when your aunty goes out and buys that big TV on layby and then can't make the repayments, so someone comes along and repossesses the TV." And the first replies, "Yeah? Why would we want to be like that? What would we be if we did that? Why would we want to be like a repossession agent out there? Those people are the enemy, aren't they? They're a problem for most of our households, aren't they?" And I thought that was quite profound. Ae—if we're framing ourselves as repossession agents, aren't we adopting the mentality and the mindset of the very practices that we want to reject?

There have been many times in this project where one or more of us has critiqued the neoliberal, materialistic, or economistic discourses in repossession, and particularly in its lay definition. But that questioning of the very concept is at the heart of this book. It has been important for us to evolve our understanding of repossession toward multifaceted strategies that are both uncompromising and grand, yet also peaceable and modest. We will conclude later that Indigenous environmental repossession is notable for its diversity, and that conclusion has come to us because of our willingness to debate online small details over great distance.

Despite the physical distance that separates us and our reliance on Zoom during the pandemic, we are bound through a range of deeply relational processes that extend across social and ecological dimensions. The oceans connect humanity in many ways beyond their visible and spatial coverage. Beneath their surface, our intercontinental connections are strengthened by a series of remarkable migrations by turtles, eels, tuna, and salmon. Salmon, for example, move across vast oceans, traveling thousands of miles from one destination to the next as they carry out their feeding and spawning practices. In each place they visit, they bring with them profound meaning to local people who eagerly await and celebrate their seasonal return. Among Indigenous nations across the northern hemisphere, the cyclical movement of salmon is foundational to Indigenous foodways, and they figure centrally in social, cultural, and spiritual structures and practices of coastal Indigenous peoples (Newell 2016). Salmon are a revered staple in the traditional food systems of Native people from the Pacific Northwest, among the Japanese Ainu, Saami Norwegian coastal areas, and Indigenous peoples of the Russian Far East. Despite their geographic separation, those nations are culturally connected through their strong ties to salmon.

As Indigenous people, we are deeply connected in our desire to protect the wellness of the lands we live on. The land provides the essentials of life: food, medicines, warmth, drinking water, and shelter. By protecting, caring for, and nurturing the land we live on, Indigenous peoples have been kept safe, nurtured, and well. This reciprocal relationship between people and environment is entangled with Indigenous knowledge, Indigenous lifeways, and the land-based wisdom embedded in Indigenous cultures, languages, and practices. Winona LaDuke (1999) describes Indigenous knowledge as the culturally and spiritually based ways Indigenous peoples relate with one another and with the land. This knowledge is deep and sacred, and it is foundational to a way of living that is specific to places and peoples. It is shared across generations, often through direct observation, but it is also carried through song, story, dance, and many other everyday practices (Daigle 2019).

Indigenous knowledge is learned through practice, by being with others on the land and observing what is taking place in both natural and social worlds (McGregor 2004). In Hawai‘i this practice is known as *kilo*, describing observation, examination, and forecasting, as well as a person who is an expert in those skills. It is foundational for *Kānaka ‘Ōiwi* (Native Hawaiian), henceforth shortened to *Kānaka*, understanding of how the natural environment responds to the movement of the sun and moon, rain and wind, tide and current. This determines how Kānaka activities can be adjusted to complement those seasonal and cyclical time frames to ensure the *‘āina* (land; literally, that which feeds) can sustain us into the future. Indigenous knowledge is transformed through practices that help us to understand how to be a good person, a good family member, a good community member, and a good ancestor—how to take care of one's relations. Indigenous knowledge is grounded in principles of love, kindness, and compassion for the land, and for one another (Dudgeon and Bray 2019). Fulfillment of these responsibilities of care is returned to us as gifts of wellness and belonging. Indigenous knowledge is not a bundle of observational data, but rather a set of relations and a dynamic treasure that Indigenous communities want to sustain; hence, they are eager to preserve and defend that treasure, motivating the environmental repossession that is the focus of this book.

Who We Are and How This Book Came to Be

We offer this book to demonstrate community-led practices of land protection and occupation, which form powerful forms of resistance to ongoing legacies of dispossession. Environmental repossession refers to the social, cultural, and political practices in which Indigenous communities engage to assert their rights to their lands, and in support of wellness, healing, and belonging (Big-Canoe and Richmond 2014). The concept parallels global conversations about Indigenous resurgence, decolonization, self-determination, and the need to recenter Indigenous knowledge and everyday practices to sustain distinct cultures.

We are Indigenous scholars, community leaders, and activists who are actively engaged in or lead environmental movements currently taking place in Hawaiʻi (Kānaka), Aotearoa (Māori), and Canada (Biigtigong Nishnaabeg). For several years, we have been engaged in an international project to explore the concept of environmental repossession with Indigenous communities across three very different cultural and geographic contexts. As a team of authors who live continents apart, this book has been written in a highly collaborative way but through online discussion and weekly Zoom meetings. Much of our conceptual work and negotiations with our case studies occurred prior to the onset of the COVID-19 pandemic. From early 2020, however, and as detailed in the very first pages of this book, subsequent collaborations have necessarily occurred in a digital landscape.

This research was funded by an Insight the *Social Sciences and Humanities Research Council of Canada*. As we are Indigenous geographers, the work reflects the emergence of Indigenous geography as a relatively new sub-discipline (Coombes, Johnson, and Howitt 2012). Indigenous geographies are infinitely place-based, they are community-engaged, and they operate within a relational ontology that emphasizes the deep connection between people and the land (Daigle 2016; Daigle and Ramírez 2019). Those relations form the essence of who we are as people, and they evoke responsibilities and obligations to human and more-than-human kin (Johnson and Larsen 2013). In respect of research, the agenda for Indigenous geography is to recognize and support Indigenous sovereignty, be of service to Indigenous communities, and to advocate for Indigenous lifeways (Richmond, Coombes, and Louis 2022). This collection adds to existing scholarship on Indigenous geographies but, as it is led by three Indigenous scholars, uniquely it avoids many of the ethical challenges in such transcultural approaches as community-based participatory research (Castleden, Morgan, and Lamb 2012). Only through greater leadership of Indigenous participants can Indigenous agendas be properly foregrounded in academic research, enabling Indigenous voices to be heard in self-determining projects (De Leeuw and Hunt 2018).

For this book, we lead research with communities and groups in which we hold established relationships, or to whom we belong. Although working with our own families and communities produces unique problems and challenges, there are multiple benefits, and we believe it should be the preferred option in all research with Indigenous communities. Working with a researcher's own families or communities may reduce the likelihood of knowledge misrepresentation or appropriation, and it may lead to greater scrutiny or even a higher probability of converting knowledge into transformation. We are committed to our task because we write on matters that fundamentally concern us; first as members of our communities, and secondarily as Indigenous scholars. In Chapter 1, we share how relational ontologies and Indigenous environmental philosophies inform our repossession work. In Chapters 3, 4, and 5, those concepts assist us to shift the lens to highlight Indigenous community perspectives, voices, and experiences in various acts of land protection and environmental guardianship.

Environmental Dispossession

Indigenous connections with our original places, knowledge, and ways of doing are shaped, and continually threatened by processes of environmental dispossession that sever or reduce access to lands and environmental resources (Richmond and Ross 2009). Land loss, assimilationist policies, pollution, and climate change compound those forms of dispossession. However varied they may seem, those processes intersect to create vulnerability for Indigenous peoples' health because they threaten our relationships with the land, disrupt the continuity of our cultural practices, and view the land primarily as a commodity (McGregor, Littlechild, and Sritharan 2022). Within such worldviews, there is no consideration of the wider relational networks that land may be connected to, nor of the depth of social, cultural, and spiritual meanings that the land and its resources hold. Environmental dispossession threatens the very core of Indigenous knowledge, lifeways, and collective wellbeing.

Indigenous experiences of colonization represent the most significant, most destructive, and globally unifying form of dispossession (Farrell et al. 2021). In the time since colonization, Indigenous knowledge, Indigenous languages, and many Indigenous cultural practices have declined. The tools of colonization have been used to dispossess Indigenous peoples of their lands, to disrupt Indigenous ways of knowing and doing, and to break families and communities apart. The most horrific examples come from the forced removal of children by nation states and the churches in Canada, the United States, Australia, and New Zealand. Colonial and religious missions have been enforced mercilessly, often maintained through violence, and upheld today through racialized biases that are deeply entrenched in nation-state structures, including health care, justice, and education systems (Deloria et al. 2018).

When Indigenous peoples cannot access their lands and relations, they risk losing their places and practices of knowing, belonging, and identity (Wexler 2009). For example, processes of dispossession lead to reduced access to and consumption of traditional foods and medicines (Richmond et al. 2021; Tobias and Richmond 2014); fewer opportunities for land-based education and knowledge sharing (Alfred 2014; Greenwood and Lindsay 2019); reduced opportunities for language acquisition (McCarty, Romero, and Zepeda 2006); and strains on social cohesion and connections (Harper et al. 2015). They also diminish the distinctive spiritual, place-based relationships many Indigenous peoples hold with the lands, animals, plants, and waters that are essential components of cultural identities (Arsenault et al. 2018; Cunsolo Willox et al. 2012). The holistic nature of Indigenous health and wellness means that the impacts of dispossession can extend far beyond affected individuals, families, and communities. These impacts reach across generations, and their outcomes are visible in physical, cultural, social, and mental dimensions of wellness (Mergler and Da Silva 2018; Philibert, Fillion, and Mergler 2020). In this book, however, we report hopefully on community projects that resist *dispossession* through practices of Indigenous environmental *repossession*.

Environmental Repossession

The concept of environmental repossession emerged from a community-based study with youth from Biigtigong Nishnaabeg, a First Nation reserve in Northwestern Ontario, Canada. This work grew from the Master's research of Katie Big-Canoe (2011), and was focused on understanding Nishnaabeg youth's notions of health and wellness, including how their social relationships and connections to the land are incorporated into those concepts. A notable finding from Big-Canoe's (2011) research was that young people were particularly worried about their community's health and wellness. Specifically, the young people spoke about how their collective disconnection from the land had both affected their sense of Nishnaabeg identity and wellness, but also their knowledge and abilities to go out on the lands of their traditional territory. Youth expressed concern about the limited time they have with their community Elders and how that had impacted their capacity to hunt or learn about traditional foods. By engaging more often with Elders in these land-based activities on their traditional territory, Biigtigong youth believed they would have greater opportunities to learn and practice Nishnaabeg knowledge, values, and ways of knowing. They insisted these interactions would instill stronger Nishnaabeg identities among Biigtigong's next generations.

Since the concept of environmental repossession was introduced in 2014, it has been applied almost exclusively in the First Nation reserve-based context. Primarily, that was through community-based studies linking Anishinaabe youth, Elders and other knowledge holders in land-based gatherings meant to restore social relationships and learning. Drawing on the Anishinaabe concept *gimiigiwemin*, meaning the exchange of gifts, Tobias and Richmond (2016) used sharing circle methodology with Nishnaabeg Elders from Biigtigong Nishnaabeg and Batchewana First Nation to identify four key strategies for environmental repossession:

1. continuing focus on Elder/youth relations,
2. increasing time spent on traditional lands,
3. encouraging activities that improve physical health, and
4. generating activities that strengthen identity and foster community pride.

In 2018, members of Biigtigong Nishnaabeg canoed the length of the *Biigtig Ziibii* (Pic River) for the first time in a century. The purpose of the journey was to reclaim places (e.g., mountains, rivers, portages) along the route in *Anishinabemoen* (the Ojibway language) and to restore community history and stories of the river and its meanings. A secondary goal of the journey was to support land-based learning about healthy relationships and *mino bimaadiziwin* or "the good life." Mikraszewicz and Richmond (2019) interviewed canoe participants about what the journey meant for them. They described the canoe trip as a critical opportunity for learning and practice of Indigenous knowledge, including from the river and land; navigating currents, building fire, and finding drinking water. Knowing how to respond and act with care for the group formed important spaces of relational learning and development. Finally, the trip offered unique opportunities to get to know the land. Some participants had never been out in Biigtigong's broad territory, and for many it was a deeply spiritual experience. Learning and being on the land and waters that their ancestors had previously travelled offered connections with their families and enhanced cultural pride as Nishnaabeg people.

Within Nishnaabeg's territory, there are key cultural places that the community has become disconnected from over time. One of these places is Mountain Lake, which is located along the western boundary of the territory (see Figure 5.1 for a map of Biigtigong's territory). Biigtigong's leadership constructed two cabins on the lake to support its members to return to this place. In summer 2019, the community planned a youth and Elders gathering at Mountain Lake. Nightingale and Richmond (2022) participated in the gathering and subsequently interviewed several participants about the meaning of the cabins and the gathering for restoring relationships with this place. Doing the work of reclaiming access to Mountain Lake required multiple and interconnected steps: clearing land, planning the gathering, inviting the people, designing activities, meal-planning, and transporting people to and from the site. Each step required specific knowledge and relationships between people and with the land. This gathering was not just about reintroducing the community to this place; it was a purposefully designed interaction to engage community members in a process of remaking community relationships with one another and with the land. These spaces enhance belonging, connection, and overall wellness (Nightingale and Richmond 2022). As one participant explains:

> When you come together in these kinds of environments people do have a good time. They have fun. It's like whatever is going on in their lives for that moment, it's gone. Because when you're out there

you have an opportunity, it's almost like you're cleansing your body when you're on the land in an environment that you're so familiar with. That's what I noticed down there, people were just, they looked so at ease. They looked like they were relaxed. Was it being in the bush? Probably. Was it being around people that you don't see very often? Probably, yes. But just taking the time and appreciating the environment, but also making those reconnections with family and friends and sharing tea and telling stories or doing activities that are going to make you forget life for a moment.

(Staff 4: 7)

Collectively, the cases raise important questions about the sustainability, planning, commitment, and responsibilities entailed in repossession efforts, especially regarding budgetary and cultural knowledge needs. Nightingale and Richmond (2022) reflected on these questions with staff members from Biigtigong Nishnaabeg's Department of Lands and Sustainability, those who have been primarily responsible for Biigtigong's environmental repossession efforts. Conversational interviews with seven current or former employees highlight the importance of everyday and long-term practices of environmental repossession, and the strength of modeling these efforts from Nishnaabeg principles and knowledge. Participants point to the everyday work of the department as building the foundation for community self-determination over land, life, and wellness. By renewing its land-based history, knowledge, and practices, the department also works to support the resurgence of Biigtigong Nishnaabeg culture and identity.

To date, the concept of environmental repossession has been adopted primarily within Indigenous health geographies and related studies. That sub-discipline critically examines the relationships between the places in which Indigenous peoples engage on a daily basis, and the meanings and impacts they hold for health, wellness, and healing (Richmond and Big-Canoe 2018). Expanding the concept of repossession to the Arctic, Robertson and Ljubicic (2019) worked with Uqsuqtuurmiut (people of Uqsuqtuuq) on local priorities for caribou and relational wellbeing. Notably, they emphasize how the practice of Uqsuqtuurmiut environmental knowledge and norms—with people, land, animals, water, and sea ice—supports a wider relational, interdependent sense of unity (or freedom) and happiness. This concept has also been applied in the urban context, with First Nations youth of Winnipeg who seek connections with the land in practices of "land-making" (Hatala et al. 2019; Morton et al. 2020).

While many Indigenous communities maintain connection with their traditional territories and have access to their knowledge and languages, there are many more who do not. Globally, Indigenous peoples are significantly urbanized (Stephens 2015), with the United Nations (2016) reporting that more than half the world's Indigenous population now live in urban areas with projections estimating 66 percent by 2050. Displacement and migration mean that many Indigenous peoples now live in places that are located at great distances from their traditional territories (Trujano 2008). There are broad possibilities for expanding the concept of repossession into novel spaces of healing (Peach, Richmond, and Brunette-Debassige 2020), incarceration (Ambtman-Smith and Richmond 2020), and digital landscapes (Reitmeier 2022). In a variety of ways, these case studies show how contributions to environmental repossession enable reconnection for those who cannot otherwise connect with their traditional territories.

Indigenous Resurgence and the Need to Account for Environmental Repossession

The growing body of research on environmental repossession also aligns importantly with a wider global discourse about Indigenous resurgence and reclamation of Indigenous land, culture, and lifeways (Corntassel 2012; Corntassel and Hardbarger 2019; Simpson 2016; Wildcat et al. 2014). Corntassel (2012: 88) describes resurgence as acting in ways that "reclaim and regenerate one's relational, place-based existence by challenging the ongoing, destructive forces of colonization." The relational nature of Corntassel's concept of resurgence provides the foundation for our work on environmental repossession, which seeks to restore Indigenous place-based relationships and practices, including those relating to land. We have witnessed multiple examples of Indigenous communities that, despite challenging circumstances, have reactivated everyday practices of resilience and resistance to protect relations in nature. For those reasons, it is important to document the work of those communities so that others may learn from them.

Despite the ongoing violence and harm perpetuated by processes of environmental dispossession, Indigenous peoples remain resilient, hopeful, and strong in their efforts to reclaim, protect, and celebrate their unique relationships with the land. Their role as protectors of the land remains as relevant as it ever has been (Goodyear-Kaōpua 2017). In November 2012, the *Idle No More* movement was initiated to protest impending parliamentary bills that would have eroded Indigenous sovereignty and environmental protections in Canada. In what began as a series of "teach-ins" in community centers in Saskatchewan, Canada, the message of Idle No More was brought to life through a global social media campaign that led to peaceful demonstrations, spontaneous round dances in shopping malls, rail and road blockages in Canada, and activities around the world (Kino-nda-niimi Collective 2014). At the root of this movement was the need for increased discussion and public education about Indigenous land issues, and a general desire to create public spaces for Indigenous peoples to exercise their concerns about their environmental futures and dishonored treaty rights. Similar practices of Indigenous reclamation are evident in such parallel movements as *Land Back* and the renewal of water guardianship (refer to Section 2.1).

This book is about Indigenous people's relationships with the land and the importance of strengthening and protecting those relationships through land-based cultural practices. Both on a global level, but also with respect to the ways we know and relate to the lands of our own traditional territories, the purpose of this book is to showcase how Indigenous communities from different cultures and ecologies are engaging in action to protect their lands and to restore the relational practices that support wellness for their peoples. It is our goal to build a more practical and also hopeful account of Indigenous community-driven work that details Indigenous practices of repossession. To meet this goal, in Chapter 1 we ground our research in the relational principles that motivate repossession strategies in Hawai'i, Aotearoa, and Canada. *Kapu Aloha* is a code of conduct informed by Kānaka ontologies and epistemologies that aligns with Kānaka cultural practices and notions of the sacred and delivered through non-violent direct action. Among Māori, *kaitiakitanga* is a form of guardianship, but it has been habitually misrepresented only in environmental terms. A kaitiaki is a guardian, not only for environments but also for community interests and across generations. Among the Anishinaabe, *mino bimaadiziwin* is a philosophy that outlines "the good life," and considers Anishinaabe connections and responsibilities with the physical, social, ecological, and the spiritual.

Through engagement with those relational principles, the widest goal of this book is to broaden both theoretical and applied concepts of environmental repossession, and to empower Indigenous communities who similarly desire to assert their rights to land. But we also seek to challenge common misconceptions about what Indigeneity looks like, including where Indigenous connections to land take place, how they are practiced, and what rights-making can look like in a modern context. This reconceptualization urges us to consider a variety of Indigenous environments, including urban spaces, gardens, the digital, mountain tops, rivers, and university classrooms, among many others, and a range of practices that encapsulate the diverse ways in which Indigenous peoples are contemporarily exhibiting their rights. Moreover, this reconceptualization moves beyond North America, and beyond Indigenous health geographies, and into Indigenous places and movements where Indigenous rights-making occurs through varying methods, including everyday actions but also large-scale, direct action events.

Book Outline

In this book, we will demonstrate that Indigenous environmental repossession is a diverse and "messy" suite of related practices that share the goal of reconnecting Indigenous peoples with environments and practices of importance to them. The lay understanding of repossession emphasizes assertive protest to reclaim material objects and other assets. We will prove, however, that its definition should be extended to subtle practices and the enactment of everyday routines which unsettle settler society expectations and means of social control. Our case studies suggest that direct actions and modest, daily change-making are necessarily connected strategies rather than alternatives. This introductory chapter has offered a broad understanding of key concepts central to environmental repossession, including Indigenous knowledge, environmental dispossession, and resurgence. We have introduced the concept of environmental repossession, noting its diversity and how it has been used to date. In the rest of the book, we build from this small base of existing research to enrich discussions about where repossession is happening, and what repossession practices look like.

Chapter 1 unfolds across two key sections. In the first section, we introduce and interrogate the concept of relational ontology, as it is understood in our home discipline of geography, and specifically so among Indigenous scholars and communities who draw upon relational ways of knowing to guide their research and within other environmental movements across the globe. This section also discusses the related concepts of kincentric ecology and kinship relationships. In the second half of the chapter, we outline the relational knowledge we know and understand, as Kanaka, Māori, and Anishinaabe scholars, respectively, as they pertain to our roles and positions in the repossession projects described in this book. This is the place where we introduce and describe who we are—as authors, scholars, and community people—and where we demonstrate our relationships to the work described in the book.

In **Chapter 2** we acknowledge that repossession overlaps with a variety of other strategies that inform Indigenous activism. First, we review Indigenous experience with occupations and blockades that contest the expanding petrochemical superstructure, highlighting how direct action remains central to Indigenous strategies of resistance. Second, though, we shift scales to consider how the everyday rehabilitation of lifeways maintains connections between cultural practices and relational systems of care for the environment. Third, we counter the assumption that Indigenous resistance and resilience is always separatist, demonstrating a long history of strategic alliances and how that is currently expressed through collaborative research. Last, we modernize a historical academic preoccupation with Indigenous cultural production and art, revealing how it has become another approach to making and drawing attention to environmental claims. In other words, we review a broader range and scale of methods and practices that Indigenous communities experiment with to make and sustain important political projects.

The first of our empirical chapters, **Chapter 3**, showcases an Indigenous art exhibit—*Kūkulu: Pillars of Mauna Kea*—and how it has enabled Indigenous communities in Hawaiʻi to contest construction of a Thirty Meter Telescope (TMT) on the summit of Mauna Kea. Kānaka objected to the environmental and cultural impact of a massive eighteen-story, five-acre telescope complex on sacred land. As a traveling art exhibit, Kūkulu was curated conscientiously by a contributor to Chapter 3, Aunty Pua Case, as a response to the questions posed by our research team. Her most important goal for the exhibit was to "bring the Mauna to the people." She believes that "before there can be repossession, there has to be reconnection." Using guiding principles for establishing ancestral alignments, Aunty Pua transformed a vacant room into a space made safe to delve deeply into difficult conversations through culturally implemented and contextually relevant participatory engagements.

In **Chapter 4,** an explicitly urban context reveals the relevance of repossession to less conventional circumstances for Indigenous politics. In lay discourse, Indigenous peoples are willfully associated with fixity, stasis, and propinquity. In reality, however, many Indigenous communities and tribes have experienced significant diaspora, involuntary resettlement, or displacement. If the concept of environmental repossession is to be useful for Indigenous communities, therefore, it must speak to urban Indigenes and urban indigeneity. Taniwha Club is a youth program for Māori and other Polynesian children who live in south Auckland. Their neighborhoods are lively and diverse, but they also experience diverse challenges. Some of its Māori communities live within their tribal *rohe* (boundaries), but the city has expanded over their once peri-urban environs. In other instances, significant rural-to-urban migration has transplanted Māori into foreign territory, where pursuit of Treaty of Waitangi rights may be unrealizable. Accordingly, the leaders of Taniwha Club asked early questions about what Indigenous reclamation and decolonization should look like in those contexts. The Club emerged as an Indigenous art project but rapidly transformed into a guerrilla gardening ensemble. For its members, "staking a claim" within the city is, therefore, both literal and figurative, so their practices represent a bold prototype for actioning environmental repossession in the most challenging of circumstances.

In Chapter 5, the social, cultural, and political significance of everyday gathering for wellness are considered in Biigtigong Nishnaabeg, Canada. The chapter focuses on gathering practices as strategies of environmental repossession among Biigtigong Nishnaabeg, a First Nation community in Northwestern Ontario. Located on the north shore of Lake Superior, the community of Biigtigong Nishnaabeg is physically surrounded by varying industrial developments and interests that threaten Biigtigong's capacity to live well and be self-determining in its territory. For more than forty years, Biigtigong has engaged in a pathway of hope and healing, through which the Nation aims to restore its original cultural practices and knowledge. Alongside a lengthy land claims process, Biigtigong is re-establishing many of its original gathering practices to support reconnection and cultural resurgence for community members. Described through the lens of connection, this chapter emphasizes three specific repossession efforts: gathering around the moose hunt, returning to the Mouth of the Pic, and reconnecting our social relations with one another. In this chapter, engaging in Nishnaabeg gathering practices is fundamentally about living and being in *mino bimaadiziwin* ("the good life"), and demonstrating Nishnaabeg capabilities to create spaces that offer healing, belonging, and a self-determined future.

The final chapter of this book, **Chapter 6**, returns to the questions raised in this introduction. We contemplate the ways in which Indigenous communities engage with their Indigenous knowledge to reconnect with one another to protect their lands. We also evaluate the practicalities and challenges for repossession strategies, and how efforts to protect the environment support healing and wellness. The diversity in narratives of repossession defies generalization, but our case studies nonetheless infer strategies for communities which face similar histories and processes of environmental dispossession.

As scholars whose passions lie in the various interconnections between Indigenous peoples and the land, we offer this Indigenous-led, community-engaged research in support of an exciting body of work that places Indigenous people's priorities at the center of the narrative. We intend for those voices to be central for future learning and thinking about the usefulness and expansion of environmental repossession in both academic and community contexts. This matters especially in a time when Indigenous communities are increasingly engaging in action on the key matters affecting their Indigenous rights and overall wellness. Indigenous communities and their knowledge and experiences are rich and unique, and much can be learned when the appropriate space for the sharing of gifts, knowledge, and experience is created. The global nature of this book is fundamentally important as it offers insights into the unique yet shared experiences of Indigenous communities to forces such as colonialism, climate change, and capitalism. It is our hope that this book offers space for Indigenous communities to tell stories about what the land means to them and how they have protected it for future generations.

Chapter 1

FOR ALL OUR KIN: A RELATIONAL UNDERSTANDING OF ENVIRONMENTAL RESPONSIBILITIES

We offer this chapter on relationality with the land as Indigenous scholars from distinct places and cultural orientations, but with similar philosophical principles about who we are and about the roles we play in matters related to land protection, Indigenous rights, and the wellness of Indigenous peoples. The first half of this chapter introduces and explores the relational principles we draw on in our academic work of environmental repossession, including relational ontology, kincentric ecology, and kinship relationships. These concepts figure centrally in the field of Indigenous geography, and especially so among scholars and communities who draw upon relational ways of knowing to conceptualize Indigenous environmental justice (Whyte et al. 2016), water protection (Wilson and Inkster 2018), and other movements to protect Indigenous lands and rights. These concepts also form key theoretical guides for research and community work examining Indigenous relationships with the land (Bawaka Country et al. 2016; Daigle 2016; Whetung and Wakefield 2019), and they have featured centrally in our own research examining interconnection from cultural, political, cartographic, and wellness-based perspectives (Coombes et al. 2011; Louis 2017; Richmond 2018).

In the second half of this chapter, we offer our personal narratives about how we know and understand our Indigenous relational ontologies as Kanaka, Māori, and Anishinaabe scholars. We share our individual narratives to highlight the multiple positions and responsibilities we hold as Indigenous scholars, or more accurately to what Sarah Hunt (2014) describes as "dancing between worlds," and of the opportunities and complexities these positions can present. In our aspirations to support our communities to do their environmental repossession work described in Chapters 3, 4, and 5, we necessarily navigate a number of ontological and axiological tensions associated with the varying people and places we dance through, and especially so as Indigenous peoples who have chosen to work for our communities but from within academia. Our relationships with the people and places we come from shape our dedication to these matters. While we recognize our relationships to these peoples and places are characterized by our various experiences of colonialism, still these connections hold a depth of knowledge, memory, and practice that continue to steer us today in our respective bodies of research, and especially so in the community-based approaches we take to our environmental repossession projects.

Relational Ontology, Kincentric Ecology, and Kinship

Across the globe, Indigenous peoples inhabit unique ecologies that range across varying ecosystems, including prairies and deserts, rivers, islands, mountains, and many more. In these places, Indigenous peoples have developed sophisticated knowledge systems and ways of living that support and strengthen their cultural identities, belonging, and wellness (McGregor 2004). Indigenous peoples use the terms "Land," "Earth," or "Country" to refer to all animate and inanimate pieces of their natural world, which encompasses living and non-living features of the physical environment, including land, waters, air, fire, and all who inhabit those elements. Common among Indigenous peoples is a relational way of knowing that is deeply connected to the land.

A relational ontology is a way of knowing that views all life to be interconnected and related, including humanity and all beings that inhabit the Earth, including more-than-human elements such as the animate and inanimate pieces of the natural world (Abram 2012). A relational ontology expresses these more-than-human elements in their broadest interpretations, including and exceeding human societies, and recognizes that complex webs of interdependency are formed between the countless beings that share the natural world (Abram 2012).

Indigenous worldviews build on the concept of relational ontology through an emphasis on the kincentric nature of associated interdependencies (Lloyd et al. 2012; Wright et al. 2018). A kincentric ecology emerges when humankind views the life around them, including the more-than-human beings, as kin or as relatives (Salmón 2000; TallBear 2011). The reorientation from "nature as other" to "nature as kin" necessarily involves consideration of the value-based practices and behaviors we engage in to uphold our relationships with the land. Enrique Salmón offers the Raramuri concept of *iwigara* (kinship of people and plants) to demonstrate the distinctly place-based nature of ideas, ways of thinking, and doing among the Raramuri. He (2000: 1328) likens a kincentric ecology to "sharing breath with our relatives," noting that everything that breathes has a soul, and that everything that breathes shares the same breath, including plants, animals, humans, stones, and the land.

Kinship relationships with the land are an embodied relationship whose quality and wellness depends on an ethic of care and respect (Hunt 2014; Tynan 2021), which is governed by a spiritual reverence for the land (Archibald 2008). "Indigenous kinship systems are not merely descriptions of relationships, but also describe ways of living well, laws for strengthening human and more-than-human life and restoring and nurturing social-ecological well-being" (Dudgeon and Bray 2019: 3). Kinship relationships in the human context are upheld through such everyday behaviors as sharing, helping, communicating, and feeding. Within an Indigenous context, kinship systems are also upheld through a number of distinct cultural and spiritual practices (e.g., words said to open meetings, feeding Elders and children first, or preparing an ancestor dish). Together, these practices demonstrate care and belonging. Over generations they form lessons and expectations for how to live well with one another to demonstrate mutual care and reciprocity among people.

In *Braiding Sweetgrass*, Robin Kimmerer (2013) devotes considerable attention to the concept of the "honorable harvest," which refers to the ethical reciprocity we, as humans, ought to show to the land in exchange for the countless gifts it provides. Through various stories about her own relationships with maple trees, the strawberry plant, and the pond in her back yard, Kimmerer demonstrates her own caring practices and ways of offering gratitude to the Earth. She also raises the notion of consent—what practices should we engage in before taking from the earth, and how we should listen for answers from the Earth before we take. Notably, Kimmerer details several principles that acknowledge the agency of the Earth: consent, sharing, gratitude, minimizing harm and waste, reciprocity, respect, and willingness to defend. Reo (2019) draws from *Anishinaabe inawendiwin,* an Anishinaabe concept of interconnection, to further elaborate on rights, responsibilities, and accountabilities of the land, and of the ways he has upheld these principles in his own research with and on the land. In practice, this means engaging in ceremony and acknowledging the spiritual connections imbued in our kincentric ecologies with one another and with the Earth.

This worldview is a values-based perspective that sees all components of our ecologies as deserving of respect for the roles they contribute to the wellbeing of our social and ecological system as a whole. Among Indigenous peoples, one of the clearest examples of this kincentric relationality comes from our stories. Creation stories, for example, span across cultures, and they offer rich and varied narratives that embed human origins in broader cosmologies, migrations, and other journeys to interconnect human beings with spiritual, and animate and inanimate features of the land. Across many Indigenous nations, creation stories share understandings of where we come, and they also offer teachings meant to guide people in times of confusion or conflict (McGregor 2004).

There are many versions of the Creation Story that describe the origins of Turtle Island, a term Indigenous people often use to describe North America. One version of the story is that the Creator, also known as Gitchi Manitou, placed Nishnaabeg on the Earth. Over time, Nishnaabeg began to fight with one another, and they disobeyed their original laws about living well, including sharing, practicing reciprocity, and recognizing their responsibilities to one another and especially with the animals. Creator flooded the Earth as a means to purify it, and many Nishnaabeg and animals died. Basil Johnston's (1976) version of the story talks about Sky-Woman (the original human) who survives and comes to rest on the back of a great turtle:

> Gladly, all the animals tried to serve the spirit woman. The beaver was the first to plunge into the depths. He soon surfaced out of breath and without the precious soil. The fisher tried, but he too failed. The marten went down, came up empty handed, reporting the water was too deep. The loon tried. Although he remained out of sight for a long time, he too emerged, gasping for air. He said that it was too dark. All tried to fulfill the spirit women's request. All failed. All were ashamed.
>
> Finally, the least of the water creatures, the muskrat, volunteered to dive. At this announcement the other water creatures laughed in scorn, because they doubted this little creature's strength and endurance. Had not they, who were strong and able, been unable to grasp the soil from the bottom of the sea? How could he, the muskrat, the most humble among them, succeed when they could not?
>
> Nevertheless, the little muskrat volunteered to dive. Undaunted, he disappeared into the waves. The onlookers smiled. They waited for the muskrat to emerge as empty handed as they had done. Time

passed. Smiles turned to worried frowns. The small hope that each had nurtured for the success of the muskrat turned into despair. When the waiting creatures had given up, the muskrat floated to the surface more dead than alive, but he clutched in his paws a small morsel of soil. Where the great had failed, the small succeeded.

(Johnston 1976: 14)

This excerpt contains many teachings and interpretations, but one of the most significant lessons is a reminder that everyone and everything in Creation has a role to play, despite their size or strength. For Nishnaabeg, this story reminds us that we, as humans, are one piece of much larger spiritual and natural systems that are in constant connection, and sometimes conflict. Thus, we are reminded of how to carry ourselves with humility, and above all to recall that we are but one small part of a large and dynamic system that deserves our continual respect.

Mele ko'ihonua (Hawai'i cosmogonic genealogies) form the foundation of Kānaka worldviews and express a kincentric connection Kānaka share with the 'āina. Through the mele ko'ihonua relationships are established, described, and reinscribed between the land, ocean, and sky; *Akua* (divine natural entities and processes who are our kinfolk) and *ali'i* (chiefs); and ali'i and *maka'āinana* (general population). Although Kānaka have several mele ko'ihonua that sometimes contradict one another, perhaps suggesting regional distinctions, they all share a common element, the genealogical relationship between 'Āina, Akua, and Kānaka.

The best-known mele ko'ihonua is the Kumulipo, a 2,000-line chant of origin and ordered evolution that details the emergence of the 'āina, the first living organisms, the birth of the Akua, and later generations upon generations of Kānaka. It emphasizes *pono* (balance), in the pairing of ocean and land creatures, further illuminating Kānaka understanding of the interdependence between land and sea. It is also the most encompassing of all mele ko'ihonua because it maintains strands of other mele ko'ihonua within it. One such strand is the mele ko'ihonua of the primal pair, *Papa* and *Wākea* (earth mother and sky father).

Papa and Wākea emerge in the twelfth *wā* (epoch) of the Kumulipo where Wākea procreates with *Haumea* (divine natural entity considered to be a progenitor of all life on earth) and his daughter, *Ho'ohōkūkalani* (divine natural entity considered to be the generator of stars in the heavens). When Wākea procreated with Papa, who is also a manifestation of Haumea, their offspring were the islands, with

Hawai'i Island being the firstborn and Maui soon after. When Wākea procreated with Ho'ohōkūkalani, their firstborn was an unformed fetus they named Hāloanakalaukapalili. They buried the fetus and from it sprang the first *kalo* (taro plant). Their second born was a human child they named Hāloa in honor of his Elder brother.

Among the major implications of this mele ko'ihonua was the establishment of "an ecologically integrated evolutionary genealogy of Kanaka Hawai'i." Specifically, it bound Hāloanakalaukapalili, the kalo-child, as the Elder sibling to Hāloa, the human child. With this connection comes the familial responsibilities of the Elder sibling nourishing the younger sibling and in return pays attention to the older sibling's needs ensuring a perfectly *pono* (balanced) "reciprocal relationship, wherein each party sacrifices a part of themselves for the other. The kalo surrenders itself to the Kanaka Hawai'i who cultivates, plants, waters, weeds, and feeds the plant. Each grows from the other's sacrifice" (Louis 2017: 54).

Anchoring Environmental Repossession in Our Own Relational Ontologies

Doing the work of environmental repossession calls Indigenous peoples to be on the land together, whether in their traditional territories or in cities, maybe even in hospital environments, with others in such a way that stories, knowledge, and other pieces of our histories can be shared, practiced, and passed on to younger generations. The remainder of this chapter draws on a storied approach to share how we understand our relationships with our lands, and the philosophies that underlie these relationships. In doing this, we first introduce ourselves and our origins, local traditions, and ways of knowing and understanding. We share stories and perspectives about the relational ontologies we know as Indigenous peoples who come from geographically and culturally distinct places and ecologies.

We offer our narratives to speak truth to the breadth of Indigenous relational ontologies that exist today. We do not wish to contribute to a body of literature that essentializes Indigenous ways of knowing, or to romanticize Indigenous relationships with the Land. The colonial context is pervasive across our personal and professional lives, and our own experiences with colonialism in academic and other contexts have powerfully shaped how we know and live our respective Indigenous ontologies, which are inclusive of our own kincentric ecologies and kinship relationships. Those experiences underlie how we know and understand some of the key relational ontologies that guide us in our work with Indigenous peoples of Hawai'i, Aotearoa, and Biigtigong Nishnaabeg.

Kapu Aloha

Aloha mai, greetings, 'o Mauna Loa a me Mauna Kea ko'u mau mauna, my mountains are Mauna Loa and Mauna Kea, 'o Kanilehua ko'u ua, Kanilehua is my rain, 'o Waiākea ko'u wai a me ko'u ahupua'a ma ka moku o Keawe, Waiākea is my waterway and my district on the island of Keawe (an affectionate term for Hawai'i Island), 'o Waiuli ko'u kai, Waiuli is my sea.

Aloha is one unifying concept uniquely "of Hawai'i." Though oversimplified to mean love or a daily greeting, the actual term itself is best explained as the sharing of breath, *ha*, face to face, *alo*. It is the most fundamental of all reciprocal relationships between human and non-human kinfolk. Kānaka consider the air we breathe a *kinolau* (body form) of Lono (a divine entity associated with socio-geophysiological concepts such as fertility, peace, and recreation, as well as the wet season and its accompanying atmospheric and terrestrial disturbances). To inhale is to accept the divine element into your physical body and the exchange in the exhale, where your body reciprocates by breathing out the nutrients plants need to survive.

People's knowledge of the world depends on how they engage with it. For Kānaka, "Aloha is the intelligence with which we meet life." Aunty Olana Ai shared this nugget of wisdom with Aunty Dr. Manulani Meyer. Learning this changed my understanding of why the 1970s Hawaiian cultural renaissance used the term "*Aloha 'Āina*" (love of the land) as a guiding principle that became a slogan associated with Kānaka nationalism and patriotism.

As a concept, Aloha 'Āina dates back to mythic times and can be found in several Hawai'i cosmologies, including the most renowned, the Kumulipo. As a practice, the profoundly intimate bond nurtured between Kānaka and 'āina is found in *mele* (Hawai'i song), *hula* (Hawai'i dance), *mo'olelo* (Hawai'i historical narrative accounts), as well as in daily life ways of farming and fishing. During the Hawaiian cultural renaissance, the Aloha 'Āina movement focused on land struggles between Kānaka and landowners. Demonstrations during this era are discussed further in the Hawai'i chapter, Kūkulu (Chapter 3).

While still a moniker for returning to a kin-centric relationship with 'āina, the term evolved to focus on kalo culture. Kalo culture directly relates to Kānaka wellbeing. Many Kānaka are returning to traditional dietary practices, resuscitating the decimated lands and polluted waterways necessary for kalo cultivation to reverse high rates of heart disease, diabetes, and many cancers. Aloha 'Āina advocates today are focused on restoring the holistic health of Kānaka communities by reconnecting Kānaka ancestral relationships to 'āina.

Kapu Aloha is a term relatively few people were familiar with before the Mauna Kea movement. People did not need to know the term unless they were involved in a cultural practice that used it as protocol. I came to know Kapu Aloha in 2013 assisting Aunty Luana Neff, a Kanaka nationalist, and Aunty Pua Case, a contributor to Chapter 3, organize the first *E Ala E Apapalani E* ceremonial event at Pu'u Huluhulu (a hill situated in the saddle between Mauna Kea and Mauna Loa). It was strategically timed to correspond with the weekend after the annual Merrie Monarch, the internationally acclaimed hula competition held after Easter Sunday. In a flyer we composed as a *kahea* (call) to gather. The first bullet point under the guidelines was "Kapu Aloha—all participants must treat each other with aloha and respect and be mindful of the surrounding environment we are entering."

I remember the day we were going to scout the area surrounding Pu'u Huluhulu. That meant we were going there to ask permission and make our request for a gathering to the Akua. Aunty Luana chanted; she invited me to walk with her and envision the hillside filled with a thousand people playing *pahu* (Hawai'i drums) and other instruments. The scene that filled my visionscape was palpable. The future presented itself before us. A portal of what was to be in 2019, which is now in the past, opened to reveal a community of young and old, Kānaka and non-Kānaka, embracing, chanting, dancing, and standing in unity, celebrating and connecting with our sacred places with ritualized ceremonies.

I never doubted what I witnessed. It was not my first visionscape; not even the first I have shared with another person. I knew it was going to happen. That made working to make the event a success even more daunting because now I knew the Akua were watching. We recognized it was a time for profound transformation and change. The gathering was meant to honor our kupuna, Mauna Kea, through traditional pule and cultural practices. In the flyer, we asked "all cultural practitioners to lend a collective voice; a voice of great reverence, a voice of love, a voice of regeneration, a voice of restoration, a voice of ancestral memory, a voice of deep wisdom." We hoped the venue would serve as a place to teach future generations the value of creating a deeper relationship, a kinship with the natural world in a ceremonial space.

On the day of the event, I awoke at 3 a.m. Sunrise was mere hours away. I had loaded up my truck the night before with the tables, chairs, water, and toilet paper. Puʻu Huluhulu only had a portable toilet at the time, and the nearest flushing toilet was a five- to ten-minute drive to the State park. I made some coffee and drove down to pick up people wanting a ride to the event. We drove up with the usual small talk until we neared the venue. It was an unspoken knowing that we had entered a sacred space.

Everyone helped to unload the truck and set up for the event. Slowly, the parking lot filled with dozens of Kānaka who came for the opening ceremony. Strangely enough, there was no noise louder than a vehicle passing by. Not until Aunty Luana raised her family *pū* (conch shell) at five minutes before sunrise to mark the moment the ceremony began. *Kumu Hula* (Hula Teachers) and their *haumana* (students) came with their instruments to *kani ka pū* (blow the conch shell), *oli* (Hawaiʻi chant), and hula every hour on the hour from sunrise until noon.

Aunty Pua Case was one of the practitioners who assisted in coordinating the ceremony that day and as always brought her family with her. They abided by Kapu Aloha because they were among chanters or dancers and ceremonial people who already knew what it meant. She explains:

> Whenever we went there, we made sure to abide in Kapu Aloha because we were in a ceremonial space. It was simple yet profound. There was no need for instruction or interpretation, or definition. It was just what you did when you were in a ceremony interacting with the environment and everything that is of that realm. It was just that simple. It never needed an explanation.

It wasn't until the ceremonies were opened to people who did not come from those backgrounds that explanations became necessary. For a general description of Kapu Aloha, we look to the online video of Aunty Hōkūlani Holt and Aunty Pualani Kanahele sharing their *manaʻo* (thoughts) on the Mauna during the 2019 occupation entitled *Kapu Aloha: Remember Your Ancestors.* Aunty Hōkūlani explains Kapu Aloha in relation to conduct and behavior:

Kapu Aloha is always thinking about others, thinking about place, thinking about relationships, and how to best have that habit and to keep yourself in that disciplining of thinking that what I want is not the most important thing if it does not align with these ways of behaving well with each other and with the place that we are in. So that is, at its simplest level, how we want people to be here.

Aunty Pualani Kanahele explains the terminology:

Kapu has two English definitions that are usually used. One word is prohibited, and the other word is sacred. In the case of Kapu Aloha, it means both in the idea that the way you behave should be sacred to yourself and the people around you. It is prohibited because you're prohibited to act in a certain way. The aloha part has many different meanings one of them the greater meanings that everybody uses as aloha is love … So when we talk about Kapu Aloha, we're talking about a prohibition, a way to act with the idea of exuding a particular level of love.

Aunty Pua Case adds:

During the movement, Kapu Aloha only applied on the Mauna. We were not telling people what to do when they went home. That would be overstepping into people's personal lives. But some terms fit precisely at that moment in the place they are at. If we did not have that term, and the practices that aligned with it, and guidelines that could still be connected to the term from ancient times to present day, we would not have been able to get as far as we did. Every cultural movement needs at least one term that is going to assist in establishing a code of conduct that includes protocols and behavior expectations. A term that is a value and principle. If you find that term, you ground your action, your ceremony, and your stance.

In truth, the term evolved to fit the needs of the movement. It is now the guiding term by which *Kia'i* (guardians, protectors) and Kānaka conduct themselves. That was not the original intention. It became more than how it was initially used and incorporated into ceremonies. There needed to be a term with a high-level value for the movement to proceed as it did. A term that, once uttered, all would know, this is what you can do and how you interact.

Kaitiakitanga—Land as Pedagogy and a wanaka at Wanaka

Ko Moponui te maunga
Ko Waitete te awa
I mua, no Pūrākaunui ki Ōtepoti ahau
Ko Kati Māmoe rāua ko Ngāti Kahungunu aku iwi
Ko Brad Coombes ahau

Place and natural icons are clearly important for Māori cultural identities. That we commence our oratory with a *pepeha* (identity statement), as above, with references to our *maunga* (mountain) and *awa* (river) is revealing. It is also significant that those pepeha include our place of upbringing—for me, the small village of Pūrākaunui near Dunedin at the south of the South Island of Aotearoa New Zealand. It is not common, however, to dangle *i mua* (in the past) within the locational details of our pepeha. I do so because I have not lived in the South Island for twenty-five years and *i mua* flags the uncertainty in any expectation that I have a specifically landed identity.

Accordingly, it seems inauthentic to write a section on *kaitiakitanga*. I seldom use the word, in part because it has an ambiguous status within my own tribal lexicon. While dialectical variation within *te reo Māori* (Māori language) is minimal compared with other Indigenous languages, te reo Kati Māmoe represents a partial outlier, most notably in our use of K rather than Ng (Kati rather than Ngati; significantly for what follows, *wanaka* rather than *wananga*). The *kai-* prefix emphasizes the subject of an action; *tiaki* is the verb to watch; and as a nominalizing suffix, *-tanga* often connotes an abstract noun. Hence, kaitiakitanga is a practice of being one who watches over and safeguards important dimensions of social life. Although I will problematize it further, kaitiakitanga overlaps with guardianship and, therefore, with debates about the rise of Indigenous protectors in environmental politics (Dodson and Miru 2021; Reed et al. 2021). Compared to other *iwi* (tribes), Kati Māmoe has few words that end with—*tanga*, perhaps suggesting we have no humor for abstract thinking nor neologisms that resemble *Pākehā* (non-Māori) world views. We value *kaitieki* (sp. Kati Māmoe), but we do not complicate their role through an abstract noun or by assuming a timeless, reified practice of being in the world. Yet, kaitiakitanga is modish within academic and policy-forming communities, and it has status within such legislation as the Resource Management Act 1991, where it was once translated as, before repeals that mean it now merely parallels, "the ethic of stewardship" (Section 7(aa)). It is reasonable to ask whether a kaitieki can practice kaitiakitanga, and such dilemmas may prompt additional questions about who may aspire to such roles. I never aspire to be a kaitiaki, but I have had the label imposed upon me in circumstances which were troubling. I will recount one of those occasions because it signals the exclusionary forces that delimit non-local or "urban" indigeneity and, thereby, it prefaces my later case study (Chapter 4).

I am slow to discern the significance of coincidences, so I did not at first contemplate the irony in reading a special journal issue on *Land as Pedagogy* (*Decolonization: Indigeneity, Education, Society* vol. 3, no. 3) while flying from Auckland, where I work, to Otago, where I was born. I was travelling from a *wananga* (university)—specifically, the University of Auckland—to the town of Wanaka to perform as kaitiaki. Few of the tourists who visit Wanaka for skiing, hiking, and water sports will know of its original function as a site of several wanaka/wananga. Now that multiple Pākehā and Māori conquests and migrations have erased most Kati Māmoe connections to that area, tourists are unlikely to recognize how infrastructure established for them impacts the vestiges of Kati Māmoe heritage. Two others from my *hapu* (sub-tribe) and I were tasked to advise on a consenting process for a mobile phone tower, something ordained for the site of a former wanaka near Wanaka to improve the safety of outdoor enthusiasts. Traditionally, wananga served on a continuum between informal institutions for addressing everyday educational needs to deeply spiritual sites for intergenerational transfer of specialist knowledges. As I alternated between *Land as Pedagogy* and briefing notes about the wanaka near Wanaka, I marveled at the socio-cultural significance that our universities were once outdoors, but I failed to appreciate the possible connections between the two sets of documents.

Although little is known about the wanaka near Wanaka, it is regarded as one of the most *tapu* (sacred). It had been a training camp for elite warriors and *tohunga* (experts, priests), so the prosaic intrusion of a communications repeater was controversial. The three who were to meet with the proposal's developer and consenting authority had never been to the site, knew of it only by reputation and could not be briefed as to its importance because Elders with requisite knowledge had passed before informing the next generations. A kaitieki should be anointed by their own people, but rather we had been sampled by a *tauiwi* (foreign) system of resource management and were asked to provide "a kaitiakitanga perspective as tangata whenua" (landed peoples). All three had lived outside our tribal *rohe* (boundaries) for decades, and all sensed incompetence to act as kaitieki.

I read innocently the *Land as Pedagogy* articles as an escape from thinking about whether it was legitimate for me to be a guardian for any wananga. Mostly, the articles impressed me with their repudiation of the recognition politics that benevolently yet destructively opens spaces for Indigenous "participation" in non-Indigenous practices. I applauded, highlighted in yellow and underlined in red, Wildcat and colleagues' contention that because the "violent separation of Indigenous peoples from our sources of knowledge and strength—the land" (Wildcat et al. 2014: III) was the hallmark transgression of colonization, thus "decolonization must involve forms of education that reconnect Indigenous peoples to land" (p. I). Yet, I also quivered at Simpson's (2014: 1) influential assertion that reclamation of land as pedagogy requires "generations of Indigenous peoples to grow up intimately and strongly connected to our homelands" because Indigenous education "comes through the land" (p. 9). Similarly, her claim that decolonization demands "a generation of land based ... intellectuals and cultural producers" was a burden to consume (p. 13). There is scope to misinterpret her intent because what comes *through the land* does not necessarily need to be learned *on the land*. Besides, current land titles will never erase the lived reality of continuing Indigenous presence, so "our" land is omnipresent and its pedagogical oeuvre is pervasive. Nonetheless, Simpson's arguments were received personally, as if my Indigenous credentials had been declared ersatz because I had wandered from home. I have no responsibility for, nor agency thereafter, the waves of North Island Māori who forcibly removed Kati Māmoe from its *rohe potae* (homelands). It was their sales of our *turangawaewae* (place of standing) to the Crown and the later redistribution of those land estates to Pākehā farmers that had amputated Kati Māmoe ties to the wanaka at Wanaka.

Today, Māori are 86 percent urban, with over two-thirds living outside the ancestral lands recognized by their grandparents (Te Whata 2021). Although there are notable countertrends, differences in health, housing, education, environmental quality, and other cross-cultural disparities are regularly attributed to the landlessness and spatial displacement of Māori (Metge 2021; Te Karu et al. 2021). Urban Māori are considered "out of place," leading to denial of rights and disenfranchisement, so they "experience cultural conditioning about where they should live, what rights to which they have access, and the quality of environments that they can expect" (Coombes 2013: 351). Just as kaitiakitanga may be a concession for those few who have retained access to land-culture relations despite colonial transformations, *Land as Pedagogy* may be a privileged expectation for relatively few Māori. I am conflicted about kaitiakitanga and too embarrassed to perform as kaitieki, even if that role resonates with my academic engagements in Treaty of Waitangi settlements, environmental justice, and biocultural restoration.

As Kati Māmoe had not utilized the wanaka in over 130 years, the three commentators did not know what to think of it, nor our part in what could have been a moment of cooption. At site visits and subsequent hearings, it was clear that the decision on the communications array was in the balance. Fervent evidence from a Crown advisory service, Heritage New Zealand (formerly the Historic Places Trust), attested to the importance of the site, even though that service had not consulted with any iwi or hapu. For reasons of safety and disaster preparedness, some recreational groups and resource management agencies entreated for extension of mobile coverage into gaps where public recreation and tourism were expanding. Evidently, our opinion as kaitieki would guarantee a particular outcome, and all, it seemed, anticipated we would vote with the environment and against the phone tower. We did not. What little we did know about our role included the notion that kaitieki should not guard anything in a selfish manner to the sole advantage of our hapu, but rather should consider the common good. Moreover, if this was a living wanaka its function would evolve over time, so public safety, communications, and networking were modern functions of relevance to a knowledge-sharing facility.

Heritage New Zealand and environmental groups were outraged, labeling us traitors and imposters. Along with the original RMA legislators, they had presumed that kaitiakitanga is solely an environmental ethic.

> kaitiakitanga has become almost locked into meaning simply "guardianship" without understanding of (or in the case of the Crown, providing for) the wider obligations and rights it embraces. Māori interpretations of kaitiakitanga as guardianship can be far greater than non-Māori interpretations of it (p. 351) ... Kaitiakitanga is, therefore, more than managing relations between environmental resources and humans; it also involves managing relationships between people in the past, present and future [and it ...] cannot be interpreted as simply an ethic whose relevance is found only in relation to the bio-physical environment.
>
> (Kawharu 2000: 352)

Early assumptions that kaitiakitanga was equivalent to stewardship or reducible to environmental guardianship were misplaced. First, kaitiaki are responsible to their communities as well as for the environment, and therefore kaitiakitanga is also deeply relational within economic, socio-cultural, and family life. Second, Te Whiti Love (2003: 36) offers an "objection to stewardship" because "by nature a steward is not also the 'owner' of the resource but is acting on someone else's behalf—this is not the case for a kaitiaki." Setting aside the irony in a postcolonial use of a term popularized during the enclosures of the United Kingdom, this objection is significant for the current meaning of kaitiakitanga. Te Whiti Love suggests that celebration and legislative recognition of Māori as kaitiaki is a manipulative and assimilative strategy that simultaneously disavows land repatriation.

Kaitiakitanga is currently being reclaimed in a radical process that indigenizes conservation, economic development, and conventions about expertise and leadership (Barnes et al. 2021; Harcourt et al. 2022; Reihana et al. 2021). Yet, the rearticulation of kaitiakitanga after the RMA 1991 is a shallow semblance of what it should mean that continues to dominate, so those who pursue a wider, evolving understanding of the term are labeled traitors and imposters. My engagement with the wanaka near Wanaka taught many useful life lessons, including the need to avoid fashionable academic concepts, especially when they are framed within an environmental thought-silo that obscures the relational philosophies of Indigenous resurgence. At the end of that trip south, I returned to Auckland with determination to work harder for Māori wellbeing and rights in the places I presently occupy rather than on lands to which I belong but have seldom revisited. Not long thereafter, I joined Taniwha Club—the case study for Chapter 4—as one of its founding trustees, and I commenced work on this project about (environmental) repossession. At times, though, I do wonder whether repossession is as privileged and unrealistic an expectation as is *Land as Pedagogy*.

Mino Bimaadiziwin: An Anishinaabe Philosophy for Living the Good Life (on the Land, in the City, and in the University)

Geeziskwe dishnikaz mukwa dodem, Biigtigong
Nishnaabeg ndoonjiba.

My name is sun woman and I am from the bear clan. I am Anishinaabe of Biigtigong Nishnaabeg. As an Anishinaabe woman, I have been taught that when introducing ourselves, it is customary to acknowledge our name, clan, community, and language. We do this to honor our place in the world and to demonstrate our kinship, family, responsibilities, and helpers. This helps others to know where we come from, and who we are related to. The ability to introduce myself in Anishinabemoen represents a loving commitment to my family and ancestors, who stood strong and bravely so that I can be here today.

From a young age, I was taught about principles of mino bimaadiziwin. Mino bimaadiziwin is a spiritual and relational way of knowing that Creator has provided the gifts we need to live well on this land. These gifts include other people, shelter, food and medicine, our songs, histories, knowledge, language, and ceremonies. These gifts nurture our wellness as whole people, including our physical, social, mental, and spiritual wellness. This relational way of knowing respects the interconnections between people, the earth, and the wider spirit world (Leah 2016) and acknowledges that Nishnaabeg wellness is rooted deeply in the ways we interact with and care for the relationships that support our way of life (Borrows 2016; Goudreau 2006; McGuire 2013). These relationships are maintained and strengthened through our ceremonies (Debassige 2010).

For me, coming to understand and live in mino bimaadiziwin is both a simple and a complicated story. It is simple because I know my family, where I come from, and I have a strong sense of belonging therein. This privilege is sketched into my mind and heart such that when I am on or near my home territory, I can feel my connection to this place; here, my senses peak and my heart is full. This is the place where my ancestors have always lived, and it is the place that they cared for and protected because they knew I was coming.

My home sits along the north shore of Lake Superior, the largest freshwater lake in the world. The spiritual, geographic, and economic importance of this place signified a critical role for Nishnaabeg people, as it placed us at the center of an important network of families, clans, and connections that persist today. Our territory is a place of immense beauty throughout the year. In the spring and summer, it smells like earth and dew. There is rarely a time when you cannot hear or feel the vastness of the lake, which crashes constantly in the background. If you cannot hear the lake, it may be a calm day when instead you are wrapped in its foggy clutches like a cold, wet hug. Biigtigong territory stretches the length of the Biigtig Ziibii, and roughly a few hundred kilometers on either side of the river. Here, we sit in the heart of the Boreal Forest, which is as rugged as it is beautiful. Giant bedrock rises from the lake and through the soil. White, green, and orange mosses hang from these rocks. The rock is deep red and brown, sometimes it is black; other times you can see white veins seep through. The bedrock is covered by pine and birch trees, moss, lichen, sand dunes, and a lot of swamp. Moving inland, the soil is deeper, the bush thicker, and the bugs, flies, and insects a lot more present.

As a people, we come into the strength of our Nishinaabeg identities because of the learning we do on the land. The land teaches us that we must respect the cycles of life that are ever present in the natural world, and that we must constantly think about how our decisions will affect future generations of beings to live in mino bimaadiziwin. The land teaches us that all life is precious. That life is always present. When the wildflowers bloom and the loons sing noisily. But also in the stillness of winter. When the trees lie dormant, when the river has frozen over, as the bears sleep. The spirit of life is ever present.

As a family, we gather in these places to share food and stories, tea, and laughter. We share heartache too—loneliness, grief, sorrow, and loss. However we are in this place, we know that the spirits of our ancestors are alive in the rocks, animals, and waters that surround us. They are present in the wind, the trees, and in the skies above. Their continued presence comforts us to know that we are not alone in this world. But their presence is not just a comforting quality; their presence demands accountability from us. We have an accountability to live our lives in a way that accounts for their teachings, love, and sacrifice. We have a responsibility to know and appreciate our ancestors' commitment to this land and the humility and reciprocity they have shown. For me, these two strands—our Anishinaabe people and these wonderful Lands—are one and the same, and together they form the basis for my identity as an Anishinaabe woman.

It is my experience that being an Anishinaabe woman in this world is also tremendously complex. My mother, Diane Richmond (born as Diane Michano), was born and raised in Biigtigong Nishnaabeg. My father, Reginald Richmond, was a settler from Newfoundland. He and my mother met and fell in love in the city of Toronto, Ontario, Canada. They married in 1970 and had three daughters. When my mom married my dad, she lost her Indian status as an Anishinaabe woman, and all legal rights and obligations permitted under Canadian law. The reality of my identity, having been born to an Anishinaabe mother and a Newfoundlander father, means that my identity as an Anishinaabe person has been shaped in powerful ways by colonial laws designed to dispossess me and my family from our lands, family, and the beauty of the knowledge systems contained therein.

The most extensive and direct impact of colonialism on my life is the fact that I have lived my entire life as an off-reserve Indian, where I was dislocated from other Nishnaabeg, except for some of my cousins, who also lived this reality. I understand that these complications are related to colonial definitions of recognition, yet the impacts of these laws were devastating for my mother. The gendered implications of the Indian Act are extensive, cruel, and intentional; they reach across time and place (Lawrence 2004). The social, emotional, and cultural rejection that so many women (and their children and grandchildren) have endured, and continue to endure today, is immense (McIver 1995; Paul 2010). Indigenous women and their children were unable to live with and be among family. Nishnaabeg were unable to learn immersively through language, song, ceremony, and the many important land-based practices central for wellness and belonging. This has been both destructive and dislocating for those affected. It has led to cultural loss, and the continued fraying of families, tradition, and overall ability for communities to live, know, and practice *mino bimaadiziwin* in their everyday lives (Royal Commission of Aboriginal Peoples 1996).

That I know and connect with my family and traditional territory so strongly today is due in large part to my mother's healing journey and her determination for us to belong, and to understand our place as Nishnaabeg people. Yet I recognize today that our community, and my own family, has suffered tremendous cultural loss because of Canada's colonial project. There are many more people like me across the lands known as Canada who have been dispossessed of their rights to know and love the land as our ancestors meant for us to.

As a teenager, I was given my traditional name *Geeziskwe* by the late Dave Courchene. I have always loved my name, which translates into Sun Woman. I was proud to be given a name associated with the sun as I imagined my likeness with its radiance, light, and warmth. It was not until many years later, through teachings with one of my greatest Anishinaabekwe helpers, Liz Akiwenzie, that I came to understand that this name carries significant responsibility, and especially so in my work as an Anishinaabe scholar.

I come to academia as a curious and critical learner. I know now that this system of learning was not created with the intention of supporting the sorts of knowledge sharing, ideas, and methods that are critical for the resurgence of Indigenous lands, cultural identities, and belonging. Yet many Indigenous learners *do come* to university and they *do find* those very gifts in this place. In the fourth year of my undergraduate degree at McMaster University, I had a single elective course to fill. I chose to take introduction to Indigenous Studies, taught by Dr. Rick Monture. On our first day, he introduced himself, and then invited each student to do the same. Row after row, these introductions took a long time. In his very special way, Dr. Monture took opportunities to look for connections with us; "Oh you're from [place name], did you ever know [name] who used to play on the baseball team?" His gentle smile encouraged us all to engage, to share freely, and to know that this was a place of belonging.

I had never before been in a class where the professor went to such lengths to make connections with their students, and to help them feel both welcomed and that their presence mattered. *And it did matter.* This simple practice of opening relationships was critical for developing the space needed for our class to subsequently dive into the many sensitive subjects, topics, and concepts we would engage in: stolen land, broken promises, cultural appropriation, collective grief, but also healing, diversity, relationships, and pathways forward. That simple but effective practice of seeing, hearing, and engaging individuals on their learning pathway was one that I have since used in many classrooms over the past twenty years. To know that I could be welcomed into academia, and that what I had to say as an Anishinaabe person would not merely be tolerated, but welcomed, was not an experience I had yet known. I was grateful for this small gesture.

Twenty-something years later and having now taught and mentored hundreds of undergraduate and graduate students myself, I am coming to appreciate and embody my responsibilities as *Geeziskwe*. Much of my teaching revolves around the substantive matters covered in this very book: Indigenous relationship with Land, Indigenous concepts of health and wellness, and processes of environmental dispossession. My students and I navigate these complex matters through talking, reading, watching documentaries, learning from visitors, and thinking about how these matters have impacted our own lives. Students are asked to think about their own relationships with land, with creation, with their families, and with their cultures and knowledge. I ask my students: in what ways are your understandings and experiences similar and/or different from that of the peoples and communities we are learning about? Over several months, I see the learners light up. They come to know that they too have special relationships with the land, with their families, and with their ancestors. But what I had not expected was the level of guilt and shame that so many students also express. They ask me: "Why did it take 20+ years for me to learn about this?" From their anger and guilt comes compassion and gratitude. The learners ask: "How do I become a helper? How do I support Indigenous peoples and communities? What is my role in making this place a better, more equal place?" I share some of my own stories and experiences with my students, and I compile many more from other Indigenous communities for them to learn from. I ask them to see and understand these experiences through a lens of shared humanity. In exchange, I urge them all to apply their new-found knowledge and compassion broadly moving forward.

Over the years I have come to see that my responsibility as *Geeziskwe* is to bring light and perspective to these spaces. Especially in that complicated space when I am working with Indigenous students, many who have stories and experiences like mine—filled with trauma, disconnection, shame, and grief—I draw from the teachings of mino bimaadiziwin to help them see that this can be a place of belonging, learning, and transformation for them. I support them to view these experiences for the memories they also contain, including a whole lot of beauty and wonder, generosity, and above all, hopefulness. That is, while the university was never created with the ambition of making life better for Indigenous peoples, still we find ourselves here. We are here, using the tools, resources, and people we encounter to come back into our cultural and spiritual strengths as Indigenous peoples. To be in this place does not mean that we forget our original teachings or responsibilities. Nor does being in this place mean that we are not also spiritual people. In this place rather, and especially in the company of other Indigenous peoples, we cling to these knowledge more fervently to do the work entrusted to us in our original stories, and from the people who worked so hard so that we could be here today. To me, that is the wonder and beauty of mino bimaadiziwin, and it is also the promise of environmental repossession.

Chapter Summary

As Indigenous peoples, we are connected by a common and beautiful, yet often complicated, relationship to the land. Among Indigenous peoples across the globe, there are many broad-scale similarities and shared philosophies that articulate how Indigenous wellness is reliant on one's connections with the land. Our relatedness to the land is deep and it is old, and it is founded in our understanding that all of creation has purpose and thus forms an interconnected web of life. As peoples, we see ourselves as an integrated part of this web. We appreciate the gifts the earth provides us, and we understand that we have responsibilities to support, strengthen, and carry this web of life into the future. As Elders, parents, siblings, and mentors, we bear a responsibility to demonstrate and share these philosophies with those we care for, especially those who follow in our footsteps.

The ways we come to know our unique identities are shaped strongly by our kinship relationships with the places and people we have grown from. These ways of knowing, and the values we attribute to them, are central to how we practice environmental repossession. While some Indigenous people and communities continue to live on the original lands of their ancestors, others are displaced from these original places and have since formed relationships to new lands and territories. Regardless of how one is connected to the land, Indigenous relationships to land are upheld by culturally significant, often spiritual, dimensions of care, including love, respect, humility, and many others that are shared through our relational ontologies and kincentric ecologies.

Chapter 2

THE PRACTICES AND PRAXIS OF INDIGENOUS ENVIRONMENTAL REPOSSESSION

This chapter focuses on the social significance of interrelated Indigenous strategies for reclaiming environmental connections with places of importance. We recognize that environmental repossession does not act alone, but rather overlaps with a broad variety of decolonial strategies. Therefore, it is appropriate to identify and differentiate those strategies, and to discuss Indigenous engagement with each of them. Here, we present several analogs for repossession—direct action, rehabilitation of everyday practices, alliance building, and cultural production. We maintain that there are commonalities to those strategies, the understanding of which can be enhanced by (re)analyzing them from the vantage of repossession; that is, to assess their capacity to assist Indigenous reconnection with preferred environments.

Too often, the Indigenous intent in such practices as direct action or everyday food gathering is misconstrued, with presumptions that they have either excessive or no political purpose. Hasty supposition about an Indigenous appetite to tear down colonial structures leads to disregard of the futuristic, self-educative, and community-affirming aspects of occupations or blockades. Likewise, if Indigenous communities are framed as separatist minorities, the social significance and extent of Indigenous alliance building is overlooked. The role of cultural products and practices in influencing the external environment will be ignored if they are analyzed solely as goods and services for satisfying intramural needs. Scholarly analysis underestimates the intent of *big* and *small* Indigenous agency, so here we emphasize the transformational characteristics of multiple forms of activism and at multiple scales.

Occupations, Blockades, and Resistance Camps: Indigenous Direct Action as Repossession

Even though our case studies in Chapters 3, 4, and 5 express such subtle actions as artistic defiance and children's gardening, there are functional relationships among those case studies and forms of Indigenous direct action. Two of the case studies are inseparable from high-profile occupations, while another involves cultural camps that serve multiple functions. For those reasons, it is important to discuss our case studies in the light of Indigenous leadership in occupations, blockades, camps, and boycotts. The weighty media and academic emphasis on such North American examples as the Dakota Access Pipeline (DAPL), Pacific Trails Pipeline, Keystone XL, and Trans Mountain Expansion (TMX) conceals similar disputes in Peru, Ecuador, Bolivia, Nigeria, and Indonesia, so there is need to focus on other places and practices (Canning 2018). While our own case studies are not about resistance to petro-hegemony, similar processes are involved, so we attempt to learn from occupations against controversial pipeline projects. In doing so, we differentiate aggressive tactics from the more subtle forms of activism that are also associated with landed occupation. It advantages the state if occupations can be framed as hostile events because that masks the historical violence upon which petrochemical infrastructure is predicated. Even though Indigenous communities are much more likely to be affected by pipeline spills than other groups, many NGOs and some governments have refused to view those problems through the lens of Indigenous sovereignty (Hurlbert and Datta 2022). Instead, those agencies often position all debate about petrochemical extraction and distribution on a continuum between national interest and environmental wellbeing, privileging either corporate or environmentalist agendas.

The potential ambiguity in the social significance of land occupation is deepened through the complexity, overdetermination, and overlap among analogous terms. For instance, North America's *#landback* movement also emphasizes the importance of "being present for" the land (Landback 2023). Yet, early appraisals of *#landback* over-applied Tuck and Yang's (2012) plea for decolonization to be more than a metaphor with an associated over-emphasis on the material act of land repatriation (Schneider 2022). At ground level, however, practitioners of *#landback* typically differentiate title transfer from a wider manifesto:

> But when we say "Land Back" we aren't asking for just the ground or a piece of paper that allows us to tear up and pollute the earth. We want the system that is land to be alive so that it can perpetuate itself, and perpetuate us as an extension of itself. That's what we want back: our place in keeping land alive and spiritually connected.
>
> (Longman et al. 2020: 2)

Discussions of *#landback* therefore mimic our earlier plea to frame repossession as an act of reconnecting with land and environs rather than as a venal act of land seizure. Indeed, the assumption that *#landback* is solely devoted to land repatriation masks the movement's spectacular but often unheralded investment in capacity building for ethical environmental leadership (Pieratos et al. 2021). Repatriation of land is necessary for but insufficient to repair land and environments in settler societies; so where healing is a principal goal of decolonization, *#landback* must also include "the full restoration of Indigenous land relationships" (Schneider 2022: 453). It is also significant that the *#landback* movement understands its role as upscaling grassroots action across space rather than replacing grassroots resistance—"to provide the unifying and organizing meta narrative … which will become many voices and movements within one" (Pieratos et al. 2021: 52). This attests to the need for multiscale Indigenous action, which is also the principal emphasis of this chapter. Despite the diversity of experiences and within the many terms that have been used, it nonetheless seems that *#landback* is one of many trends heralding a revival in land occupation as a political strategy of Indigenous peoples.

Initially, the resurgence of landed forms of direct action was unheeded in academic analysis, with the presumption that they are remnants of an Indigenous response to the age of exploration or bygone models of capitalist accumulation. Despite rural-urban migration and myriad new socio-economic structures, however, "Frontiers are Still Frontlines" and, with an expansion in resource extractivist industries in recent times, the social role of camps and blockades has expanded (Armstrong and Brown 2019). Yet, their reemergence represents an echoing of, rather than a new, history, with such well-known cases at Fort Mackay, the Oka Crisis, and more recent blockades of tar sands "fighting the same old battle" against land appropriation and environmental abuse (Audette-Longo 2018). Resilient, enduring occupations are needed because the structural power of settler society is similarly omnipresent and durable. Working the land is central to both Indigenous identities and to the liberal, Lockean notions of land rights in settler societies, so occupying land is essential both for protecting associated cultural relationships and defending it against homogenizing practices (Atleo and Boron 2022). Associated with such supplemental activities as artistic interventions, skills acquisition, and intergenerational learning, occupations and camps are a form of "generative refusal" that develops momentum for change. They are often incomprehensible for the monitoring apparatus of the nation state and, therefore, they are a primal source of public and governmental anxiety (Simpson 2017).

The important relationship between occupations and blockades, on the one hand, and petro-hegemony on the other is also critical for understanding the social significance of Indigenous direct action (Burrell, Grosse, and Mark 2022). Occupying the land in defiance of petrochemical facilities disrupts "critical infrastructure," sometimes providing Indigenous communities with an unprecedented form of leverage in modern politics (Bosworth and Chua 2022). We note that the state's heavy-handed reactions to Indigenous protest at Mauna Kea (Chapter 3) and Ihumātao (Chapter 4) were also influenced by a perceived need to privilege critical infrastructure for telecommunications, exploration, and housing development. Hence, Indigenous direct action extends beyond mere resistance and is a deliberate, political response to state facilitation of corporate capitalism. Occupations often present alternative visions for human existence which contradict capitalist expansion and climate-wrecking orthodoxy (Estes 2019).

Occupations, boycotts, and camps are also acts of countersovereignty which interweave the sacred with the political (Braun 2020; Coulthard 2014). The "Wetsuwet'en [sic] struggle against the Coastal GasLink project" in British Columbia is not "simply a protest. It is a conflict of law"—or, at least, a conflict between Indigenous values of respect for genealogical orders and neo/colonial legal norms that support ongoing petrochemical extraction (McCreary 2020: 126). But the goals of direct action are not restricted to transforming colonial structures; rather, they also realize the same relational ontologies of care that we introduced in earlier chapters. Importantly, while finding fora or venues for implementing those relationships is generally difficult for Indigenous communities, associated philosophies and practices thrive in culture camps or blockades (Temper 2019). The lasting impact of the Witsuwit'en "Gateway Camp" was its living proof of the need to and methods for "breaking down the dualism between humans and nature" (*ibid.*: 105) and its "assertion of responsibility through active presence" (*ibid.*: 108).

The way occupations disrupt "critical infrastructure" and "national interest" unsettles the assumed "universally beneficial … objectively good outcomes" of pipelines or facilities within extractive economies (Proulx and Crane 2020: 52). They discredit the assumed sovereignty of settler states because they center attention to the colonial violence upon which today's resource extraction is predicated. That explains the recourse of such states to criminalization of land protectors, and why white governments attempt to obscure their racialized militancy as non-racialized policies for public security (Bosworth and Chua 2022; Castillo Jara and Bruns 2022). Occupations are thereby associated with precarity, violence, and harm. Globally, over 200 Indigenous environmental activists have been reported murdered during each of the past four years, but that is an underestimation because post/ colonial nation-states have no incentive to maintain official records (Global Witness 2022). In one year, 240 mostly Indigenous activists were arrested at Burnaby's blockades of the TMX. As Simpson and Le Billion (2021) conclude, those acts of rough justice were not *law-enforcing* techniques but rather *law-establishing* procedures designed to facilitate petrochemical hegemony and disrupt Indigenous laws, lore, and jurisdiction. Land-based protests reveal the unfair origins and violent foundations of settler societies, so they are subject to brutal retribution. Yet, occupations are also an unmanageable inconvenience for settler nations because they exceed the state's capacity to normalize current economic practices as fair or to obscure their origin in colonial legacies (Gergan and McCreary 2022).

Arguably, however, settler states created the conditions for protest through "state-corporate-crime," suspending ordinary forms of public participation to secure pipeline developments (Bradshaw 2015). The failure of settler states to resolve land claims before corporates initiate pipeline projects intensifies conflict between extractivist industry and Indigenous communities, so it is disingenuous to frame those communities as the source of conflict (Canning 2018). With so many possibilities for land claims settlement blocked, Indigenous leaders adopt such informal approaches to activism as blockades or boycotts to protect their interests. Their relative success in such initiatives suggests that those informal modes of governance may be crucial in the grander transitions required to properly resolve Indigenous environment claims into the future (Gobby et al. 2022).

Academic and media sensationalizing of camps and occupations as hostile, quasi-criminal activity leads to disregard of such other roles as territorial monitoring, learning, and renewal (Audette-Longo 2018; Grote and Johnson 2021). Kluttz and colleagues (2021) reveal the scope of intergenerational learning and transcultural dialogue that emerged at the Oceti Sakowin camp near Standing Rock. For them, the informal learning of Indigenous histories and ways of relating to the environment may have a greater long-term benefit than the direct impact of the physical presence. Earlier Geographical understandings of Indigenous blockades did focus on their promotion of dialogue (Blomley 1996), but that important role has also been obscured in recent scholarship. As Armstrong and Brown (2019) contend, direct actions, culture camps, and traditional living are accessible forms of contestation that counteract the expense and capacity dilemmas of battling formal state or corporate structures. Being on the land is an important means of rehabilitating Indigenous ontologies of care for people and environment (Pasternak 2017; Spiegel 2021). Occupations are grand and spectacular, but they have other characteristics. The significance of camps associated with activism against petro-hegemony extends to cultural revitalization and wellbeing initiatives—or, "to maintain hope and express ideas for a better world, to practice culture … and enliven the land in respectful and fun ways" (Armstrong and Brown 2019: 23).

Vernacular Sovereignty in the Everyday

The non-aggressive elements of occupations have been underestimated. That may also reveal a more profound disregard for Indigenous strategies of reclamation that are unmistakably subtle, peaceable and everyday:

> While large-scale actions such as rallies, protests and blockades are frequently acknowledged as sites of resistance, the daily actions undertaken by individual Indigenous people, families and communities often go unacknowledged but are no less vital to decolonial processes.
>
> (Hunt and Holmes 2015: 158)

Subtle Indigenous activism may be comparatively successful at revealing the contradictions in, and foundational violence of, colonial structures, practices, and norms. Colonization is neither inevitable nor implacably robust—it is "unfinished" and therefore vulnerable to resilient cultural practices that reveal its incompleteness (Proulx and Crane 2020). To counter the logic of settler societies, *existing* and *persisting* is just as important and effective as *resisting* for Indigenous peoples (Kauanui 2016). Yet, that should not imply strategies of mere survival and, affirming our emphasis on everyday practices, many Indigenous academics have recently focused attention to *survivance*—neither survival nor resistance in isolation but the intersection of both (King, Gubele, and Anderson 2015). We argue that despite its association with aggressive action to reclaim material objects, Indigenous repossession must also stress the intersections among practices of being (on the land) and practices of taking (back the land). It represents a continuum of activities from subtle resilience to belligerent repatriation. Accordingly, we do not suggest that Indigenous communities abandon direction action in favor of everyday practices. As Coulthard (2014) has concluded, direct action retains its importance because without the peril of large-scale protest settler states will compromise only so far as reconciliation politics and collaborative governance (refer, also, to Keisch and Scott 2023). While that argument is important, however, we suggest that diversified Indigenous responses to colonialism that include everyday resistance are needed because it is also too easy for the nation state to dismiss Indigenous action if it is exclusively confrontational and large-scale.

Too often, though, Indigenous activism has attracted attention solely for its grand character—courtroom dramas, highly visible protests, and nation-to-nation dialogue. Yet, it is just as important to ask "what does decolonization look and feel like, what does it entail in our daily actions … " (Hunt and Holmes 2015: 155). For most Indigenous persons, neo/colonialism does not happen in a courtroom nor before the news media, so decolonization must also be a lived experience that is based on daily, personal, and practical activities. It flourishes in intimate spaces; it is often scaled to the level of family, households, and neighborhoods rather than at the level of national polities. Everyday activities revitalize kinship in all its meanings, which may be the most important carrier of Indigenous influence into the future (Daigle 2019). Nonetheless, there are manifold threats to those activities and to their influence on social life, with a significant concern that they may be captured within reconciliation politics or "rights" discourse (Paquette 2020; Willis 2021). For instance, the *UN Declaration on the Rights of Indigenous Peoples* may seem like a landmark recognition of Indigenous interests, but it offers little more than "a cultural right to be Indigenous" (Johnson 2021; c.f. Nagy 2022). Indigenous everyday practices are reauthorized through such measures, but they are concurrently separated from political rights to act or to self-determine. Prior informed consent, property-based and intellectual protections for cultural production and practices are mere concessions that threaten to delimit the socially transformative momentum in everyday Indigenous resurgence.

Formalized rights-making has become a post-political distraction for many Indigenous communities, with claims settlements seemingly miring them in a politics of recognition (Borrows 2017; Coulthard 2014), diverting attention from Indigenous demands for meaningful autonomy outside the state's influence (Betasamosake Simpson 2016). Just as the human rights literature is increasingly doubtful that constitutional reform can achieve human fulfillment (Armaline, Glasberg, and Purkayastha 2017), the legalism and formality of treaty or land claims processes threatens to override everyday practices. Nonetheless, there are limits to the capacity of rights-making as reconciliation to circumscribe Indigenous agency. Any attempt to delimit Indigenous interests in rights discourse may perversely cause Indigenous everyday activism to flourish (Coombes 2018a). Precisely because the politics of containment that attempts to relegate Indigenous peoples and their practices to the cultural sphere have failed before, there is hope for resurgence through land-based practices. For instance, the state's ineptitude to deal with wicked environmental problems heralds an era of post-statist politics in which vernacular governance will prosper (Ince and Barrera de la Torre 2016; Lightfoot 2021). Environmental disorder discredits state centrism while also validating more everyday approaches to resource management and sovereignty. Notably, *de facto* rights in place may be better suited to managing planetary crises than are *de jure* entitlements, creating space for Indigenous alternatives or traditional modes of environmental care (Kröger and Lalander 2016). Rather than relying on the historical justice and conciliatory capacities of the courtroom, parliament, or claims tribunals, increasingly the space for Indigenous peoples to make real gains is outside the formal state apparatus and within the everyday.

It is tempting, therefore, to assume that the forms of transitional justice that may inspire fair dealing within the future of settler societies will be based on legal experimentation with new hybrids and social compromises. Yet, Park (2020) maintains that a formula for transitional justice is more likely to be derived from Indigenous micro-politics that survive colonial violence through Indigenous refusal and tenacity. Refusal to compromise or accept reconciliation, along with refusal to abandon vernacular traditions, may be the most progressive options for Indigenizing the future. Therefore, the restoration of everyday lifeways is one key to Indigenous resurgence and a better future for all because they combine habits, practices, and relational philosophies within mutually reproducing forms of collective action (Corntassel and Hardbarger 2019). The rehabilitation of such lifeways provides for "land-centered literacies" which are needed for adapting to change, mobilizing for action, and advancing Indigenous causes (Goodyear-Ka'opua 2013, 2018):

Examined in this light, something as seemingly benign as pulling invasive plant species from Indigenous homelands deemed "public parks" becomes a significant action towards regenerating Indigenous *food systems* ... and land-based relationships. It is these often unseen or unacknowledged everyday actions, such as regenerating Indigenous plants and food systems, that represent important sites for renewing relationships with community, family and homelands.

(Corntassel and Hardbarger 2019: 89)

Thriving Indigenous lifeways teach and affirm the practices that are fundamental for Indigenous communities to *perpetuate* and, in turn, that generate a platform for sustainable self-determination (*ibid.*). Practicing everyday lifeways is an act of recommitment that renews personal and collective relationships with territory, heritage, and nature (Corntassel 2012).

Renewal of everyday practices is also associated with multiple indirect benefits. Everyday lifeways are dynamic, diverse, and spontaneous and, from the external gaze of colonial systems, seemingly disorganized. Apparent chaos in Indigenous resource use is a threat to the colonial affinity for orderly, predictable conduct, so the mundane, quotidian practices of Indigenous communities and families materialize as *The Art of Not Being Governed* (Scott 2009). Everyday customs are more immune to the calculating and disciplining functions of settler societies and, therefore, are a principal means by which Indigenous peoples have evaded colonial erasure. Indigenous food sovereignty openly displays the indirect benefits of everyday praxis, motivating and shaping Indigenous mobilization through informal provisioning and care systems (Daigle 2019). Because Indigenous food provisioning systems demonstrate survivance, they also complicate the settler state's understanding of its social license and sovereign power. For many Indigenous cultures, food is not merely a commodity, so the care and reciprocity involved in everyday food provision subverts capitalist valuation and draws attention to the benefits of systems based on gift exchange. In Aotearoa, Māori defiance toward the criminalization of food and fiber gathering practices has unsettled the preservationist and aesthetic principles upon which its parks and reserves were founded (Coombes 2018a). It is often too embarrassing for the state to police rigorously as poaching the nominally illegal harvesting regimes of Māori communities, leading to involuntary compromises that undermine broader systems of neo/colonial authority. Again, it is the *persistence* of those regimes that most troubles the settler state, thereby yielding more transformative power than is at first obvious.

Alliance-Making and Collaboration with Others

Because Indigenous environmental activism is often placed-based, there is an associated assumption that it is secessionist and only place-based, with local clans presumed to operate in absolute independence. In our case studies, however, pan-tribal and multiethnic allies participated in important ways. Indeed, it could be argued that any success for Indigenous protests against the TMT (Thirty Meter Telescope on Mauna a Wākea; Chapter 3) and against the spread of medium density housing over cultural heritage sites at Ihumātao (Chapter 4) was dependent on internationalization of and alliance building for the respective causes. Allyship has long been important for Indigenous repossession, particularly because of the increasing need for Indigenous communities or nations to "jump scales" to secure their interests (Diver et al. 2022). The wicked environmental problems and associated post-sovereign governance mentioned earlier, along with the incompetence of some nation states, have required chief-to-chief, pan-Arctic, or cross-Pacific initiatives (Bennett 2020). The depletion, size, or vast distances associated with land returned under customary title in such countries as Australia complicates its subsequent management. In turn, that has required complex interactions with supportive and combative stakeholders who operate at multiple levels and may enjoy greater resourcing (Hunt et al. 2021). Indigenous communities need to counter those dilemmas with cross-spatial networks of their own.

Although transcalar alliances are increasingly important for, they are not new to, Indigenous politics. Bypassing colonial states, Indigenous leaders were early attendees at the *League* and *United Nations*, and they have been prominent in global forums over the last decade (Lightfoot 2016; Lightfoot 2021). Events leading up to and multiparty allegiances at Bolivia's *World Conference on Climate Change* also prove the extent and influence of Indigenous transnationalism, with many countries adopting rights of nature legislation in the years after attendance by Indigenous representatives (Coombes 2021; De La Cadena 2010). Because non-Indigenous academics assumed that Indigenous interests and agency are restricted to the local, the global reach of Indigenous activism has been underestimated, but it is indeed significant.

The "unprecedented levels of solidarity" at Standing Rock confirm the genuine strength of bonds created in this era of Indigenous alliance-making (Canning 2018: 15). However, the occupation there was also riven with gendered, eco-centered, and other divisions (Christiansen 2021). For many of the tribes involved, water protection had been the domain of women, but environmentalist partners often disregarded those traditions in their eagerness to support activism led belatedly by Indigenous men. Even where transcultural partnerships are successful, they are sometimes based on convenience and may, therefore, be temporary. We conclude that there are place- and time-specific drivers of these strategic partnerships, and that failure to understand those drivers may reproduce a presumed solidarity.

Yet, there should be space retained for cross-cultural affiliation or companionship within the concept of Indigenous environmental repossession. First, "Indigenous conceptions of responsibility and autonomy provide lessons about how to ground activism in place-based politics," and organizations with civic ambitions that support Indigenous agendas require that grounding to empower their community projects (Coombes, Johnson, and Howitt 2013). Second, if colonization is about the attempted erasure of Indigenous peoples, then decolonization needs to be founded on interpersonal allyship that armors Indigenous persons from sustained attack (Hunt and Holmes 2015). A corollary to that understanding is that non-Indigenous partners must recognize their role as supporters of Indigenous activism, and not presume a right to lead, but that requires more than mere recognition of researcher positionality (Hemsworth et al. 2022). Notwithstanding that concern, friendship, intimacy, and cordiality among allied Indigenous and non-Indigenous partners is an underappreciated best practice for decolonial initiatives (Bawaka Country et al. 2022; De Leeuw, Cameron, and Greenwood 2012).

In what follows, though, we discuss the injustices that may emerge when allyship is artificially constructed. Concerns about collaborative research with Indigenous peoples reveal a need to decolonize solidarity itself, to unsettle its paternalistic assumptions of necessary assistance across cultures and to reveal its actual rather than intended beneficiaries (Kluttz, Walker, and Walter 2020). That there is a dark side to allyship suggests that there may be times or issues for which it is better for Indigenous leaders to act alone, meaning that Indigenous/non-Indigenous alliances may be subject to termination or disappointment. Allyship is unlikely to provide comfort for its non-Indigenous collaborators, especially for those who fail to acknowledge their privilege (Kluttz, Walker, and Walter 2021).

It is important that the limits to and complications of partnerships are clearly understood, and this is particularly the case in respect of transcultural research collaborations. Such partnerships often reflect more the needs of outsiders, and they may be based on "assumed affinities" (Barker and Pickerill 2012). In other instances, anxieties about uncertain environmental futures prompt non-Indigenous researchers to collaborate with Indigenous communities who may hold important knowledge because of past experience with environmental disruption (Latulippe and Klenk 2020). Although that can at times provide a genuine platform for rapprochement, it may have no benefit for Indigenous knowledge holders or those with developmental aspirations (Diver et al. 2022). At its worst, debasing—although often benevolent—understandings of an Indigenous need for assistance motivates collaborative research partnerships (Chapman and Schott 2020; Krusz et al. 2020). The authors of this book have regularly been asked to comment on conference sessions or special journal issues about CBPR (community-based participatory research). In many of those instances, speakers or authors were singularly non-Indigenous, the dominant methods were insensitive (e.g., telephone interviews), and Indigenous voice was barely audible. Our role was restricted to a demeaning opportunity to "provide an Indigenous perspective" but, by commenting at all, we may have been complicit in providing social license for fallaciously collaborative approaches.

Non-Indigenous researchers are slowly becoming attuned to the challenges in working with Indigenous communities, but that generates new problems. Remorseful, non-Indigenous introspection about mandates to work with Indigenous communities dominates academic discussion of research collaborations so—by association— matters of importance to Indigenous scholars are not being published. The necessary differences in research involving *whānau* (family) and *kaumātua* (Elders) are absent from conventional academic discourse, but they are a significant source of anxiety for Māori scholars (Keelan et al. 2022). Brad evaded research with his wider whānau for the first twenty years of his academic career because of internecine disputes about whether to log forests on whānau land (Coombes 2018b). Later, he applied participatory drama with school-aged children to assist competing parties to envision new forest management practices, resulting in a contested, though majority, decision to cease logging. Many commended the approach, and some noted in a *hapori* (community) newsletter that it correlated with their expectations for *Kaupapa Māori Research* (KMR, or by Māori for Māori research that addresses "Māori purposes"). Notwithstanding that support, Brad's own uncles resized excerpts from the newsletter, plastering billboards in highly visible places with the heading, "**Don't Believe Kaupapa Māori Research.**" *Kupapa* was a name given to traitors who fought on the side of colonial forces during the New Zealand Wars, and it is the deepest insult that one Māori can serve to another. Along with the scarcity of commentaries about how to incorporate family commitments, environmental obligations, and community responsibilities into research, there is seemingly no academic interest in how Indigenous scholars navigate such difficult terrain. There is similar indifference toward situations where Indigenous academics must act as cultural intermediaries between their communities and non-Indigenous colleagues, learning to wear two or more ill-fitting hats. Priorities in relevant literature are misplaced because they often reflect the apprehension of white majority researchers.

KMR is a descendant of Freirian PAR (participatory action research), which has strongly influenced Indigenous research precepts the world over (Ginn et al. 2022). Yet, because of white anxiety about research involving Indigenous communities, two epistemological voids have emerged. First, the evolution in research—previously *on* but increasingly *with* or *for* Indigenous peoples—is stillborn unless there is also movement toward more research by Indigenous representatives (McGregor 2018a). Unfortunately, Indigenous leadership in research encounters passive-aggressive defiance or ethnocentric habits that inhibit meaningful partnerships. It is unrealistic to expect infrequent encounters that are labeled collaborations to generate lasting relationships. Rather, researchers can only expect to derive mutually supportive partnerships from frequent "doings" together—micro-practices and projects that include but are not limited to research and which establish affective bonds to sustain multifaceted relationships (Barker and Pickerill 2020). That important conclusion sustains the core argument of the second section of this chapter, revealing that collaborative research itself must be a normal, *everyday* practice. The value of everyday, less formal research will become apparent in Chapters 3, 4, and 5, but those chapters will also highlight the benefits of research collaborations that are among kin, friends, comrades, and aligned clans.

Performative Action: Cultural Production and Indigenous Activism

The second research void associated with current apprehension about the ethics of collaborative research is that most discussion about PAR has focused on **P**[articipation], with comparatively little concern for **A**[ction] (Coombes 2018b). As an authoring troupe, we have suggested before that the active and performative dimensions of certain approaches to research are <u>at least</u> as important for representing Indigenous interests as is collaboration (Richmond, Coombes, and Pualani Louis 2022). Even where dialogue and the capacity to speak and interweave narratives is a key goal in PAR, that is more often facilitated through action research rather than through mere discussion (Bryan and Viteri 2022). Indigenous communities involved in "bucket brigade" monitoring of the petrochemical industry are more likely to trust, act upon, and implement their findings because their own actions generate the air quality samples (Wiebe 2016). In genuine PAR, it is the opportunity to do and to learn from the doing that is fundamental, but too often community-based research treats Indigenous participants as mere knowledge sources, engaging them solely in verbalized knowledge transfer (Chapman and Schott 2020; Latulippe and Klenk 2020).

The hands-on, generative practices associated with such performative approaches as community-based monitoring, participatory video, arts-science encounters, and dance-based communication are enlivening, thought-provoking, and worthwhile for Indigenous participants (Rao, Narain, and Sabir 2022). Alternatively, **p**articipation ***without*** **a**ction echoes the sterile, passive extraction of knowledge in colonial science, providing no opportunity for Indigenous participants to learn for themselves. Action-centered approaches to research enable participants to communicate matters of importance for their communities that are more concerned with *affect* than with the *effect* of change, and they enable Indigenous peoples to use their creative talents to engage all the senses (Dowling, Lloyd, and Suchet-Pearson 2018). Research with and ***by*** Indigenous peoples "should value freedom of self-expression, creativity and artfulness as means to proclaim, access or experience Indigenous values" (Richmond, Coombes, and Pualani Louis 2022: 91). That is why performative activism is often matched with performative research in our case study chapters, with research conforming to artistic praxis (refer, for example, to the overlap between art and activism in Chapter 3 and to the interaction between Māori guerilla gardening and Māori art competitions in Chapter 4).

The reconfiguration of research as (collaborative) performance may have wider benefits. Whether they are collaborative or not, the best forms of research for Indigenous application are embodied and embedded. Informal but frequent interactions provide confidence for allied partners to share on an emotive and affective level, potentially evading misrepresentation (Barker and Pickerill 2020; Hemsworth et al. 2022). Renee (in Richmond, Coombes, and Pualani Louis 2022) contends that conventional research will only overcome its anthropocentric tendencies through greater adoption of posthuman ontologies. As that runs counter to a long history of objectivist and rationalizing approaches to research, however, it may only happen through transcultural research partnerships with Indigenous leadership. Where the "Indigenous demand for leadership within research … is realized a more creative, spontaneous and intersubjective approach to research methods will follow" (Richmond, Coombes, and Pualani Louis 2022: 894). An expanding range of planetary threats which affect Indigenous and non-Indigenous participants alike require that degree of intersubjectivity but that, in turn, requires Indigenous leadership.

Those lessons from performative research also suggest a role for Indigenous cultural production in environmental repossession. In line with earlier arguments of this chapter, we reject any conjecture that (Indigenous) art serves only aesthetic and internal group needs and is, therefore, apolitical. Because they represent diverse and sometimes superior forms of expression, artistic pursuits, cultural production, performance arts, and even such cultural routines as *pow wow* (gatherings) or *hui* (meetings) are a medium for both group continuity and persuasive resistance. "Performance is a 'doing'—an action or set of activities—that proposes something new and then works to create that new reality" (Snider 2021: 2). Within the social sciences, and with a focus on arts-science collaborations, there is renewed interest in the role of art as a generative practice that provides affective connections and transformative motivations (Clark et al. 2020). For instance, the need to surpass mere "public understanding of science" has generated new possibilities for human engagement and action through artistic creativity (Marizzi and Bartar 2021). Notably, Indigenous artists are adept at blending public contemplation of ecosystem science with communication of Indigenous interests and evidence for the damage caused by neo/colonial practices (Blackmore 2022). This emotive, provocative, and galvanizing role is also witnessed in other forms of cultural production and is central to Hawaiian art exhibits (Chapter 3) and Māori gardening (Chapter 4).

Artistic representation informs what Chazan and Baldwin (2021) refer to as "institutional memory work," and that correlates with Indigenous demands to place moments of decision-making in their appropriate temporal context. Indigenous art is deeply connected with intergenerational transmission of important cultural knowledge and goals. It engenders both collective remembrance, thereby mobilizing group agency, and provides confidence to the artist, yielding robust modes of individual agency for fighting back against colonial structures (Guntarik and Harwood 2022). Visible connectedness through cultural production provides validity for Indigenous groups whom society otherwise declares inauthentic. For instance, Indigenous Hip Hop from Chicago is a unique outlet for combatting discourses of urban decline and associated abandonment of its Indigenous casualties:

> In a settler state designed for the perpetual dispossession of Indigenous people, it is difficult to make Indigenous people and their particular problems visible. This is doubly hard for urban Indigenous people when, in general, their life in the city appears contrary to their supposed placement on a reserve/ation. However, Indigenous Hip Hop, as a culture, with its creative energy and ingenuity, has the potential and possibility to alter that discourse.
>
> (Mays 2019: 475)

Cultural production can raise the profile of Indigenous causes in ways that bypass the colonial disciplining techniques considered in the first section of this chapter. Moreover, out of all the Indigenous approaches to repossession, cultural production is perhaps most likely to promote healing because it relies on self-reflection rather than acts that might be perceived as cross-cultural retribution. Malika Ndlovu (2020: 17), a Xhosan poet, maintains that "Listening is a foundational aspect of all healing practices" and that "listening is essential for a range of decolonial ... methodologies." Auditory or visual stimulus is important for delivering a message across cultures, and sometimes the material properties of cultural production themselves mimic the complexity of Indigenous political arguments. It has become commonplace to speak of Indigenous social and biocultural relations as "entangled," so there is no better analog for promulgating such relations than (counter)weaving (Hamilton Faris 2022).

Weaving has become a premier mode of communicating the need for "intercultural climate justice" across Indigenous peoples of Oceania (Hamilton Faris 2022: 130). Collectively, the climate interventions of Pacific artists constitute an "active and interactive endeavor to enhance awareness, modify perceptions, and effect meaningful change in people's climate responsiveness" (Mangioni 2021: 56). Of equal importance, Indigenous art against climate change draws attention to the technocentrism and coloniality of climate mitigation narratives, while also being "generative in its capacity to imagine and act otherwise" (Wander 2021: 156). Pacific climate stewardship confronts the challenge that its Indigenous champions are often invisible within the settler societies to which they have migrated (Mangioni 2021). White fatalism about climate change leads to apathy and inaction, so confident and imaginative approaches to Indigenous cultural production are a rare possibility for promoting trans-Oceanic solutions to whole nations. For Tongan-Australian performance artist Latai Taumoepeau, her interventionist art is as much about "imagining potential futures" as it is about mourning present conditions or "highlighting histories of resource extractivism" (Mangioni 2021: 35). Hence, a careful "weaving" of futurism and learning from the past has been deployed in the interventions of Indigenous artists, and that is a more balanced position from which to address climate change.

Art is received dynamically, leading to multiple interpretive positions. To increase further the range of interpretive possibilities, some Indigenous artists from Canada use walking in the performance of their art, and that is "fundamentally pedagogical because it enables interactions with the place-world that inform reflections and intentions" (Feinberg 2021: 165). The activist intent of the art is foregrounded, with the additional performativity increasing the possibility that decolonial messages will be received. Likewise, walking while viewing together allows for the sharing of stories and, therefore, generates transcultural solidarity through points of connection and critical reflection. Useful transdisciplinarity of that nature is evoked in multiple ways. Indigenous artists experiment with forms of "autobricolage—mixing art, activism and ethnography … as a decolonising strategy to centre Indigenous ontology" (Guntarik and Harwood 2022: 257). Again, that awakens the imagination to new ways of reading and countering colonial practices, elevating the probability that new thoughts will produce new actions at a societal level.

Unfortunately, however, conventional approaches to exhibiting Indigenous art are framed through a colonial lens. When walking into a museum, there are often rote narratives of people and timeframes, displayed and created by people looking in from the outside. Whoever tells the story has the power to shape the perspective of the observer. Later, we assess what happens when Indigenous people tell their own stories, framing their lifeways and worldviews in ways that affect interaction with sacred and historical landscapes.

The *Kūkulu: Pillars of Mauna a Wākea* traveling art exhibit, which features in Chapter 3, turns the colonial tide, with a story told with, for, and by Kānaka and spearheaded by Aunty Pua Case. She dedicated the exhibit to the "Protect Mauna Kea Movement" with the intention to bring the Mauna to the masses because she believes that repossession of Mauna Kea requires establishing or strengthening a personal connection to the mountain. Unlike museums that merely provide display spaces for "dead and gone" histories told through the lens of an outsider (Kreps 2015), Kūkulu is more than an exhibit—it is a living invitation to experience the sacredness of Mauna a Wākea through the lens of Kiaʻi (guardians). Stories of resistance line the walls as art, photographs, and objects honored and remembered by mountain protectors. Each serves as a vehicle for autonomous storytelling woven into the fabric of collective lived memories of resistance. Kūkulu transforms exhibit spaces to accommodate honoring, paying tribute, cultural safety, and human activation, along with calls to action, pride, and learning, where experiences erased and ignored by the US colonial state live, thrive, and are welcomed and centered.

Through careful thought and consideration, the exhibit layout reflected, portrayed, and emanated the spirit of the Mauna. Exhibit rooms became landscapes of time and place, in which the Kūkulu Research Team placed the artwork, images, and objects provided by the community. Foundational pieces were chosen by Aunty Pua and community members. Grassroots networking channels were used to invite and grow a community of contributors through social media outlets, flyers posted at central gathering spaces, phone calls, and face-to-face talk story. In this way, the exhibit was not merely constructed with an object-based epistemology, as we often see in westernized museums. Instead, Kūkulu represented a multidimensional, alive, and culture-based epistemology.

Kūkulu is an example of Indigenous museology in its most alive form (Kreps 2015; 2008). The curator's attention to protocol, local history, culture, spirituality, politics, and the environmental significance of Kānaka demonstrate their connection to a land base they recognize as a genealogical ancestor—Mauna a Wākea. Kūkulu also serves as a record of events, created and curated by those who participated in them, thereby making them responsible for their own image. Kūkulu centers the experiences of the community, the Mauna Kea ʻOhana (family), and tells their stories, but also creates an exhibit space for those outside of the movement to learn what the Mauna Kea ʻOhana wants to share and hopefully becomes a framework to take back to their communities.

Chapter 3

KŪKULU: PILLARS OF MAUNA KEA EXHIBIT

... e welina mai nei ... welcome ...

Hawaiʻi—one of the most remote locations on the planet. Surrounded by the Pacific Ocean, the Hawaiʻi archipelago is over 3,600 kilometers (over 2,200 miles) from the nearest landmass, the tip of the Alaska Peninsula. Long before humans set foot on these islands, they were formed by natural processes specific to their unique geography. Born of *Papahānaumoku* (divine natural entity considered to be earth mother who births islands and a manifestation of Haumea), each island emerged several million years ago from the depths and darkness beneath the ocean floor and reached up into the open and bright expanse of the atmosphere. Here the winds, rains, and clouds shaped each island, creating unique ecological spaces that support diverse biological beings. Each island became host to an array of flora and fauna for over a millennia. Slowly the islands began vibrating with life.

With great effort, human habitation and occupation occurred comparatively recently in just the last few millennia. Talented ocean people found and settled on each island's nearshore, lowlands, and nearby valleys. Among those who arrived on these islands were my ancestors. When those Pacific Islanders first stepped foot on the islands, they found fertile lands capable of supporting their island lifeways. Bigger and more expansive in almost every way than most islands in the Pacific, the human population grew, and with it, so did the need to form social structures of leadership.

Generations passed and eventually, an enigmatic woman and man, Papa and Wākea, rose to legendary status. Their life experiences continue to be celebrated in stories, songs, and dance. Their contribution to social reformation was ecologically infused into the landscape. The value of their contributions is recognized as the very apogee, the highest point of the islands, Mauna a Wākea.

Shortened to Mauna Kea, and sometimes referred to as "the Mauna," human perception of its nobility has taken many forms. As one ascends its peak, the vegetation becomes sparse, the air thins, and excessive movement can make one nauseated. These limiting physical conditions are only part of why the summit is considered unsuitable for long-term human habitation by Kānaka. As a result, only a tiny subset of the population was trained and prepared to access the highest elevations, considered the *Wao Akua* (realm of divine entities and energetics). Those few trained to be in the Wao Akua built *ahu* (altars) to honor the Akua, performed rites to initiate acolytes, and organized ceremonies of recognition and gratitude. Another important reason for limiting human activity in the Wao Akua is the recognition of its ecological role as the core energizing force of the island ecoverse. It is the island's generator of life, the guarantor of generational existence. Its revered status is noted in several documented accounts (Hitt 2019).

The arrival of colonial expansionists decimated Kānaka populations and disrupted their lifeways. All too quickly, less than two centuries, the turmoil of colonial contact ultimately led to the illegal overthrow of the Hawaiian Kingdom and the illegal annexation of the current settler colony known as the State of Hawai'i into the United States of America. Today, Hawai'i continues to be portrayed as an exotic island paradise, a strategically important location for US national security, and one of the most ecologically diverse places on the planet. Every generation has placed a new lens with which to see these islands.

I remember learning about the era when the slogan "Hawai'i is a melting pot" came into being. This lie began as a theory in the 1920s by Romanzo Adams, a social scientist and founder of the sociology department at the University of Hawai'i. It was perpetuated by the State of Hawai'i Tourism Authority. It promotes Hawai'i as the ideal "tropical vacation destination infused with an always welcoming Hawaiian culture … encouraging the public in and outside of Hawai'i to downplay the ways that Native Hawaiians continue to face both individual and structural forms of racism and colonialism in their own home" (Arvin 2019). The State of Hawai'i used this perception of Hawai'i as racially harmonious to boost tourism and draw in potentially lucrative forms of development like astronomy.

As an Indigenous geographer, I am naturally drawn to land, life, and community origin stories. As an Indigenous cartographer, I embrace performances as the primary form of communicating spatial knowledge and engaging with spatial phenomena. As a Kanaka, I live every moment in gratitude for those who came before me and nourish my connection with the Akua as often as possible. As the narrator of this chapter and the academic advocate for this project, I carry the honored responsibility of unfolding the brilliance of the team who curated the focus of this chapter, the *Kūkulu: Pillars of Mauna Kea* traveling art exhibit.

Aunty Pua Case (henceforth, Aunty Pua) conscientiously curated Kūkulu as a response to the questions posed by the research team. Her most important goal was to "bring the Mauna to the masses." Aunty Pua was born and raised on the Island of Hawai'i. She is a Kumu Hula and an educator of Kānaka lifeways, culture, and traditions. She holds multiple degrees and was a public-school teacher for more than thirty years. However, today, she and her family work to protect their ancestral spaces from destruction and desecration.

This chapter also chronicles the courage, challenges, and strategies used by Kānaka who protect the summit of Mauna Kea from the construction of the proposed Extremely Large Telescope (ELT), the Thirty Meter Telescope (TMT). They object to the environmental, cultural, and spiritual impacts of a massive eighteen-story, five-acre telescope complex on sacred land. To be sure, this is only the latest protest in a decades-long history of Kānaka who demonstrate to ensure there is a sacred landscape left intact for future generations to continue practicing ancestral alignments on familiar ground.

Before I outline what is to come in this chapter, I feel compelled to share that this project expanded and transformed my understanding of Kānaka cartographic engagements. I now see them as a living, daily dance of our relational responsibilities to our ancestral alignments. It should come as no surprise that this chapter will be a blending of voices within a recurring vernacular of performing Indigenous cartographic acts of repossession. We begin with a *ka'i* (a chant during which dancers enter onstage before their hula performance) composed by Aunty Pua prior to the creation of the exhibit. She prefaces the chant with a personal sharing that immediately situates you on Mauna Kea in an early morning hour when line upon line of *Kia'i Mauna* (Mountain Protectors; henceforth abbreviated to *Kia'i*) stood in formation to protect the Mauna from further desecration.

Ka'i Kūkulu: He aha la he kūkulu

On June 24, 2015, we stood gathered before dawn on the mountain. In the darkness, we heard a voice say, "I will lead Line 1," and another, "I will lead Line 2." Yes, we were readying for how we would stand to protect our Mauna that morning. Then the voice of a female called out, "I will lead Line 3, but that line will be only *wāhine*, only for women," and the tone of her voice and the words that she stated brought tears to my eyes. The lines that day formed clear up to the top of the Mauna. And we stood, protected by our mountain, surrounded by rock altars, strong as the boulders, shoulder to shoulder as people, as pillars. That early morning and the way we stood that day inspired the words and the motions of this ka'i. We were pillars that day, and pillars we are still!

—Pua Case, Mauna Kea 'Ohana

Ka'i Kūkulu: He aha la he kūkulu?

He aha lā he kūkulu?
He mauna!
He aha lā he kūkulu?
He ahu!
He aha lā he kūkulu?
He pōhaku!
He aha lā he kūkulu?
He Kānaka! (×3)

What is a pillar?
A mountain!
What is a pillar?
An altar!
What is a pillar?
A rock!
What is a pillar?
A person! (×3)

Hānau Ka Mauna, the Mountain Is Born

Mauna Kea is a *piko* for *Kānaka*. The word *piko* can be broadly explained as "navel; navel string; umbilical cord; blood relative; genitals; center; summit or top of a hill or mountain; crest; the crown of the head; place where a stem is attached to the leaf, as of taro" (Pukui and Elbert 1986: 328). As the *piko*, the Mauna is also the center, the navel, the umbilical cord, and a blood relative. Peralto (2014: 234) explains that there is a direct genealogical connection between Kānaka and Mauna Kea:

> The mountain-child of Wākea. Born of the union between Papahānaumoku and Wākea, Mauna a Wākea is the Elder sibling of Hāloa, the *ali'i* (chief, chiefess, officer, ruler, monarch). As such, both the Mauna and Kānaka Maoli are instilled, at birth, with particular

kuleana (right, privilege, concern, responsibility) to each other. This relationship is reciprocal, and its sanctity requires continual maintenance in order to remain *pono* (goodness, uprightness, morality, virtuous, in perfect order) or balanced.

This genealogical relationship binds, nourishes, and sustains Kānaka to' the past, present, and future (Peralto 2014: 233–5). From this perspective, the Mauna is a literal, genealogical ancestor of the Kānaka.

This relationship with the Mauna is a source of life for many cultural rituals and practices on the Mauna and at the ahu on her slopes. Perpetuating these practices and protecting her sacred slopes for intergenerational equity, so future generations have the right to continue practicing ancestral alignments on the Mauna, is one of many motivations made clear by Kiaʻi and Kānaka who were forced to engage with legal strategies and became court petitioners. Their hope is to leave this sacred place in a natural condition, thereby respecting the culturally grounded pono relationships each Kānaka continues to nurture between Akua, ʻāina, and ʻohana.

The summit is in the Wao Akua, recognized as a space for the elements to be left undisturbed, where spiritual engagements can occur (Winter and Lucas 2017: 461). Kānaka have been holistically practicing science, spirituality, and culture on the Mauna for generations (Maly and Maly 2005). However, the Wao Akua was not considered a place for daily human habitation activities. Kānaka cultural practitioner Emalani Case explained that "while Hawaiians could access the Wao Akua, and other regions above that for particular purposes, they knew they needed to live in the *Wao Kānaka* (place where humans lived and cultivated), below the gods" (Case 2019: 176). It is recognized as a temple of the highest order and was constantly used by those mentored into ancestral practices.

In one example, an Uncle, who prefers not to be named, shares that, according to his father's and grandfather's journals, his family was one of the honored few who had access to the Mauna for initiation rituals. They were a family of *Lua* warriors dedicated as babies to the Akua by those who would mentor them into the art form to become the bodyguards of the Aliʻi. *Lua* is a Hawaiʻi style of hand-to-hand combat. The upper elevation of Mauna Kea is sacred beyond the understanding of colonial conditioning, and that is why continued desecration was certain to evoke conflict. In turn, that is a conflict that forces Kānaka to remain idle no more and vigilantly work to raise awareness at a local scale while making a difference on a global scale.

Historical Acts of Kānaka Resistance

Before 1968, the summit of the Mauna was a marginally altered cultural landscape, utilized primarily by cultural practitioners who interacted in spiritually significant ways with their ahu and by those quarrying adz stones (McCoy et al. 2012). Now, there is a visitor center, parking lots, multiple access roads, increasing foot traffic on the Mauna, and a general lack of reverence shown by many people spending time on this sacred summit. The first observatory was built on the summit in 1968 by the US Air Force and then given to the University of Hawaiʻi at Hilo (UHH) after the State Board of Land and Natural Resources (BLNR) issued a 65-year general lease to UHH in 1968. Shortly thereafter, another telescope was built in 1970, and three more in 1979. By 2000, there were thirteen telescopes with supporting infrastructure (KAHEA 2016).

The increased intensity of activity was unsettling for Kealoha Pisciotta, one of five petitioners in the 2015 contested case hearings discussed below, a cultural practitioner, and a former technician at the W. M. Keck observatory for twelve years. She describes her experience watching the escalation of building on the Mauna in an interview with PBS News Hour, "When I began to see the landscape being taken over, that's when I realized, whoa! This is no longer man operating in a natural landscape, its man dominating the natural landscape, and that's where it started to shift for me" (PBS NewsHour 2016). TMT would be the fourteenth observatory and the largest, towering eighteen-stories high. In 2015, Kānaka and supporters halted the project through occupation, specifically "by camping out and blocking the road to construction crews for months, until the Hawaiʻi Supreme Court officially stopped construction in December 2015" (Arvin 2019).

This was not the first time Kānaka protested the loss of lands and lifeways via occupation and demonstration, nor was it the first time they faced other Kānaka. In 1971, thirty-two Kānaka were arrested in Kalama Valley in East Oʻahu while protesting the evictions of local pig farmers from land owned by Bishop Estate. Bishop Estate was and still is the largest private landowner in the State of Hawaiʻi. The *estate* was created in 1884 by the will of Bernice Pauahi Bishop, the great-granddaughter of King Kamehameha the Great. He was credited for uniting the Hawaiian Islands during the eighteenth century. When Princess Pauahi died, she left the bulk of her estate "to erect and maintain in the Hawaiian Islands two schools, one for boys and one for girls, to be called the Kamehameha Schools" (Kaʻiwakīloumoku 2022).

During the protest, Kānaka demonstrators were singing, and saying to police officers, "Hey, you guys are Hawaiian. You should be up here with us" (Tenbruggencate 1971). Haunani Kay Trask (1987), professor of Hawaiian Studies and staunch Hawaiian rights activist, identifies these evictions and arrests as the beginning of the Hawaiian cultural renaissance.

Perhaps the most famous example of Kānaka activism prior to the TMT was in 1976, when Kānaka faced the US Military to regain control of the island of Kahoʻolawe, the smallest of the eight main Hawaiian Islands situated about seven miles southwest of Maui. The US Military had been using the island for bombing practice since 1953 and even simulated a nuclear bomb eviscerating the water table beneath the island. It took decades and cost two Kānaka lives. However, control was returned to the State of Hawaiʻi with a $300 million budget to clean up the unexploded ordinances (UXO) from the main areas of access. Unfortunately, UXO remains scattered across a majority of the island. Visitors must remain within cordoned areas and are warned against walking around unaccompanied.

The TMT protest was not even the first for Hawaiʻi Island. In 1978, Kānaka and allies occupied the Hilo International Airport to protest numerous injustices against Kānaka including the *Kahoʻolawe* bombings, the disproportionate incarceration of the Kānaka men, and alleged mismanagement at Bishop Estate. Of the fifty people who voluntarily submitted to arrest, nine were from the media. Decades later, on March 25, 1990, the Pele Defense Fund organized 1,500 *Pele* (divine entity associated with magma) practitioners and supporters to attempt to enter the drilling site at Wao Kele O Puna rainforest and conduct a religious ceremony. Although 141 people were charged with trespassing, the demonstration was considered one of Hawaiʻiʻs largest acts of civil disobedience and the largest single act of peaceful disobedience in the United States to save a rainforest (McGregor and Aluli 2014).

These precursors to the TMT protests not only informed the Kiaʻi of the method and dedication necessary to move forward but also showed that Kānaka were both actively protesting and capable of elevating the way they demonstrated for decades. It also shows that Kānaka have always used occupation, music, chanting, and dancing as effective strategies for demonstrating against the continued dispossession of land and lifeways.

In the next section, a second contributor, Loke Aloua, Kiaʻi, and community researcher for the project with a Master of Arts in

Archeology from Simon Frasier University, shares some of the strategies used from the courtroom near sea level to the crosswalk at 9,000-ft elevation. She begins with a personal sharing of how she was called to the Mauna.

Ku Kiaʻi Mauna, Mountain Protectors Rise

Loke: I was called to the mountain shortly after returning home from studying abroad in Canada for a Master of Arts in archaeology. I returned home knowing I wanted to be of service to Hawaiʻi. I thought archaeology was the pathway where I would make this difference. I was hired by an archaeological firm and during an excavation a pōhaku (rock) toppled, crushing the fingers on my right hand. I remember feeling my hands trembling with pulsing pain and removed my field gloves to find thick red blood dripping from my fingertips. At that moment, I wished I had kept my gloves on. In a state of panic, my supervisor rushed me uphill to the nearest doctor. Luckily, x-rays determined I only fractured one finger and would heal. During my time off, I helped with organizing efforts for the mountain and attended community gatherings remembering the sacredness of our Mauna. One day while praying at the ahu near Puʻuhuluhulu, a group of Kiaʻi stopped by to offer prayers before heading up the mountain. Unknowing what was unfolding, I was told that construction equipment was advancing to the Northern Plateau. They were heading up to coordinate with others like Lanakila Mangauil, who had reached the summit by foot. Without hesitation, I jumped in the truck. As the mountain winds swirled around us and the image of the ahu dwindled, I had no idea what I was doing, but I knew the Mauna needed help.

Several weeks later, my hand was healed, and it was time to return to work. I eventually called the firm owner, asking if I could be granted the flexibility to help keep our Mauna safe. With no delay, I was told "no," and had to choose. Either continue on a path that could build my career in archaeology, or resign and stand with the ʻān a (land). I chose ʻāina.

Looking back, I thank the pōhaku who changed my life, leading me to Mauna Kea. The time I had to heal my hand was a time I was gifted to remember.

Multiple strategies have been used to protect Mauna Kea from desecration. Since TMT was introduced, multiple court cases have been filed since 2010. These cases questioned the adequacy of environmental assessments and management documents, actual cumulative impacts, proper use of conservation land, impacts on natural resources, desecration of cultural structures, public consultation process, protection of traditional and customary practices, administrative rules and rulemaking, enforcement, and jurisdiction legitimacies. Though I have never been a petitioner for Mauna Kea, I have entered into land and water litigation downslope. While each individual experience varies, I have learned that being a petitioner is a sacrifice. Offerings of time are made to dedicate to cases that could otherwise be spent with loved ones, places, and self. The energy that could be used for nourishment or collective health is redirected to protection efforts. Financial security is threatened with donated time, while opposing parties often have highly paid attorneys with academic training to pursue legal cases. When compounded, personal health and wellbeing fluctuate with the highs and lows of the *kuleana* (responsibility).

Simultaneously, litigation was often unfolding and increasing while face-to-face standoffs took place. As kānaka took the project to court in two rounds of contested hearings from 2011 ending with the Supreme Court ruling in December 2015, at 9,000-ft elevation across from Hale Pōhaku, they utilized the public space to perform acts of civil disobedience like walking across a crosswalk to slow construction efforts. Over a series of weeks, hundreds of individuals constantly walked across the legal pathway preventing construction equipment from accessing higher elevations. These efforts utilized public spaces to create encampments for 24-hour protection efforts. The encampment became home for those who answered the call remaining for days, weeks, and months, providing a watchful eye over access roads. Here, strangers became friends, and groups became a community who were fed and provided for by donated food, water, medicine, and goods.

On October 7, 2014, a groundbreaking ceremony was scheduled for the TMT at the proposed site. Lanakila Mangauil, Kiaʻi, Kumu Hula, and creator of the Hawaiian Cultural Center of Hāmākua (HCCoH) confronted the crowd at the groundbreaking, canceling the international gathering (Big Island Video News 2014). Several dozen Kiaʻi and Kānaka arrived behind Lanakila in a peaceful standoff performing an oli and engaging groundbreaking attendees in impassioned dialogue. The disruption of the TMT groundbreaking ceremony and subsequent direct action altered the history of the movement forever. Soon after, the Kiaʻi Mauna community embraced various social media platforms. Their call-out for the protection of the Mauna became increasingly public with a strong response. From this time forward, a great deal of footage, photographs, and writing is available on YouTube, Facebook, Instagram, in blogs and articles, and through music and art, as many more people were documenting the resistance efforts on Mauna Kea.

Social media served multiple roles. With real-time postings, calls to action were and still are made instantly to global, international, and local communities. Energy is harnessed at an earth-wide scale for prayers, calls for support, and donations. Indigenous allies sharing struggles and successes, relationships with scholars interested in supporting, and friends offering food, water, and rest are opened. Narratives often controlled by mainstream media are met by the voices of those they tried to silence. These bodies of records are reclamation spaces where Kānaka write, record, and assert their own histories and voices regarding the Mauna.

On April 2, 2015, hundreds of Kiaʻi gathered near the Mauna Kea Visitor Center at the 9,000-ft elevation, creating a roadblock in and around the crosswalk on the summit to stop construction vehicles from proceeding to the project site. That day, there were thirty-one arrests of peaceful protectors, men and women, who stood throughout the years, who had taken those frontline positions that day as they had done so over so many years for so many other Hawaiian issues and actions. They were bound and hauled off to jail for protecting their rightful lands, familial burials, and spiritual practices. The arrests gained international attention, especially on social media, where the Kiaʻi already had a following and gained thousands more globally to support this movement via social media platforms and donations. This event also prompted 53,000 people to sign the Mauna Kea Petition that was delivered to Governor David Ige on April 20th (Hurley 2015).

June 24, 2015 was another monumental day for the movement. When TMT attempted to move more construction equipment up the mountain, more than 750 peaceful protectors arrived to line the roads and prevent construction vehicles from arriving at the summit. Kānaka and non-Kānaka arrived. With oli, hula, *lei* (floral garland), and pōhaku, arm in arm, they lined the roadway. There were twelve arrests that day of peaceful protectors. In the months to follow, there were many ceremonies and land occupation actions on the Mauna to keep the access road blocked to construction vehicles. These were also accompanied by actions occurring off the Mauna.

While human intervention has helped with delaying and often stopping construction, the watchful eyes of bystanders simultaneously served as a means of protection for those who stood face-to-face with law enforcement officers. These witnesses to the events provide accountability measures, influencing the treatment of arrestees and the militaristic tactics that have been deployed (and undeployed). For example, in the 2019 face-to-face standoffs, the LRAD (Long-Range Acoustic Device) sound cannon was brought forward before the wāhine line, while women, children, Elders, and news media outlets watched. Additionally, the capabilities of portable recording devices carried in pockets grow the eyes watching with livestream capabilities.

Loke's real-life experiences are palpable, and her assessment of the strategies used by Kānaka is both encouraging and serves as a warning. If you go to these kinds of Kānaka-led occupational demonstrations, you need to decide if you are willing to be arrested or a witness to the events. Both are necessary. Next, we introduce Kūkulu, a traveling art exhibit created as another pathway of the movement to protect Mauna Kea and begin by clearly situating it as a strategy of Indigenous Repossession.

Kūkulu and Indigenous Repossession

In Summer 2015, while Kiaʻi were occupying the crosswalk on the Mauna and courtrooms, I approached Aunty Pua with a research project idea. She reviewed the Hawaiʻi portion of the draft research proposal in the summer of 2015 and hesitatingly agreed to participate as her life at that point was focused on frontline actions and court cases. Things really came together when Chantelle came to meet with Aunty Pua and me at a local Hilo eatery in October 2016. Chantelle explained everything from theoretical concepts to project implementation and budget. Aunty Pua invited Chantelle to Puʻuhuluhulu, where Kiaʻi and allies gather for planned and impromptu celebrations of historic victories with *pule* (prayer), oli, and hula. Often, participants made offerings of *wai* (freshwater) or *lei*. Chantelle made an offering of a traditional song from her homeland. Less than a year later, in April 2017, Aunty Pua and her daughter, Hāwane Rios, came to Boston to present at the American Association of Geographers Annual Meeting and to meet face-to-face with the other Indigenous community leaders and team members who also agreed to work on the project.

At the meeting, the community leaders decided to proceed as separate but interconnected projects serving local purposes while answering a set of more prominent project themes they composed. The two themes that blossomed from the discussion about Environmental Repossessions were "reawakening our Native values" and "revivifying intergenerational awareness of sustainable practices." While Aunty Pua had the idea of creating an exhibit before she agreed to participate in the project, after the Boston meeting, she began including the concept of Indigenous repossession as part of her creative process. She said, "Before we could repossess anything, before any strategies could be implemented, we had to identify what was the necessary ingredient … because … we need to first connect what we desire to repossess with the people who are going to do that work. Before there can be repossession, there has to be reconnection."

While there may have been hundreds of Kiaʻi occupying the crosswalk on the Mauna, there are several thousand Kānaka whose only real relationship with the Mauna was limited to their field of vision. Aunty Pua explained that:

> Most Kānaka may live 45 minutes from the Mauna, but so few have been up there, and it is not even in their mindset. When they look up at the mountain, they may know it is important, or it is said to be sacred. Others may know that Hawaiʻi navigators learned the celestial star gazing skills and practices there. But all of these could be taking place far away in some distant lands if it is not connected to you and you are not connected to it.

Aunty Pua and others who were closely connected to the Mauna worked diligently to ensure that Kānaka were provided with opportunities to reconnect because she knew they would be needed for the duration of the stance to protect the mountain. In order to have them come to the Mauna when the kāhea went out, or to support the movement and, in some way, participate, they made that extra effort to connect the Mauna to the masses.

Kūkulu and Community Working Groups

Aunty Pua has been curating community art exhibits on Hawaiʻi Island for many years and understands the importance of alliance building and networking at the community level. She sits on various educational and cultural boards, including the Waimea Hawaiian Civic Club, Waimea Community Education Hui, and is the Lead Coordinator and Project Director of Mauna Kea Education and Awareness. When she sits at the table with community members, she shares the exhibit's purpose and listens to their concerns, hears their suggestions, and welcomes their feedback, allowing the community to have input as each exhibit is unique to each location. She is also seeking pertinent knowledge from those with a genealogical or ancestral connection to the 'āina, a knowledge that descendants retain, and often have no idea how important sharing a family story is to Aunty Pua; like my grandmother said "this" about "that chant" or these are the traditions we followed in this place. That is the kind of information she needs to listen for when meeting with community groups.

Moreover, she does this no matter if she already has deep ancestral roots in the community, as with the Honoka'a community where the first Kūkulu exhibit was displayed. Her mother was from Haina camp in Honoka'a. However, that does not mean she can overstep meeting with the community. It was the same with the Kohala community where her Kānaka father is from, and which houses the eighth exhibit. If anything, her deep roots and understanding of protocol meant it would be expected that she hold community meetings for every location. According to Aunty Pua:

> Networking at that level is really important. Then we can look at the bigger picture and network with supporters, sponsors, and funders, especially the ones who are going to extend funding through the grants we receive, for without that we could not have done it. So, we really had to be sure that the community network was set. Then we could go out to the supporters, the *Kia'i*, to make the "ask," which is the request to participate.

The first "ask" for contributions of artworks, photographs, and other precious items for the exhibit was very important. She had to define for the entire Island community that this first exhibit was to honor the pillars of Hāmākua and Kohala, two of six districts on Hawai'i Island because the Mauna is located in the Hāmākua District and therefore the art would also need to come from the Kia'i there. There would be an opportunity later for each district to host their expression of the exhibit. With the foundation of Kūkulu embedded in an interconnected network of social and spiritual significance, we focus on the first and longest-standing Kūkulu exhibit which lived at the HCCoH and will address the other exhibits in the discussion at the end.

The following section was part of cartographic presentations on Kūkulu shared across several academic venues. Aunty Pua consented to the presentation's content acknowledging that it is examined through my understanding of the cartographic expressions embedded in the design of Kūkulu. It is not an attempt to provide insight into her thoughts, observations, or expertise. Using a cartographic lens, I share how the Kānaka spiritual realities manifested in the physical space, inviting exhibit attendees to embrace, engage, and associate with Kānaka worldviews in a safe and accessible mode. I opened with a recording of the *Oli Kūkulu*, a chant composed by Aunty Pua, which she performed on opening day, so her voice was the first thing attendees heard while they viewed a slide of the translation. Here the chant is prefaced with Aunty Pua's sharing of its inspiration.

Oli Kūkulu

Aunty Pua: Oli Kūkulu began as a rallying cry and was composed in a call-and-response style. The words were inspired by the responses to the first stances for Mauna Kea from 2014 to 2017, the year this chant was created. The vision before my eyes at the time was the *hoa ʻāina* (the natives of this place), my homeland in Waimea, the ancient chiefs and warriors from Puʻukapu to Pololū, had stood there before our time and in their footsteps, the guardians and protectors were standing now. In 2019–20, for nine months on the Mauna, Oli Kūkulu ended every *Aha* held three times a day, led by native voices of all ages. The chant sealed a collective commitment to protect the mountain and invigorated and inspired the masses who came to the mountain. There they became one, rising together like a mighty wave.

Oli Kūkulu

Kāhea	PANE
E nā hoaʻāina e	
E nā hoawelo like e	
E nā hoapili e	
E nā hoaaloha e	ALOHA ʻĀINA!
Kūkulu e,	
Nā Kūkulu ʻehā e.	KŪKULU!
He mau maka koa e	
Nā maka kaʻeo	EŌ!
E Hū e,	HŪ!
He Kū Kiaʻi Mauna,	KŪ!

He Pōhaku kū,	KŪʻĒ!
He ʻiliʻili kapu,	ALOHA!
He koa wai e ola,	OLA!
E Hū e,	HŪ!

Call	**RESPONSE**
Relatives of the big ocean of Kiwa	
Relations of the first nations of Turtle Island	
Friends, supporters from around the world	ALOHA ʻĀINA!
Pillars, the four cardinal points	KŪKULU!
We are beloved warriors,	
We are strong (wearing our top knots on our heads)	EŌ!
Rise!	HŪ!
I am a mountain guardian,	KŪ!
A standing rock,	KŪʻĒ!
A sacred stone,	ALOHA!
A water protector,	OLA!
Rise!	HŪ!

—Pua Case, April 2, 2017

Kūkulu as Evolving Kānaka Hawaiʻi Cartography

Aunty Pua: In 2018, Kūkulu, a traveling art exhibition and
heartfelt tribute to the Pillars of Mauna Kea was installed at
the Hawaiian Cultural Center of Hāmākua by Mauna Kea
Education and Awareness. It was inspired by this chant,
the boots I wore on the mountain, and the photograph
which exemplified the spirit of the exhibit; the photo
of a young *mana wahine* (spiritually powerful woman),
Kaleiʻohuʻolumakua Kaheanakahailiopua Keliʻipio "Tita"
Sleightolm, offering her water at Puʻuhuluhulu to Poliʻahu.

The HCCoH is a cultural center and museum established, operated, and
was stewarded by Lanakila Mangauil at that time as "a space for residents
to deepen their connection with Hawaiian culture through community
classes in art, *hula*, language, history, agriculture, philosophy, and more"
(Hawaiian Cultural Center of Hāmākua 2018). The HCCoH provided

two main areas for the exhibition. The Kūkulu Room was the main entry hall and the Kū'ē Room was a smaller area connected through a doorway on the northwest wall. Here I focus on the Kūkulu Room.

The Kūkulu Room was organized around the Mauna hand symbol, a triangle formed with the index finger to index finger and thumb to thumb with palms outward (Figure 3.1). Laying the symbol over the floor, the right corner of the room is spiritually anchored by Pu'uhuluhulu. Here, an ahu held the pōhaku from the 2017 *Hōkūle'a Mālama Honua* worldwide voyage. *Hōkūle'a* is a traditionally designed and navigated double-hull canoe. The pōhaku from the summit of the mountain is the one thing in the exhibit that touched all parts of the earth and provided a presence of a well-traveled friend. In the left corner, Kia'i knowledgeable in building *hale* (Hawai'i house) built a *Hale-o-pili* (Hawai'i house of native grass thatching) to symbolize the *Hale Kū Kia'i Mauna* (the name of the original hale constructed in 2015 during the Mauna Kea occupation). Bringing voyagers into the exhibit exposes attendees to a Kānaka understanding of the Mauna as more than just the summit we see. The Mauna extends to the ocean with no separation. The point of the triangle is a replica of the crosswalk Kia'i occupied. Each of these elements triangulates the Mauna energetics within the exhibit floor plan allowing participants to be part of those special "Mauna moments."

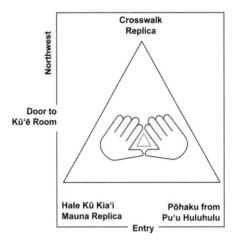

Figure 3.1 Kūkulu room design: Imprinting a sacred framework into the floor plan.

Illustrator: Renee Pualani Louis/author's original composition.

Once the sacred setting was emplaced, four pillars were raised to anchor it in the physical setting. Going clockwise from the left (lower left in the schematic diagram below), Aunty Pua explained the symbolic significance of each pillar (Figure 3.2). The first pillar, closest to the *Hale Kū Kia'i Mauna*, anchors the room to the Wao Kānaka realm and represents the masculine energy that is Kū Kia'i Mauna. The next pillar takes us into the Wao Akua and the realm of Wākea and Poliahu, divine entities of male and female energy. The third pillar adds more divine feminine energy with the presence of Haumea and Mo'oinanea. The last pillar returns us to the Wao Kānaka and the masculine energy of the Northern Plateau, which crosses into the ahu at Pu'uhuluhulu and connects back to the pōhaku. Once the horizontal alignments were settled in place, Aunty Pua could focus on vertical alignments. The four pillars focus the Mauna energetics brought in from the imprinted floor plan. Their placement invites learning about sensitive subject matters in a space made safe through culturally implemented and contextually relevant participatory engagements.

Aunty Pua identifies the space above the head, including the upper walls, as the *Wao Akua* and arranged symbolic meaning according

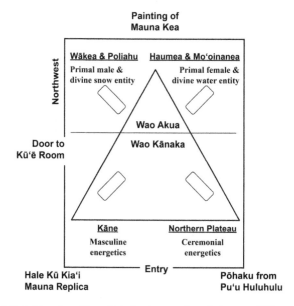

Figure 3.2 Setting the pillars: Reinforcing our foundations and lifeways.

Illustrator: Renee Pualani Louis/author's original composition.

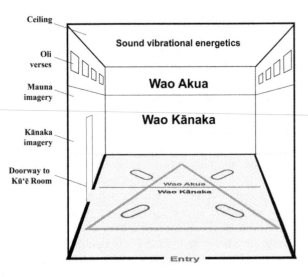

Ceiling

Sound vibrational energetics

Oli verses

Wao Akua

Mauna imagery

Wao Kānaka

Kānaka imagery

Doorway to Kūʻē Room

Wao Akua
Wao Kānaka

Entry

Figure 3.3 Elevating awareness: Wao Akua/Wao Kānaka.

Illustrator: Renee Pualani Louis/author's original composition.

to a Kānaka understanding of ecological protocols (Figure 3.3). The ceiling was adorned with banners of the names of the mountain deities: Poliʻahu, Lilinoe, Kāne, Kukahauʻula, Moʻoinanea, Kahoupokane, Līhau, and Kūauli. The three upper walls were adorned with verses from the genealogical chant that mentions the creation of the Mauna. Directly below this layer, the middle-upper portion of the walls was filled with landscape images and art of the Mauna. This layer represented tangible components of the Wao Akua decorated with framed landscape paintings and photographs. In Aunty Pua's words, "every place you look, you can see the Mauna." The lower portion of each of the three walls represented the Wao Kānaka and is filled with photos, facts, artwork, and other items that honor the people involved with the movement.

Awakening Ancestral Alignments: Opening Day Performance

On opening day, hula dancers spread out through the exhibit and began chanting to call attendees into the exhibit, enveloping all in a modern Kānaka cartographic engagement. Aunty Pua led performers through the *mele hānau* (birth chant) for Kamehameha III (which can be found in Nupepa Kuokoa (1866: 4)), specifically identifying Mauna Kea as genealogical kin. Each verse was associated with a different sound and rhythm ranging from clapping hands to using *kala'au* (sticks), *ipu* (gourd instrument), pahu, *'ili'ili* (small smooth stones), and various oli styles. Aunty Pua explained that sound is a vibration capable of penetrating beyond the physical limitation of the highest elevations.

At the opening, two community researchers began reaching out to two subsets of attendees, *Kia'i* and Allies, to fulfill the student research component of our grant. Months earlier, Aunty Pua met with Loke Aloua and Abby Laden, a University of Hawai'i at Hilo Anthropology Master's student and a third contributor to this chapter, to oversee their research design. Theoretically, they aligned with Lassiter's (2005) Collaborative Ethnography Model and Aloua's (2014) reflections on culturally relevant Community-Based Participatory Research (CBPR) in Hawai'i. Methodologically, they employed what Margaret Kovach describes as a "conversational methodology" where "both parties become engaged in a collaborative process, [so] the relationship builds and deepens as stories are shared" (2010: 43). They had "conversations" with their focus groups during Summer 2018 and shared their research with the community in a subsequent Kūkulu installation at HCCoH. In the next section, Loke shares the knowledge she received from the Kia'i with whom she collaborated.

We begin with a walk-through, highlighting featured pieces in the exhibit, then move clockwise from the northwest wall (Figure 3.4). As noted previously, each wall's top was laid out per the Kānaka ecological understanding of the Wao Akua. The lower portions of the room walls were filled with images of Kia'i and the people of the movement representing the Wao Kānaka. The northwest wall featured the timeline of events of *Protect Mauna Kea Movement*, efforts which circled clockwise to the northeast wall. When asked about his favorite piece, interviewee Kia'i 1, Kānaka ocean lover and keeper, stated his favorite piece was the photo featuring the mana wāhine line on the June 24, 2016 shutdown:

> I love the mana wāhine line. I love the crosswalk line. I love those pictures because those are our children and our women. Of course, Wahine 1 is in those photos and she is the mother of my children. I really aloha my little family as much as I aloha everybody. I *aloha* my little family. Knowing that we went up the Mauna together. You get to the point where you would rather go up the Mauna together. Those photos remind me of my family.

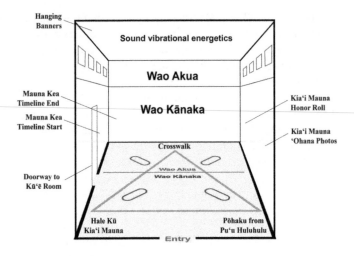

Figure 3.4 Kūkulu and elevating Kiaʻi voices.

Illustrator: Renee Pualani Louis/author's original composition.

A quilt sewn together by Pua Case's mother, Delma Case, contained patches honoring the names of Kiaʻi, and was also on this northwest wall. Maoli photographer and filmmaker, Kiaʻi 2, shared about this quilt, saying:

> I really love this quilt because it really tied in the petitioners. Aunty Delma did such a good job on it. It was so pretty. I didn't know how somebody could make all those little quilt pieces with all the writings on them. Everyone writing from the last day of the contested case hearing at the Crown Room at Naniloa. They had written so close to the edge and Aunty Delma had gotten all the squares on there perfectly. It was exactly 50 pieces and all of them were filled up. I love the quilt because that was the last day of the contested case hearing. I feel like everybody felt good about that day because it finally was over after how many months? Eight or so driving to Hilo everyday. Last minute I just grabbed this pack of quilt cloth and said, "they gotta write on em." I brought my Sharpie. I was so happy that everyone wanted to write something to remember.

The quilt was a soft and impactful reminder of the many who stand for the Mauna in the courtrooms, classrooms, and beyond—a call of remembering and lifting collective energies while still honoring each individual.

The northeast wall held a replica crosswalk with popularized movement signs and messages. It connected to the 24/7 crosswalk occupations beginning in 2015 by Kiaʻi and symbolized a foundational moment for the movement, the unity of the rising of a nation. Within the exhibit, black padding measuring the length and width of the original mountain crosswalk was brought to life by Bimo Akiona. As on the Mauna, in the exhibit, mountain supporters gathered with signs and messages to be photographed and immortalized through social media portals, documentaries, and educational presentations. The southeast wall displayed an honor roll of *kūpuna* (Elders), *keiki* (children), and allies who stood in the movement and passed on to the ancestral realm. The remainder of the wall was filled with poetry, paintings, newspaper clippings, and photographs sharing more memories of the mountain movement. Kānaka graphic designer, Auliʻi Case, referenced a collection of poems featured on this wall created by her sister, Emalani Case:

> There was a collective piece that I helped my sister with, and we split it into three pieces. She had written a blog post about Mauna Kea, and they took some of her words and made them into graphic images. I put some designs and photos in the background of these words. My sister has always been a huge inspiration for me for many reasons. Her writing has always really inspired me, spoke to me, been very moving in a lot of ways. Just within the last year she's lived in different places and traveled around the world. I know her desire to be here for the mountain. I know her and how she feels and how it's been a struggle because she hasn't been able to be here. I think for that reason her words have meant even more to me. It was important for me to include her words in the exhibit and give it another venue to be seen, heard, and felt.

The exhibit also featured contributions from global mountain supporters and those Native nations who were allies like the Winnemem Wintu Tribe, Confederated Villages of Lisjan/Ohlone, Pit River Nation, and many more in the Kūʻē Room. It was situated through a doorway on the northwest wall and expressed resistance and reclamation messages of the movement. It was filled with popular hashtags, merchandise generated to share messaging, music created for the mountain, images, and regalia of Native nations standing in solidarity, words of interviewees, powerful photographs marking points of remembrance, and objects held as symbols of resistance. Kānaka photographer, Kapulei Flores, mentioned the significance of hashtags as spreading the movement message:

> In this movement hashtags have been so important in spreading the word and connecting everyone about the same thing. When it [Protect Mauna Kea Movement] was going on then I would use the hashtags more but now I don't use the hashtags as much. You want to get your messages out there, you want to spread what you are talking about, and you want other people who agree or are on the same page as you to see what you are sharing. Hashtags are really important for that.

With the use of hashtags, the movement garnered support and enhanced reach to prospective audiences otherwise physically inaccessible.

Kānaka artist and designer, Kiaʻi 3, offered an *Hae Hawaiʻi* (Hawaiʻi flag) that she carried on the mountain. With tattered edges, worn fabric showed through fading coloration from kissing the sun, and sections ripped from high-elevation winds, the story of her flag was told through photographs of Jessica standing for Mauna Kea. Thematic, within this exhibit and on the mountain, the Hae Hawaiʻi stood as a remembrance of the past, present, and future. Photographs, art, music, and mountain gear honored components of the Hae Hawaiʻi symbolic of the Hawaiian Kingdom. Kiaʻi 3 offered thoughts regarding how she understood Kapu Aloha:

> When I first heard the term kapu aloha in my own mind I asked, "What does that mean?" I didn't understand what *Kapu Aloha* meant. I actually had to learn that *Kapu Aloha* is an old term hardly ever used and it's more of a feeling much like *lōkahi*. *Lōkahi* is not the "giving tree" or "unity" it's nothing like that. *Lōkahi* was a way of life.

Here, Kiaʻi 3 describes Kapu Aloha as a lifeway rather than a sterile moment or definition. For Kanaka Kumu Hula, Kiaʻi 4, Kapu Aloha guided conduct and behavior: "*Kapu Aloha* means to me how do I conduct myself to represent our ancestor and how he wants us to be with others." Peaceful and non-violent, Kūkulu provided a space where the voices of Kiaʻi, along with Kānaka culture in relationship to Mauna Kea, could be brought before familiar and unfamiliar audiences. It is a space where we would not be erased or neglected, where our stories could be told and retold, made, and remembered.

The Mauna movement also involved international actors and attracted all kinds of supporters. In the next section, a third contributor, Abby Laden, shares her research on the role, responsibilities, and pono relationships non-Kānaka allies played in the movement. It was especially useful at a time when clearly defined roles and responsibilities for allies were elusive. We begin with her personal sharing of how she came to this work.

Kūkulu and the Non-Kānaka Ally

Abby: I humbly come to this piece of writing as a non-Indigenous ally, a supporter of Mauna Kea and the *Kia'i*. My intention is to share how allies can stand with, and behind, those who are protecting their ancestral and ever-present, lands, rights, and sovereignty. In the words of Aunty Pua's *oli*, above, the global supporters are the hoaaloha (friends) and we must deeply understand and acknowledge our place within that protocol.

My connection with the Mauna began in 2016 at the second round of Contested Case Hearings for Mauna Kea. I had spent the six years prior to 2016 learning about a broad spectrum of Indigenous rights concerns, land rights, and spending time with Indigenous folks in service-oriented spaces. After moving to *Moku o Keawe* (an affectionate term for Hawai'i Island), I was invited to attend one of the early days of the hearings. I will never forget that day. I listened to the testimony, and it was clear to me in just one day, of the horrendous injustices occurring on the Mauna. Yet, I also experienced through the people present the profound, infinite, immutable sacredness of the Mauna. As a massage therapist by training, the only thing I knew to do was to offer what I could in those rooms: I spent the next couple of months attending the hearings, sitting in the back, and offering massage to petitioners and Kia'i, while also listening, observing, and learning. It was an honor and a privilege to be there with the Kia'i, and it set me on a path to connecting more deeply with the Mauna and the movement.

The community that stands for Mauna Kea is both local and global, and all are essential. An important part of the journey of this research was discovering how these relationships intertwine with a sense of place. In the context of this research, allies are defined as non-Kānaka supporters of Mauna Kea who were not born in Hawai'i. In this section, I offer two main intentions: to provide a quick synopsis of the words and stories of some of the local allies of Mauna Kea, and to synthesize a small quantity of information on what it means to be a non-Kānaka ally within a Kānaka-led space. This ally section is intended to support, show solidarity, and be clear that there are many varied voices standing firmly for the liberation of Mauna Kea and her people. The seven dedicated allies interviewed are Aunty Cheryl Ann Burghardt, Lily Ah Nee, Katy Benjamin, Koko Kawauchi Johnson, Hannah Sky, Jodi Mercier, and Dhiresha McCarver. Each has openly shared their experiences, thoughts, and hearts around their participation in the movement and their love for Mauna Kea. I am deeply grateful for their contribution, openness, and commitment.

While almost everyone I listened to felt a deep pull to Hawai'i or felt drawn to Hawai'i spiritually, they were also aware they were guests in a host nation. They also express a deep sense of responsibility to Hawai'i's lands, waters, and the original people of this place. In the interviews, people shared many reasons why they choose to stand in solidarity: shared values, common goals such as decolonization or protected rights, empathetic connections, community empowerment, environmental justice, and more. The primary role described was one of service and support. Lily Ah Nee called the ally role that of being a "backup singer," as opposed to being center-stage, and said, "maybe that's just my kuleana for this lifetime, you know, I don't necessarily belong here, but I can try to stand up and do the right thing for this place."

Many spoke at length about respectful (and disrespectful) ways of being, conduct, and protocol for non-Indigenous folks inside the movement. They shared their view of *how* to show up properly and respectfully, noting that the most important aspect was to look to Kānaka leadership, observe, and not take up too much space. As Dhiresha McCarver stated:

> Observe. Observe, observe, observe. Observe with an open heart, with a wide, open mind, observe, observe, observe. And don't feel like you're not valuable if you're not talking and speaking … When you're talking about actual actions, that's Kānaka-led. For me to be an ally in that situation, I will participate in the training to take a stand, but I will only do that under the guidance … Kānaka-led.

These sentiments of listening, observation, and following leadership were held by the group in the information exchange sessions and then carried forward into the interviews. In a similar vein of discussing proper conduct for an ally, Hannah Sky shared that "It's important to be an ally. Not to be, not to try to put yourself as one of them. Because you're not. I didn't endure any of what they've endured, or I don't have layers of cultural trauma." Later, Hannah also shared the importance of allies being self-reliant while inside Indigenous spaces and not expecting to be taken care of by others as another form of support and respect.

Education was by far one of the most heavily discussed topics in all seven interviews. The major emphasis was targeted to self-education for allies. While the movements themselves are Kānaka-led, there is important work to do as an ally and we need to be ready when we arrive, to the best of our ability. This also led to discussions about the roles of allies in educating other allies to take the burden from Kānaka. Katy Benjamin sees a primary role of allyship is to educate your own to prevent bad behavior, saying, "Go get your girl. Like, if you see somebody who is in your group, your race, your gender, your profession, whatever, in something that's kinda your area and they are overstepping, they're messing up big time, you need to 'go get your girl' and/or boy, quite often."

As allies share their personal experiences of direct action and standing in protection, they inevitably speak to their personal connections to the Mauna and the other Kiaʻi, and well as the very important protocol in place for all who step foot on the Mauna: Kapu Aloha. Koko shares a story of her personal experience with Kapu Aloha and how it moved her,

> And it's so sacred, isn't it? I was so touched by *Kapu Aloha*. The people, young people, keep themselves to being Aloha. One thing that I was very touched was, this Elder man, Hawaiian man, came with a truck, yelling … Very angry vibe, he came up. And he get out from the truck and keep upsetting and yelling. It's not really *Kapu Aloha* vibe, but, Kahoʻokahi [Kanuha], he just come close to this Uncle and he start hugging him. And, this man just, trying to let go from his arm and keep yelling. And another person come, start holding his energy. Then somewhere I start hearing, [singing] "*E Aloha e.*" Then everybody start chanting, "*E Aloha e.*" One by one, [singing] "*E Aloha e.*" Ahh, oh my gosh. Ahh … This really touched my heart. I was just, standing, what do you say? No words. These young people, and the Kapu Aloha, really touched my heart. And I believe that's their job, to make the world, what they call "new," a reality. Making things right [sigh]. Hew! I'm a little bit older, and I'm Japanese, so I always step aside and try to help, or support … to keep open that pathway for them.

Ally Guidelines

1. We respect and practice Kapu Aloha at all times, in all ways, with all people.
2. We recognize that this is a Kanaka Maoli-led Movement. As such, we follow Kanaka Maoli leadership and trust their wisdom for their movement, even if our personal opinions on matters may differ.
3. We are allies, not saviors. We stand in solidarity in protection, but do not come with the solutions.
4. We watch, listen, and learn while being attentive not to overstep our boundaries or overburden Kanaka Maoli. We are aware of the space we take up, and know when to step back.
5. We know it is our job to educate ourselves on issues that are important to understand in the context of Hawai'i and do not rely on others to educate us.
6. We are aware that the histories of Hawai'i and colonization can still play out in modern relationship dynamics, and therefore, we pay careful attention to our presence, actions, and words.
7. We assist where we are needed, which may not always be what we "want" to be doing.
8. We take care of ourselves in every way we can, as to not burden the Movement or those who are present to care for the Kia'i. We are as self-sufficient as possible.
9. We come to the movement knowing who we are and where we come from, careful to not appropriate the Hawaiian culture and spirituality, and participating where it is welcomed.
10. We do our best to ask for permission and consent from our alaka'i, wherever it may be needed.
11. We are aware that our main focus is to care for and protect the Kia'i, who are dedicating their lives to protecting the mauna. As such, we know we are in service roles, not leadership positions. We come to the movement with respect and integrity.

Figure 3.5 Ally guidelines, with a list of resources specific to the Mauna movement.

Illustrator: Renee Pualani Louis/author's original composition.

Koko gives us this perfect summary of the role of non-Kānaka allies, "I always step aside and try to help, or support ... to keep open that pathway for them."

Abby not only dedicated her time to learning how to navigate the tensions of being a non-Kānaka ally, but she also created specific and place-based Mauna Kea Ally guidelines from all her learning to provide something useful to the *Lāhui* (nation) (Figure 3.5). It was gifted to the *Mauna Medic Healers Hui*, a group of volunteer medical personnel, who provided a wide range of medical and mental health services at the Pu'uhonua, safe haven, located at Pu'uhuluhulu during the 2019 occupation.

By this time, the movement had gone global and was drawing an international audience, many of whom came to pay their respect and show support. Having the guidelines made it easier for the medics to help over-exuberant newcomers become energetically aligned with their roles and responsibilities while on the Mauna.

Ka'i Kūkulu—Lasting Impressions

Kūkulu was designed to be interactive, inclusive, and responsive to community needs. It created a safe place for people to connect to the Mauna. Not only is the exhibit dedicated to a movement that works toward the repossession of sacred lands and ancestral practices on Mauna Kea, but it also provides a space for others to connect with and learn about these lands so that they may participate in the process. It acknowledges Kia'i and all their supporters who dedicate their lives to the principles and practices of Indigenous people repossessing their lands and their relationships with those land entities. It has also been utilized by educators, cultural practitioners, and local knowledge keepers as a classroom space to host cultural classes, workshops on Mauna Kea chants, nonviolent direct-action training, potlucks, and special events. It hosted daily school groups, tourists from around the world, relations showing their support and solidarity, and meetings for Kia'i and allies preparing to stand once again on Mauna Kea. It offered workshops for people to gain comfort, awareness, practice, and familiarity with Hawaiian chants, hula, and prayers.

Kūkulu, and consequently HCCoH, also offered an essential space to conduct and share research stories. Cartographically, the Kūkulu Room design was intentionally laid out to evoke the spiritual first and foremost and then to create a cohesive "story" around the room that was layered with meaning, centering design around traditional Kānaka understanding of regions that extend from ocean to mountain to celestial expanse. The room and its story came to life on opening day as dancers, chanters, and musical instruments were engaged to "awaken" the artistic contributions and "invited" the deities to be present. Later, another ceremony gave gratitude to the deities and "released" the space of their presence as the day's events came to a close.

Loke's research focused on sharing connections, thoughts, and experiences of Kānaka who identified as Kiaʻi for Mauna Kea and contributed to the exhibit. Her intent was to bring forward individual voices of Kiaʻi highlighting the shared and unique tapestry of collective connections. These voices are normally silenced, ignored, or misrepresented by mass media. The talk story approach sought to humanize the term by creating a safe space for Kiaʻi to tell their stories. Contributions to the exhibit provided a common grounding space for all interviewees to expand conversations. Art pieces were pathways of meaning and memory to be shared and remembered. Abby focused on the role of allies in Indigenous land repossession and in the process of unification; what creates true unity is the knowledge and understanding of place, role, and kuleana. Allies expressed an understanding of where they fit into the picture, and that it is more than being on the frontlines.

Kūkulu was fortunate enough to have the use of HCCoH for thirty months. Aunty Pua curated no less than five new installations at HCCoH to stay current. By 2019, she recognized a shift in the people coming to the exhibit. While most people still came to connect with the Mauna and learn from the curriculum she created, more and more individuals began using it as a place to gather before heading up to the Mauna. Some even used it as a place to reacclimate with the Wao Kānaka after being on the Mauna and in ceremony for long periods of time.

As COVID-19 overwhelmed the world and the threat of construction on the Mauna has been put on pause, Aunty Pua took some much-needed time to rest, recuperate, and recalibrate her daily life. She re-emerged with requests for more Kūkulu exhibits. Initially, any proposed event associated with the Mauna was too controversial, including Kūkulu. The HCCoH was the only place that offered to host the exhibit. Now having communities reaching out wanting her to bring the exhibit to them is a testament to her careful consideration of the ancestral energies and the relational protocols she maintains, as well as the networking within the communities and the honor and respect for the Kiaʻi and the Mauna which were apparent throughout each exhibit. Here, we end as we began, with a personal sharing from Aunty Pua on the future of Kūkulu:

> I'd like to close off the chapter by saying that there is no end to *Kūkulu* Exhibits in sight. In 2022, the eighth exhibit was installed and is currently on display in five locations throughout Kohala, from Kapaʻau to Pololū, and we are in the planning stages for three Kūkulu exhibits in California, the first in Santa Cruz, another in Santa Barbara and the last set to coincide with the Winnimum Wintuʻs Run4Salmon Prayer Journey to honor our pillars in those areas. From there, Kūkulu will be available to all communities who request an exhibit as these exhibits will continue to connect generations of *Kiaʻi*, bring the mountain to the masses, and honor the pillars of Mauna Kea. As long as there is a need to protect Mauna Kea and all sacred places, there will be tributes such as Kūkulu to honor the work of the pillars here in Hawaiʻi and everywhere. We will keep rising like a mighty wave … E Hū e hū … our Kūkulu work will go on, mau a mau, kau a kau, a pau loa, (always, over and over, forever).

Acknowledgments

Loke Aloua and **Abby Laden** were students during the resistance to the Thirty Meter Telescope (TMT). During and after their studies, they were involved in research and activism associated with attempts to protect Mauna a Wakea. Aunty **Pua Case** is an educator and leader who is involved deeply in cultural and political revitalization, and she played a significant role in the Kanaka response to the TMT. She brought together the Kūkulu exhibit which is a central focus of this chapter. All contributed to the early drafts of this chapter, and they all provided narrative about their personal experiences that Renee collated, presented, and interpreted here.

Chapter 4

CULTIVATING BOUNDARY CROSSERS: TRESPASS GARDENING IN THE STONEFIELDS

This chapter is testimony of a Māori youth project, Taniwha Club—in southern Auckland, Aotearoa New Zealand—and what its members have learned about transformational change through their acts of guerrilla gardening. Because I have been a trustee of the group, I had opportunities to ground truth the idea of repossession with other trustees, parents, and *tamariki* (children). However, that concept only captured some aspects of the group's work, underestimating the significance of how children learn to be *kaitiaki* (guardians) and changemakers. The club followed my involvement in two other activist projects in southern Auckland, each revealing the restraints on rights-making for urban Māori. The first utilized participatory video alongside other forms of local resistance to a gas-fired power station which is located next to state housing for Māori and Pacific peoples and a *wharenui* (meeting house), itself built on a former landfill (Coombes 2013). The second focused on a groundswell movement to plant *māra kai* (food gardens) at urban marae. Māra are a visible and literal intercession to stake out and reclaim the city, but both projects included elements of Indigenous resurgence in the face of socially and politically difficult contexts. Urban Māori are not always permitted to function as *mana whenua* (those with customary authority over the land), so are excluded from rights which, under the Treaty of Waitangi 1840, should be available for all Māori. In that context, practices like clandestine gardening became a rare outlet for the activism of Māori residents. Gardens look good, feel good, and capture the public imagination, so they can be used politically to launch and validate other causes.

In what follows, I have been careful not to focus too much on the globally renowned case of Ihumātao where land occupations emerged after authorization of a Special Housing Area on a culturally significant volcanic landscape. Taniwha Club deliberately championed volcanic landscapes in other parts of southern Auckland because they were less well-known and even more neglected. However, it is difficult not to be drawn to the significance of the Ihumātao case, which is often compared with the work of land defenders in North America's *Trans Mountain* and *Standing Rock* disputes about petrochemical pipelines (refer to the first section of Chapter 2; Hancock and Newton 2022; Mika et al. 2022). Māori reverence for those volcanic landscapes, and their responses to the neo/colonial processes which threaten them have become a touchstone for decolonizing practices in Aotearoa. The work of Taniwha Club is related to what happened at Ihumātao, but its emphasis on generative practices in gardening and the building of youth capacity require separate analysis. It is argued here that real, material change at the micro-scale and in mundane, everyday practices is required to make positive change in the postcolonial, particularly urban, environments in which most Māori now live (see also Coombes 2018a). In their habitually retrospective framings of foregone rights, "grand" practices like court action and Treaty settlements or audacious land occupations have an important role. However, the subtlety of youth practices in informal gardening helps conceptualize new visions and pathways for transformational change. It is the critical thinking and boundary crossing of the tamariki gardeners that matter most.

Learning Repossession

Despite my critique of *Land as Pedagogy* in Chapter 1 as a possibly elite and unrealistic agenda, I also acknowledge the subsequent good work that has been completed in the field of land-based learning to remove essentialist understandings of where and how we must learn. Indeed, the practice of intergenerational learning with, on, and through the land has become an inspiring waypoint in the transition from mere survival to Indigenous resurgence (Corntassel and Hardbarger 2019; Hohenthal and Veintie 2022). Similarly inspirational trends are evident in Aotearoa where Māori have rewritten the conventions of environmental education and social learning (Dodson and Miru 2021; Moewaka Barnes et al. 2019). Māori have proud traditions of land-based learning, and they apply their skills at environmental monitoring with culturally relevant indicators to fill a void in ecosystem awareness (Moewaka Barnes et al. 2021). Such activities have been particularly important following neoliberal reforms that have accelerated environmental impacts while undermining capacity to know and protect the environment. In that context, Māori leaders raise questions that are similar to those asked by academics about how to inspire youth to embrace environmental protection, activate environmental citizenship, and encourage collective action. Intergenerational learning to be environmental protectors is a fundamental need of Indigenous communities at this time, and it has become highly integrated with other components of Indigenous direct action.

Environmental education and activation are conceived increasingly as generative practices that must flow spontaneously from engagement among human and more-than-human others (Iared and Hofstatter 2022). Reconfiguring environmental pedagogies as the capacity "to affect and be affective," environmental educators have made similar discoveries to those involved with Indigenous approaches to land-based learning (Fox and Alldred 2021). The power to discover for oneself and thereby enact life-long learning is greatly enhanced by doing together within the environment. Nature is no longer conceived as a passive informer but as an active participant in the generation of new environmental motivations and socio-ecological assemblages (Cole 2019). Accordingly, there is greater interaction among relational approaches to environmental care, rehabilitation, and responsibility, within all of which Indigenous scholars have been prominent leaders (McGregor, Whitaker, and Sritharan 2020; Whyte 2018). Place-responsive education—an objective shared in recent Indigenous, decolonial, and pedagogical literatures—results from being affected in and by the environment, so hands-on, materially grounded, and sensate learning is required (Lynch and Mannion 2021).

The need to sponsor transgressive, critical thinking is another pivotal critique within the new environmental activation literature (Morse, Blenkinsop, and Jickling 2021). Critical learning is also needed to fulfill the objectives of decolonial praxis and environmental repossession, so the *Land as Pedagogy* focus on Indigenous learning on Indigenous land is an incomplete vision. Criticality demands boundary crossing, not insularity; it needs exposure and not retreat to remote Indigenous lands as cultural safe zones. Unsurprisingly, the focus of this chapter—guerilla gardening by Māori children—demonstrates how those multiple perspectives on land and learning may be fulfilled as a strategy to achieve environmental repossession. Gardening was an important socio-cultural and economic practice of Māori communities in southern Auckland before the New Zealand Wars of the 1860s, and its reinvention today marks guerrilla gardening as an act of Indigenous reclamation.

Children use guerrilla gardening politically as a means to communicate their dissatisfaction with adults' wrecking of the environments they will soon inherit (Pâquet 2020). Yet, it is not a simple act of resistance to neoliberal encroachments on public space, but rather it is symbolic of the way claims to re-appropriate urban space coalesce with demands for new urban socionatures (Apostolopoulou and Kotsila 2022). Hence, it is a generative, creative strategy of experimentation with the power to envision new social orders and is, therefore, highly relevant to the social standing of urban Indigenous communities. Planting an informal garden over forgone ancestral lands or within municipal wastelands is not only an apex methodology for reclaiming the city, it is also a publicly visible act of re-education for trialing alternative urban futures (Mikadze 2020). There are exceptions to the liberatory powers of guerrilla gardening: its demographics vary considerably and, sometimes, white residents use informal gardens to block the return of non-white others to contested lands (Hardman et al. 2018; Kouros 2022). In other cases, however, the practice is significant for its redefinition of legal norms within property, boundary-making and privatized space, so it may easily be re-imagined as a focal instrument of decolonization (Millie 2022).

Exclusion from Joint Cultural and Natural Heritage

The urban Māori who participate in Taniwha Club are disenfranchised in multiple ways and, as demonstrated in the fourth section of Chapter 1, that process is not well-theorized in Aotearoa. Likewise, their claim that Auckland's volcanic landscapes are jointly cultural and natural heritage is also poorly appreciated. For the original inhabitants of southern Auckland, volcanic landscapes were important for horticulture, shelter, and various cultural practices, and they also became significant for rural-to-urban immigrants—*mātāwaka* Māori. Attempts to protect and raise awareness about the cultural importance of volcanic heritage through Taniwha Club were part of larger, community-based responses to social and environmental need. In all those responses, urban Māori and their friends within Pacific communities developed sophisticated and distinctive approaches to intergenerational learning and alliance building.

As demonstrated in Figure 4.1, volcanic landscapes dominate the underlying geology of the area. The phrase "stonefields" may be misleading because it has become tied to the Ōtuataua Stonefields Historic Reserve and neighboring Ihumātao, but I have adopted it

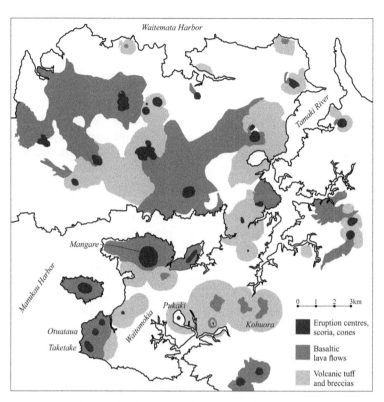

Figure 4.1 Volcanic landscapes of the Auckland Isthmus and southern Auckland as understood in 1864.

Illustration by Brad Coombes and based on a reconstruction of *Hochstetter's Geological Field Notes 1864* (Auckland War Memorial Museum, PH-NEG-B3405).

here because it is part of everyday Māori parlance in the places where Taniwha Club works. The means by which Māori lost ownership of the stonefields in southern Auckland are poorly understood. Unlike other settler colonies, *terra nullius* was not applied to Aotearoa, where the Treaty of Waitangi 1840 and the New Zealand Constitution Act 1852 presumed that the new colony was entirely Māori-owned in 1840. Nonetheless, multiple land transactions that preceded the Treaty have been an inconvenience for that view of history. From 1842, state land claims commissioners investigated all land purchases made before the signing of the Treaty. If they determined that a purchase was small and made in good faith, they had the power to validate it as a Crown grant. If the purchase was unfounded or large, excess land defaulted to Crown title, meaning that neither of the system's key mechanisms served the interests of the original Māori owners.

As demonstrated below, wars in the 1820s and 1830s partially depopulated the Auckland area, with multiple *hapū* (sub-tribes) vacating southern Auckland in fear of those *iwi* (tribes) which had sourced European weapons (Mackintosh 2021). A large area bounded by the Wairoa and Tāmaki rivers in the east and extending toward the Manukau Harbour in the west was repopulated soon after the departure of one wave of inhabitants, but ownership remained ambiguous and contested. In 1836, William Fairburn, a lay missionary, purchased 40,000 acres from a group that had no clear right to sell the land (Figure 4.2). After 1842, most of the Fairburn Purchase was invalidated in state land commissions, but very little of it was returned to the original Māori occupants (Husbands and Riddell 1993). The confusion that followed had implications for the veracity of land titles for decades and, in that uncertainty, land blocks from the Manukau Harbour in the west to the Waitemata Harbour in the east were sold and resold. Dispossessed Māori wrote multiple petitions against the Fairburn Purchase, but they were seldom successful in achieving redress (ABWN 8102 W5279/156 AUC 128). Today, those causes of land loss are difficult to address under the Treaty of Waitangi Act 1975/1985, which permits claims to the Waitangi Tribunal only for "any act done or omitted at any time on or after February 6, 1840 … by or on behalf of the Crown" (Section 6(d), Treaty of Waitangi Act; after 1985 amendment). Neither Fairburn nor those northern Māori armies that triggered the pre-Treaty flight of Auckland Māori were agents of the Crown. That the transgressions occurred a few years before 1840 is also unfortunate. Resultantly, there is little recourse to the courts or to the Waitangi Tribunal for those histories of land loss.

At the west of the southern Auckland stonefields, other forms of dispossession had a profound impact on Māori capacity to own land or utilize volcanic landscapes. The same pre-Treaty difficulties with differentiated access to European weapons, along with fearful abandonment and return to ancestral lands, were also experienced there. Pressing south from the Auckland isthmus, Ngāti Whātua iwi conquered the pā (fortified village) at Māngare on the shores of Manukau Harbour, pushing Waiohua and related hapū southwards where they centralized their economic assets and political administration at

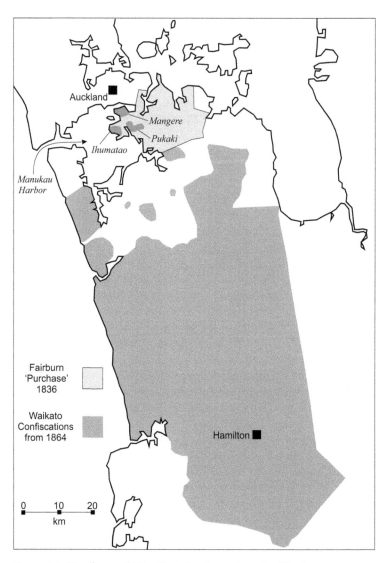

Figure 4.2 Two forms of Māori land loss in southern Auckland.

Illustration by Brad Coombes and based on a reconstruction of surveyors' guidance notes (ABWN 8102 W5279/156 AUC 129 1854; Secretary of Lands 1928).

Oruarangi, Ihumātao, and Pukaki. Later in the 1830s, both Ngāti Whātua and Waiohua partially fled the area again, fearful of yet another sortie from tribes that possessed muskets.

From the time of the Waiohua return to Ihumātao in 1836 and until 1862, however, life on the Ihumātao Peninsula was prosperous, with thriving market gardens and other forms of horticulture that served Auckland City. Mackintosh (2021) highlights how Māori horticultural skills within the stonefields were deliberately obscured in a colonial history that preferred to view southern Auckland Māori as transient rather than as sophisticated experts who raised European and sub-tropical crops. Yet, those crops were also essential for the new city's survival. As Grey and colleagues (2020) confirm, *māra* (gardens) and gardening in this area have always been political—a sometimes subtle or other times brazen form of resistance in the face of neo/colonial encroachment. By 1888, when returning Waiohua were maligned as squatter-pariahs who were trespassing on private land or public space, they replanted their gardens in a visible act of defiance until the hapū was granted a small reserve that became Ihumātao village (Murdoch 2013). The local echoing of various occupations, gardens, evictions, and protests in 1836, 1864, 1888, and 2019 attests to the political significance of gardening as an act of Indigenous reclamation. Gardening here is not a new practice but rather is long associated with a volcanic landscape that provides fertile soils, rock walls for shelter, and re-radiated heat. Complex heat-trap gardens constructed from semi-circular rock walls, along with the heat-sink properties of natural volcanic mass, were used to counteract seasonal and diurnal temperature differences to grow near tropical crops (Lawlor 2009). Two-hundred years ago, about 8000 hectares of volcanic landscapes were under Māori cultivation in Auckland, but only 160 hectares of the original stonefields remain (Rickard, Veart, and Bulmer 1983).

Because of the threats from northern tribes and with *whakapapa* (genealogical) connections to tribes in the south, Waiohua and related hapū solidified their allegiances with Waikato Tainui iwi. Their connections with Tainui were used against them, however, as a justification to eliminate their estates and economic strength within *kainga* Māori (Māori villages). Tainui was a driving force in negotiating the "Kīngitanga" and election of the first Māori king as a bastion against Māori land loss and breaches of the Treaty (Anderson, Binney, and Harris 2014). The Crown's response led directly to the New Zealand Wars of the 1860s and failed to differentiate Māori of the stonefields from Māori of the Waikato or further south. A proclamation was addressed "To the Natives of Mangere, Pukaki, Ihumatao, Te Kirikiri, Patumahoe, Pokeno, and Tuakau"—all places in the southern Auckland stonefields that are associated with volcanic landscapes and Indigenous market gardening—and it warned that:

> All persons of the native race living in the Manukau district and the Waikato frontier are hereby required immediately to take the oath of allegiance to Her Majesty the Queen, and to give up their arms to an officer appointed by Government for that purpose. Natives who comply with this order will be protected. Natives refusing to do so are hereby warned forthwith to leave the district aforesaid, and retire to Waikato beyond Mangatawhiri. In case of their not complying with this order they will be ejected.
>
> (*New Zealand Gazette* 9.7.1863: 1987)

Most refused to take the oath and were forced to leave for Waikato. Later, their villages, gardens, and other assets at Ihumātao, Pukaki, and Māngere were leveled, and those Waiohua who remained were evicted (Anderson, Binney, and Harris 2014: 234–5). "Soon their beautiful settlement became a wreck" and "old and young, the widow and the orphan, were driven from their peaceful homes. Their houses and settlements were soon pillaged of everything" (Tweedie 1864: 10). After military victories in Waikato, the government passed the New Zealand Settlements Act 1863, applying it in the two years thereafter to confiscate 1.2-m hectares of land associated with the Kīngitanga. As is clear in Figure 4.2, most of that land was further south of the stonefields, with confiscation of the enclaves at Pukaki, Māngere, and Ihumātao an exception to dissuade rear-guard insurrection. Subsequent reports presented to the Waitangi Tribunal prove that there was no evidence of any rebellious activity that could have justified the confiscations or the evictions that followed (O'Malley 2016).

It is difficult to secure rights from formal rights-making processes or to practice land-based learning on ancestral lands when a sizable proportion of those lands has been confiscated. In southern Auckland, most Māori came to the city after 1950 in waves of rural-to-urban migration; for others, the city came to them or they were expelled from it, suggesting that the stigma and victimhood that are often associated with "urban Māori" are misleading. Various groups were disenfranchised in different ways, but with similarly devastating impacts. Indeed, "Aotearoa towns and cities have always been Indigenous places," and these plural histories of urban dispossession and Māori resurgence share more commonality than difference (Kiddle 2021).

The loss of ancestral lands soon established a platform for other neo/colonial acts of environmental desolation, particularly through quarrying. An archeological report for Wiri-Māngere records thousands of heritage sites in the precinct ranging from the upper Tāmaki River to Papakura and west to the Auckland Airport and the *maunga* (mountain) at Māngere (Auckland Regional Council 2012). They include former pā, māra, and burial sites, and many of those features are associated with volcanic landscapes, debris, and stone. That legacy has been disregarded, and volcanic cones at Maungataketake, Wiri, Matukutūreia, and what became the Auckland Regional Women's Correctional Facility are now unrecognizable because of quarrying. In closer proximity to Ihumātao, Maungataketake was quarried from 1944 to 1978; Ōtuataua maunga from 1922 to 1952; Moerangi and Waitomakia between 1961 and 1965; and Te Puke Tāpapatanga a Hape from 1939 to 1967 (Auckland Council 2016; Lawlor 2009). But they were only the largest of many other quarrying sites between the Manukau Harbour and the Tāmaki River (Quarries Inspectorate R20483490 1936–88).

Some sites faced a double ignominy, with the siting of sewerage, prisons, warehousing, and industry over formerly quarried land. What little of the stonefields remained was often destroyed by subsequent farming or industrial activities, or access to them was lost because of those same activities (Rickard, Veart, and Bulmer 1983). For instance, there has been no Māori or public access to Ngā Kapua Kohuora (Crater Hill) because a private farm in non-Maori title covers all of the culturally important sites. The Pukaki crater—once a site for many Māori food gathering practices—was drained three times in forty years by Pākehā farmers who own the surrounding land (Gibb 2015). At Pukaki and other craters drowned by the sea, exclusion zones for Auckland International Airport prevent harvests of *patiki* (flounder) or access for other cultural purposes. Extensions of the airport, just south of the Ōtuataua Stonefields Historic Reserve, have eradicated burial sites or leveled volcanic structures and associated pre-European built environments (Bickler and Clough 2016).

A Catalyst for More Assertive Activism: Ihumātao and the SHA

Contributors to the earlier activist projects I was involved with in southern Auckland decided to extend their political gardening to formerly volcanic landscapes through plant bombing and guerrilla gardening. They wanted to draw public attention to the importance and destruction of the stonefields and, hopefully, to repatriate "public wastelands" (Minutes of Trustees, July 16, 2014). They learned early a need to break with conventions of guerrilla gardening and to mostly abandon food plants because of soil contamination from such land uses as quarrying. Since the first year of activity, the focus of clandestine gardening has been the native plant species that are typically used in ecological restoration rather than *kai* (food) species. There had been some protection offered to volcanic landscapes in 2001, with creation of a reserve over the best remaining specimen—the Ōtuataua Stonefields Historic Reserve, just south of Ihumātao village (Anon 2001). Yet, that was a misrepresentation of the necessary scale for protection. It was a site-specific measure when Māori had been demanding general protection throughout Auckland's volcanic landscapes.

Moreover, the range of threats increased after planning changes framed the area around Ihumātao as a new "gateway" for Auckland, leveraging the strategic location of newly available land from private sales and proximity to Auckland Airport (Evidence of W Taua, Auckland Council 2016). The rezoning of those spaces created the prospect of more warehousing and twilight industry, but it was the combination of those changes with the passing of the Housing Accords and Special Housing Areas Act 2013 that generated the definitive threat for the stonefields. The Act provides for accelerated development zones, with an intent "to exercise more permissive resource consenting processes" and thereby break the hold of municipal greenbelt regulations on urban expansion (Cabinet Minutes, New Zealand Government 13, 36–12/14). That objective sits uneasily with the headline ambitions of "contributing to housing affordability," and any need for public consultation on new developments has been diluted (Cabinet Minutes, New Zealand Government 13, 36–12/14). Joint ventures among central and local authorities, as well as corporate construction companies and tribal *rūnanga* (councils), are the preferred means for achieving growth in house numbers. Developers of subdivisions with fifteen or more housing units are required to provide one-tenth of those units at less than 75 percent of the median regional house price, something which may not guarantee affordability in an era of rapidly escalating house prices (Murphy 2016). Māori have been over-represented in groups both opposed to and supporting SHAs. Some engage with public-private partnerships of this type because Māori are significantly underrepresented in home ownership. Others reject the model because of fears that new subdivisions will either commandeer culturally sensitive areas or consume properties allocated to the land banks of the Treaty settlement process. Before the process was closed to new projects in 2019, 177 SHAs were proposed in Auckland, about one-third of which involved Māori as land donors, named beneficiaries, or providers of capital and labor (Auckland Council 2022).

SHAs may be legitimated as affordable housing but their barely concealed intent is to facilitate real estate capitalism. The 2014 Act was passed under urgency and has been associated with multiple unjust outcomes, principally because it reduced constraints on land markets while claiming to involve Māori communities in the development of social housing (McLeay 2020). At Ihumātao, the clash between corporate and cultural objectives was exposed from the start, and claims that mana whenua were willing parties to the SHA were also discredited early. There was dispute among two related hapū at Ihumātao, and after their early attempts to block the gateway project failed, some locals chose "to work within the tent" of land planners to ensure suitable conditions were imposed on the SHA (Auckland Council 2016). Adopting an alternative yet complementary strategy, a coalition of mātāwaka Māori, Waiohua activists and environmental allies asserted a vision for Ihumātao that honored its gardening traditions. They revealed the hypocrisy in the social license of those who claim corporate social responsibility in their work while profiting from social housing (Hancock et al. 2020).

Adjacent to both Ihumātao village and Ōtuataua Reserve, SHA #62 was a proposal for Fletcher Residential Limited—a local branch of a transnational construction company—to build 480 house units on only 32 ha of land. The land has significant cultural heritage value, so many locals want to expand the historic reserve over the land implicated in the SHA. It is most unusual for Māori communities to fight *for* rather than against expansion or creation of public reserves. In the face of a significant police and security guard presence, Ihumātao was occupied for most of 2019 and 2020, before a compromise was negotiated that allowed for government repurchase of the site from Fletcher Residential. A down-scaled plan for some social housing and expansion of protected stonefields is emerging at the time of writing. Images of the occupation will seem familiar to most readers, and there was considerable exchange of tactics among contemporary defenders at Trans Mountain Pipeline, Mauna Kea, and Standing Rock.

Taniwha Club: Reclaiming Focus

The SHA designation provoked multiple forms of protest, but Taniwha Club mostly formed independently of that momentum. It was established in 2014, just after the SHA was first announced, but before it reached public consciousness. The main drivers for its establishment were not the SHA but rather announcements that former quarry sites at Wiri would not be remediated as had been promised, and that regional correctional facilities would expand onto historic rock gardens. Indeed, the emergence of Taniwha Club reflected concerns that most southern Auckland stonefields were *less* protected than those surrounding the Ōtuataua reserve. An early public discussion about how to protect heritage landscapes further to the east was captured by the heartbreaking appeals of a thirteen-year-old Māori girl whose "mum is in that prison and would soon lose any views of the rock playgrounds and gardens that her *kuia* [grandmother] had cared for as a kid" (Minutes of Public Meeting, April 5, 2014). Subsequently, other tamariki also confirmed a motivation to care for the lands alongside facilities in which their relatives were incarcerated, indicating why those places became favored sites for planting days. In a discussion about guerrilla gardening as decolonization, it is not off-topic to remark that over half the prison population of Aotearoa is Māori, even though Māori are only 14 percent of the national population (McIntosh and Workman 2017).

After an initial starting point in an abandoned building, Taniwha Club grew substantially to enjoy the support of three marae and four schools, accumulating over 350 school-aged members. Regular members numbered no more than forty, however, and a key feature of the program was the capacity of those regulars to entice other children into inspirational, albeit brief, moments of activation. The Club's work is intended to be visual, visible, and creative—we hope that it is empowering to be an occasional taniwha. Because the club is for children, the trustees, artists, gardeners, and *kaumātua* (Elders) who lead activities decided not to explain the full complexities in what taniwha might mean. We glibly inform participants that taniwha are "good monsters" and "environmental guardians" and, while that would satisfy neither Māori adults nor scholars, nothing more is required for tamariki. Taniwha are not inherently good nor bad, and neither are they best understood as monsters, tricksters, or environmental advocates. Strang (2014: 126) argues that taniwha represent "a Māori bioethic of partnership with the nonhuman" but, in the childhood landscapes of southern Auckland, "good monsters" and positive role models matter more than academic codification.

The concept for group activities is simple. Every second Thursday, existing members invite friends to a revolving roster of local marae to make elaborate taniwha costumes from inexpensive felt and locally harvested *harakeke* (flax). On the subsequent weekend, they dress up elaborately and, without seeking authorization, plant native seedlings on former quarry land, vacant lots, and any liminal or interstitial spaces that provoke civic contemplation. At times, the tamariki experiment with such overseas approaches as manufacturing mud balls impregnated with seeds which they throw vigorously at publicly visible targets, but they typically default to the more sedate planting of seedlings. Review of experience is another crucial element of Club culture. The trustees run open meetings where parents and participants regularly attend to discuss the socio-cultural meaning of the activities. With my colleagues' permission, I use extensively our minutes of meetings in this chapter, and it was always intended that they be for public reckoning and reflexive meditation. All aspects of Taniwha Club emulate Participatory Action Research (refer to the third section of Chapter 2), with an emphasis on action methodologies, peer-to-peer learning, and continuous review. Children develop their own agendas and work programs and are asked to think about culturally and locally appropriate approaches to transformation. The most common debate is about the end goal of the program. With several teachers and two academics as trustees, there are clear commitments to civic education, but there is constant debate about the purpose and form of education.

The trustees attend many of the art classes at marae, coordinate guerrilla gardening at the weekend, and meet fortnightly to discuss strategies. As our meetings commenced not long before this book project was initiated, at times we chose to discuss the idea of environmental repossession. My colleagues were hesitant about the concept, noting that for the Ihumātao peninsula "the attitude of this is quite right" but as a general strategy for decolonization it was potentially misplaced: "can we repossess it when we've never possessed it?" (Minutes of Trustees Meeting, April 6, 2016). Before, and for twenty-two years after signing of the Treaty in 1840, Māori did own the land around Ihumātao, so the speaker's intent must have been a critique of treating land as a possession. On the other hand, some commentators referred again to the appropriate "attitude" or the "suitable tone in that idea of repossession":

All Māori who contribute to the Club have a teaching that people owe a debt to the land. Around here, those Pākehā who have benefitted from that debt haven't honored their responsibility, so repossession might capture the idea that they've had their turn and now it should be our turn again to see if we can make better use of the opportunity.
(Minutes of Trustees Meeting, February 8, 2017)

The complications in urban indigeneity and the status of mātāwaka peoples were also raised. As there were "more mātāwaka folk who contribute to Taniwha Club than mana whenua," it may be "rude and divisive to associate our cause with repossession. It might be a bad guess, a presumption, that they'd even want that" (Minutes of Trustees Meeting, September 19, 2018).

Discussion of repossession mimicked discussion of all paths to self-determination, with the way urban Māori leadership is impeded being a common cause of uncertainty. From the time of important case law in the late 1990s, the Crown demonstrated its reluctance to work with Urban Māori Authorities (UMA)—typically non- or pan-tribal organizations that have formed to address the needs of mātāwaka and which parallel the role of more "traditional" rūnanga. Within a few months of a groundbreaking conclusion from the Waitangi Tribunal (1998) that UMAs were fit for purpose as delivery mechanisms for state welfare programs, the High Court determined that they could not act as financial beneficiaries of Treaty settlements (Justice Patterson, in Te Waka Hi Ika v ToWFC 1998). Non-resource rights and rights to deal with one's own social disadvantage are granted to non-sessile Māori, but resource rights of potentially greater consequence are not granted to mātāwaka because it is assumed they gave up such rights when they moved to the city (Gagné 2016). Disdain for urban Māori guardians and leaders was also revealed by resource management agencies that refused to work with UMAs because they had no official status, denying urban mātāwaka standing as mana whenua and, thereby, denying Treaty rights intended for all Māori (Coombes 2013).

Such impediments skewed trustees' opinions toward informal practices rather than formal mechanisms of redress; and "Given that we won't achieve the status of mana whenua and that our UMAs are barred from acting like rūnanga, how could we hope to repossess these landscapes?" (Minutes of Parental Focus Group, September 18, 2016). This may demonstrate the appeal of guerrilla gardening by children: the more adult leaders are blocked from conventional rights-making processes, the more they may rely on alternative and informal rights-taking practices involving children. Any Māori contemplation of a new concept like environmental repossession will be juxtaposed against the Treaty of Waitangi, its promises of *tino rangatiratanga* (chieftainship) and the inadequacies of the Waitangi Tribunal's settlement process. "If you can't win in the courts or the Tribunal, you have to win hearts and minds in public. That's why the kids, their cheerful costumes and their fun with plant-bombs matter so much" (Debrief Discussion on Planting Day, July 12, 2020). Therefore, "what Taniwha Club does, I reckon, is a really clever type of public relations and you won't see repossession defined that way in the dictionary" (Debrief Discussion on Planting Day, August 2, 2020). Notably, because they dismissed any prospect of repatriating land or repossessing preferred environs, parents and trustees could only sense value in repossession if it is defined as reclaiming public focus. Ironically, because encouraging children to partake in quasi-illegal practices is swathed in ethical liabilities, Taniwha Club typically avoids public focus, shielding its leadership and participants within a warren of incorporated societies and shell entities. There is no bank account, it functions on barter and gifting, and we avoid a web presence and media attention.

Training for Next-Gen Protestors

In our activity day debriefs, tamariki of Taniwha Club often commend the "hands-on nature of our learning and our training to be *kaitiaki* [guardians] and leaders" (Debrief Discussion on Planting Day, July 18, 2021). Debrief sessions often start but go no further than a single question—"What did you learn today?"—but the answers are revealing. The most common response of the tamariki extols practical activities that use malleable earth as a canvas, but those comments always convey a wider social meaning:

> We make a māra and it lives on. I go back to the places where we plant—six months go by, a year. Some were planted five years ago. They're still there, and they've grown so much. It makes you feel good and you learn so much about the environment and how it works. But even better, it makes you feel like there's a point to trying other stuff. To do other environment work or … well … me and others who are in Club and also at my school formed a *kapa haka* [Māori performing arts] group at school. Club *mahi* [work] gave us confidence to do that.
> (Debrief Discussion on Planting Day, June 7, 2021)

I'm not good at school. I failed every science test until year 11 where I got full credits. I didn't see the point of it, but I do now. I mean, plant bombing is a practical way of learning. Seeing it. Touching it. Getting real dirty. Growing it yourself. That makes a difference. And the growing becomes a symbol, you know, a ... [prompter: a metaphor?]. Ae, that's right. A metaphor. You grow plants here, then you grow other good things there, and then you grow as a person.

(Minutes of Tamariki Council, April 14, 2022)

Remarkably, those arguments are nearly identical to the conclusions in recent academic scholarship about environmental learning. The promises of the materialist turn in environmental activation and learning theories are both feasible and culturally appropriate for growing kaitiaki/tanga in southern Auckland.

When asked about what role parents and kaumātua should adopt, one participant noted that "You adults are so funny. You think we don't know that you're training us up to be next-gen protestors. But we do know. You can be honest about this cos, like, we want this" (Debrief Discussion on Planting Day, August 2, 2020). Perhaps mimicking current arguments within social movement theories and transition methodologies, the Club prioritizes the socialization of future leaders, as well as the support structures they will need for transformational change. In the opinions seemingly of all associated with Taniwha Club, "plant bombing is a *tika* [correct, proper] thing to do because it's a constructive not destructive pastime, so our kids can stay positive and make a stand too" (Minutes of Parental Focus Group, September 11, 2021). This demand for constructive outlets and noble protest was repeated often, and it was also significant in common calls about "making places that all can appreciate because that's just the best kind of victory here" (Debrief Discussion on Planting Day, July 12, 2020). Others confirmed that "showing the way to make healthier and more livable neighborhoods has the advantage of attracting Pākehā attention to *all* things Māori," meaning that "next time, they may understand better the cultural bases of our objections" (Minutes of Trustees Meeting, November 22, 2017).

Nonetheless, the common claim that "Club is a type of training for future-proofing us with visions and leaders" coexisted uneasily with the educational goals of the trustees (Debrief Discussion on Planting Day, July 9, 2022). As mentioned earlier, many of the trustees hold passions or careers in primary, secondary, and tertiary education, but they recognized that a different mode and attitude is required from their pedagogies in this case. Again, that requirement was tied to the awkward status of urban Māori and their forms of representation:

> When you have no rights in the here and now, you need to take a slower path across the generations. It's all about education, but what type of learning and where is that to be done? It's not something for the classroom or the university. It must be on this land but that can't be a passive thing. The more we plant, the more we stake a claim, take leadership and gain supporters. If our kids can learn for themselves how to make—not to remake you see, but to make new— connections to this place, they will gain the skills and motivations to inspire change.
>
> (Minutes of Trustees Meeting, December 12, 2016)

That view supports the centrality granted to ancestral land in ideas about *Land as Pedagogy*, but—significantly—most participants were not and had never worked on their ancestral lands. There are subtle and important differences about where and why this mahi is pursued and who the target audience is. Rather than retrospective learning from the past, the ethos of Taniwha Club is palpably futuristic in its goals to envision new urban relations and to "stake a claim." Considerable hope was invested in general characteristics of land, landed-relationships, and working the land, but there was no theoretical or practical need for work on tribal land held within a clan for centuries. Likewise, Taniwha Club is a training ground for developing "new Polynesian allegiances" because the "most important thing plant bombing can do is showcase the common struggles and cultural bonds between Māori, Samoan and Tongan children" (Minutes of Parental Focus Group, August 29, 2020). One of the more astonishing revelations for the trust was that within five years of operation, tamariki Māori had become less than half of the regular Polynesian attendees, but the trust had never consciously adopted a policy for that shift. Clandestine gardening "happens in complex places, with complex processes and random fusings of different peoples" and "through such complex interactions new solutions and new ways of seeing the city emerge" (Minutes of Trustees Meeting, January 25, 2018).

Going Viral, Going Radical, *and* Going Legit

At first, attendance at Taniwha Club events declined during the COVID-19 pandemic, even in times when lockdown orders had been lifted. Later in the pandemic, however, numbers increased to new record highs. "It's the right medicine for right now. Go make yourself a garden that's natural and healthy when all else is artificial and depressing" (Debrief Discussion on Planting Day, August 28, 2020). Participants gained such strength from combatting the estrangements of the pandemic through informal gardening that they coopted and adapted the language of pandemics in their practice. "Yeah, so, that was totally deliberate. We talked about and wanted Club to 'go viral' at that precise moment so we could show that our ways are about making a better life and not just about growing plants" (Debrief Discussion on Planting Day, March 12, 2022). In other words, "it's all about community bro and right now is the right time to prove that because it will have a permanent impact. If what we do can be relevant now, it will always be relevant" (Debrief Discussion on Planting Day, April 10, 2021). What becomes clear from these playful adaptations of pandemic-speak is how fully the strategies, motivational tactics, and attunement of youthful gardeners have evolved. Their capacity to lead discussions and movements expanded through their generative gardening practices, enabling them to respond later to significant social and cultural needs. It is only through self-dependent, spontaneous capacity enhancement of this type that decolonial strategies can thrive.

While young, the tamariki were maturely aware of the need to spread their messages of care and responsibility to win support among Māori and non-Māori alike. One teenage participant who had been a leader of her peers in Taniwha Club for several years noted that:

> We talk a lot about what's transformative and the tough answer is
> … not much. Being better ourselves ain't gonna be enough. Here
> in Māngere we need the rest of society to want change. The way I
> see it, you can't manufacture that. We can be role models with the
> restoration work we do in all the fucked-over quarries and abandoned
> places, but even that seems … wrong or wrong to hope for. That's why
> we twisted the virus thing—"make-Club-go-viral." We wanted this to
> be everybody's mission, an impulse you can't stop.
> (Debrief Discussion on Planting Day, July 18, 2021)

Arguably, "going viral" is a necessary component of any decolonizing strategy, whether that must be applied during a pandemic or not. What is academically and socially significant in this case is how successful the publicly visible and creative art of guerrilla gardening has become as "a super-spreader of the good kind" (Minutes of Tamariki Council Meeting, May 8, 2021).

It is mistaken, however, to anticipate that the tamariki will always buy into environmental virtues, civic enlightenment, and an Indigenous spirit. A radical edge has emerged in their politics, and sometimes that targets the relevance of Indigenous traditions as well as confronting white privilege:

> I'm not interested in all that traditional knowledge stuff, wisdom of the Elders, ways of old—how's that shit relevant to Otara? I do Club because it's for this place and of this place. I've made a commitment to this *whenua* [land], even if that's just an abandoned section we don't own next to our state house that we don't own. I've come back to Club to help other kids think differently about their rights to this place. Our revolution starts right here and nowhere else.
>
> (Debrief Discussion on Planting Day, March 7, 2019)

Generally, the commitment to where participants live is impressive. Along with other trustees, however, I am often shocked by these moments when children demonstrate such cultural and political rowdiness. Another iconoclast grew impatient with inferences that she and her peers were the modern incarnation of earlier political gardeners: "Yeah. They grew gardens here back in the day. So what? This is different. This isn't about making old ways new again" (Minutes of Tamariki Council, January 27, 2022). Such outbursts typically immobilize the trustees and advisors who are reminded awkwardly that their initial premise for Taniwha Club was to reinsert critical thinking into environmental learning. The apparent disregard for traditional knowledge and traditional practices may represent problematic assumptions and gaps in land-based pedagogies. Irrespective of how an adult may want to interpret the land-based learning of Māori youth, their involvement may reflect a fundamentally different understanding of Indigenous needs and remedies. The futuristic gaze of participants outweighs any demand to learn from past practices. The plant bombers make a/new, so the outcomes of associated practices are unpredictable. They will not dwell on the past, so they seem uncertain about whether they can learn from it. After years of knowing these tamariki, I dimly appreciate that theirs is a better way which presents an important counter to the lingering appeal of retrospective utopia in Indigenous politics.

Neo/Colonial Transgressions and Boundary (Re)Crossing

Somewhere between "go viral" and "go radical," a new direction emerged in 2019 when the children who had been with the club for most of their teenage years proposed a new structure. They perceived a need to apply their accumulated skills in leadership, and they sought to express their leadership through different activities. A think-piece document—"Your Fruit Are Ready to Begin Life as Trees"—was tabled at an open meeting, and by its end the meeting resolved to transition the board of trustees to a board of advisors. Daily management and strategy development was transferred to a Tamariki Council. The Fruit expressed clearly that they were not dissatisfied with the Old Trees, but they had envisioned new approaches that demanded greater responsibility from them. In most ways, this was a symbolic shift because all parties complete the same work they were doing before the transition. The Fruit had long before matured and had been leading Taniwha Club for some time.

The second of the two reforms is more significant. "Guerrilla," "clandestine," "quasi-legal," and "informal" gardening fulfilled many ambitions, but the Tamariki Council was concerned about the potential for self-stereotyping to minimize their impact. "I'm Tongan and I'm dark as, but I ain't no gorilla," said one with a tell-tale grin (Minutes of Tamariki Council, April 18, 2019). The concern of the new leadership was about whether their demands for southern Auckland would be taken seriously if their work was associated only with illicit practices. These excerpts from one of the first meetings of the Tamariki Council reveal the growing maturity of its leaders:

> Doing the urban guerrilla thing was nicely confrontational for a while, but it will provoke even more thought if, now that everybody expects us to do that, we get all respectable and plant only with permission.

> One problem is that plant bombing only happens in wastelands. If we want all parts of all of our 'hoods to change we can't limit ourselves to doing things in the dark and out of the way. There are good things here in Papatoetoe and I want to protect them too. We can't do that if we're trying to revive places that are already dead.

> Weekend after weekend, I've seen it happening. They find ways to discredit you. If you're trying to sell alternatives about how to make this place liveable, but they can make the guerrilla tactics look like the same stuff that got your uncle in prison, it's a no-win situation for us.
>
> (Minutes of Tamariki Council, February 10, 2019)

The biblical metaphor to know your worth from the quality of your fruit was well-chosen for its purpose. The older tamariki had evolved into thoughtful citizens and cunning activists. As regular boundary crossers, they had now crossed even the boundaries that their Old Trees had unconsciously created for them. They have so lived critical thinking since 2014 that they know when to move beyond critical thinking or mere protest. Fostering leadership and its intergenerational transfer are preconditions for any Indigenous decolonization of the city.

The decision to practice "legit" restoration also reflected important life lessons that individuals brought back to the group from their family experiences at the Ōtuataua occupation. Just before the occupation started, Taniwha Club was gifted the inventory of a financially insolvent plant nursery. Club members utilized the seedlings in many planting projects, but because some stock was older and larger it could not be used in guerilla gardening approaches. Rather, for the first time the tamariki participated in official restoration projects, contributing their plants and labor to streamside rehabilitation at multiple southern Auckland sites. The appreciation of their work was affirming, revealing the potential of restoration to develop relationships with like-minded groups. The Tamariki Council then donated excess stock to the defenders at Ōtuataua, with some used to plant a tree in front of most police officers and security guards present at the height of the occupation. This moment of armistice led to a new appreciation of the social work that land-based restoration can do. Relationships between law enforcers and occupiers were good-natured throughout, but the unanticipated use of the club's seedlings highlighted the potential for environmental work to extend into peace offerings, healing, and conflict resolution. The Fruit wanted to explore those options more fully and openly, affirming their decision to pursue henceforth only lawful practices.

The emergent maturity in the Tamariki Council is also revealed by how they have managed setbacks since they assumed leadership. It is difficult to fight airport extensions with the plantings of children, and a further round of runway additions will soon encroach onto additional sites of cultural significance (AIA 2021). The fate of Ihumātao and the SHA is not certain, and it seems that a difficult politics will persist there. Although the club has long separated itself from the adults' disputes at Ihumātao, the tamariki are saddened and lose confidence each time they learn of a setback there. In response, they developed an art program for reconceptualizing Ihumātao as the domain of taniwha. My own entry led to extended discussion about its intended meaning. My taniwha sketches, silhouetted against a photograph of the proposed SHA site, did not look particularly durable, prompting fears that this symbolized how plantings might succumb to the bulldozers or that the work of the club may not be sustained. Reflecting the unavoidable characteristics of informal, everyday activism, they lack a sense of permanence. But learning by planting is learning by doing, and learning by doing can be life-long learning. Taniwha Club's effort will be realized sometime and somewhere, even if the bulldozers level one landscape.

In any case, the response to any disappointment has been inspirational. Club members wanted to enhance heritage landscapes at Ngā Kapua Kohuora (Crater Hill). Pākehā landowners prevented such work, and there was much disenchantment when they sought to subdivide for housing one of the few volcanic maunga which had not already been leveled. Further areas of cultural significance were subject to a private plan change that was inconsistent with the Auckland District Plan, and which once again privileged elite housing developments over the protection of heritage sites. Prevented from accessing the site, the tamariki engaged instead in participatory theatre outside of private land blocks, re-enacting the 1852 cutting of survey lines by some of their own ancestors. Other groups added their own protests and several intelligent submissions ensured that this issue was better managed in the planning system. The Environment Court rejected the private plan change, invaliding the resource consents for subdivision on the maunga. The judge's decision included a new precedent for managing the clash between real estate capitalism and cultural heritage, maintaining that "assessment of net social benefits … is at the heart of any assessment of economic efficiency" (Self Family Trust v AC 2018). Although that may seem ordinary for an overseas audience, it represents a new approach for Aotearoa. The decision was not a victory for Taniwha Club, but rather the club was part of a larger social movement that emerged after the Ihumātao dispute had raised public awareness of the stonefields' special character.

He Mutunga

Māori youth and their ~~guerrilla~~ gardening in southern Auckland is a form of decolonial praxis, but it also unsettles conventional wisdom about decolonization. It is a restorative practice in third spaces, but often it is less about ecological restoration and more inclined to socio-political restitution. It involves elements of participatory action and critical pedagogies, but the Fruit have taught the Old Trees much more than the latter have instructed the former. Mimicking the new materialist approaches to environmental activation and their emphasis on generative making, it creates new landscapes that lead to new visions. That may at times be at the expense of cultural memory for old socionatures, past learnings, and inherited cultures of knowing and being in the world. Yet, while land-based pedagogies of this type are vitally important for Indigenous resurgence, they clearly do not require an essentialized framing of ("traditional") knowledge, ("ancestral") land, or ("authentic") identities. Notably, the tamariki of Taniwha Club work for their places and their neighborhoods, but not necessarily for or on their lands. A plant bomber does not need to be on Indigenous land for the making to matter.

Both as a scholar and as a contributor to this project, I have come to appreciate a need for decolonial geographies to move beyond mere critique. It is long overdue for postcolonialism to develop its own stance on how to achieve positive change and hopeful transformation. The tamariki of Taniwha Club are making a third space of possibilities, but the few other strategies for transition within decolonial thought are too passive and too bookish. Defining Indigenous agency through the mistakes of colonizing others, as many postcolonial scholars are inclined to do, is not sufficiently transformative for a new generation who clearly know that material change must accompany any critique or theorizing. Therefore, I tender and affirm certain synergies between the intent of decolonial critique and what new materialist approaches to environmental education can offer. The mahi of Taniwha Club is a creative practice; it is the making that matters. Getting your hands dirty, leaving an imprint, making anew, and learning by doing might all be needed in an urban context where legal processes will not simply hand your rights back because of who your ancestors were. We cannot evade neo/colonialism if we hope to transform it. Repossession must be a visible practice, the act of crossing and recrossing boundaries and not hiding behind them. Even though a large group of Māori children wearing brightly colored felt costumes while plant bombing can be spectacular, it is the everyday nature of the club's work that is most significant. According to Kiddle (2021: 146), "good urbanism would allow Māori to live the lives they want to live" and "the next step is seeing Māoriness in the everyday, the mundane ... [a] kind of urbanism [which] is about re-connection and recreation of places of belonging" (p. 147). It is my expectation that tamariki of the club are contributing to good urbanism, mostly through questioning what Māori-affirming landscapes should look like and through their discernable efforts to make such landscapes for themselves.

Acknowledgments

Topi Richardson and **Ihaka Te Pou** were postgraduate students at the time of the occupation of the Ōtuataua Stonefields and at various times before, during and after the research for this chapter they lived at Ihumātao or nearby villages. Although they made no direct contributions to this book, they were such engaging students to supervise that they transferred their passions for stonefields advocacy to Brad. They were also involved as leaders, educators, and artists in Taniwha Club. Their intelligent conversations influenced key ideas that were incorporated into this chapter.

Chapter 5

GATHERING FOR WELLNESS IN BIIGTIGONG NISHNAABEG

Introduction

The Mouth of the Pic is the original gathering place of Biigtigong Nishnaabeg. It is the place where the Biigtig Ziibi (formerly known as Pic River) meets the Black River and flows into Lake Superior. In Anishinabemoen, Biigtig translates into "the place of the muddy waters," a reference to the clay that lines the shore and riverbed. The Biigtig Ziibi flows approximately 200 kilometers from McKay Lake near Long Lac, until it meets the Black River. The Biigtig Ziibi's creamy color slowly dissipates as it meets with the Black River, and then with Lake Superior. The place where these waters connect forms the life force for Biigtigong. These waters and their adjacent lands form vital sources of food and nourishment, transportation, and connection with our social, cultural, and spiritual practices as Nishnaabeg people.

The Mouth of the Pic features into the very beginnings of our community's history and creation. Everyone seems to know that the mouth was a significant meeting place for families. Generations of babies were born in this place, and many more were laid to rest here as well. Our people fished from the Biigtig Ziibi, and harvested birds and eggs from nearby Gull Island. Our people moved throughout our broad territory to follow moose and trap rabbit, but the mouth is the place we always returned to. Long before the creation of our reserve site, Pic River 50, the mouth was home to our people:

> We used to live off our land at the mouth of the Pic. As told by the Elders, this is where we used to live until Indian Affairs came in and disrupted everything. And Marathon Paper, they told the Indians: "We're going to use this place, so get out of here." We used to live in Mud Bay, the mouth of the Pic, until we were moved up this way. And they only gave us 800 acres of land, which was totally wrong.

They moved us up further inland, which was wrong because our grandparents and all the Elders, they hunted all over the country. They were here; they were there.

(Elder 2)

The archaeological record demonstrates occupancy of this place by Nishnaabeg for several thousand years, and it was used by other Indigenous peoples who travelled through the area. The Mouth of the Pic was a known destination for those traveling around Lake Superior, and it served as a gateway to Northern Canada for fur traders and other travelers heading to and from Northern Ontario. The geographic, economic, and ceremonial importance of this place signified a critical role for Biigtigong Nishnaabeg people, as it placed us at the center of an important network of families, clans, and connections that endure today, across and beyond our traditional territory.

Gathering as Connection with Places, Knowledge, and People

Biigtigong Nishnaabeg is an Anishinaabe community located halfway between the cities of Thunder Bay and Sault Ste. Marie, in the province of Ontario, Canada. Biigtigong sits along the Biigtig Ziibi about 5 kilometers north of the place where the river empties into Lake Superior. Among Biigtigong Nishnaabeg, our gathering practices strongly shape our identities and our sense of belonging as Nishnaabeg people.

Gathering is as much a part of everyday life as it is a sacred one. It strengthens our relationships with our lands, and with one another. These principles feature into an Anishinaabe concept of wellness: *mino bimaadiziwin. Mino bimaadiziwin*, as described in Chapter 1, is a relational way of knowing and living that respects the interconnection between individuals and other people, including our ancestors, our future generations, and with the earth (Leah 2016). As Anishinaabe people, our abilities to live the good life are rooted deeply in the ways we interact with and care for all of the relationships that support our way of life (Borrows 2016; Goudreau 2006). *Mino bimaadiziwin* acknowledges and celebrates these varying relationships, which are maintained, shared, and strengthened through various cultural and spiritual practices and protocols (Bell 2016; Debassige 2010; Fletcher 2017; McGregor 2018b). These practices shape the way Nishnaabeg form relationships with one another and with the natural and spiritual worlds. These practices support Nishnaabeg to enjoy the rights of belonging to this community, but they are also important reminders of their responsibilities:

> We all have responsibilities to take care of one another. We must respect that it is the whole of us that makes the community stronger. Everyone has strength and purpose. We all have a role to play in making this community a good place.
>
> (Interviewee 2)

Across the vastness of our ancestral territory and beyond, the people of Biigtigong Nishnaabeg have gathered to demonstrate our accountabilities to the wider set of relationships that make us whole and well. These gatherings offered a place for Nishnaabeg to practice and share our knowledge, stories, and teachings about how to live well in this world: how to greet the day, how to respect others, how to maintain caring relations, and how to ask for help when needed. These and so many other teachings and knowledge have been shared within our families and wider community contexts. Our job was to listen to the old ones so we would always have the knowledge and stories we need to continue to fulfill our responsibilities to the land and to one another. To do this is to live *mino bimaadiziwin*.

Over many years, our abilities to gather on our lands, and to fulfill our responsibilities as Nishnaabeg have changed considerably. While we know the importance of these connections for community wellness and securing Anishinaabe knowledge, many historic and ongoing processes of cultural and environmental dispossession have significantly disrupted, and continue to disrupt, our community's interest, knowledge, and ability to be together on the land as our ancestors did.

Like many Indigenous peoples and communities who have endured colonial violence and alienation from their lands, these processes have left our community fractured socially, culturally, and geographically (Czyzewski 2011; Tobias and Richmond 2014; Truth and Reconciliation Commission 2015). Despite the considerable harm and trauma endured by our community as a result of these disruptions, Biigtigong Nishnaabeg has engaged on an incredible pathway of hope and healing, through which we aim to restore our original cultural practices and the gifts of knowledge, belonging, and wellness that are anchored therein.

The purpose of this chapter is to detail how Biigtigong is re-establishing its gathering practices to reconnect with the lands, people, and knowledge that grow from our traditional territory. We draw from the concept of environmental repossession to describe the social, cultural, and political practices Biigtigong Nishnaabeg is engaging in to support wellness, healing, and community belonging. These efforts are described in the chapter through the lens of connection; gathering around the moose hunt, returning to the Mouth of the Pic, and reconnecting our social relations with one another. Engaging in our gathering practices is fundamentally about living and being in *mino bimaadiziwin* and demonstrating our capabilities to create spaces that offer healing, belonging, and that support our own self-determined futures.

Nishnaabeg Research Creation

The research detailed in this chapter contributes to a community-based program of research that is nearly two decades in the making. Determined locally by Biigtigong's elected leadership and supported in large part by various staff members from Biigtigong's Department of Sustainable Development, this research has been led academically by Biigtigong community member Chantelle Richmond, who has been a faculty member at Western University (London, Ontario, Canada) since 2008. In general, this collaborative research program has focused on preserving and restoring Nishnaabeg knowledge about relationships with the land, Anishinaabe wellness, and the connection between healthy lands and healthy peoples (Big-Canoe and Richmond 2014; Nightingale and Richmond 2022).

Over the past several years, this community-based program of research has engaged many Elders and knowledge keepers, elected and ceremonial leaders, teachers, administrators, and youth in discussions about key community matters, activities, and programs that revolve around health and wellness, Nishnaabeg knowledge, and social relationships. During this time, we have been afforded the opportunity to work with and train many local youths, as well as a number of Anishinaabe, and other Indigenous and allied graduate students and scholars from across Turtle Island to support Biigtigong with doing this work. This research has occurred largely on the land, and it has emphasized Elder-youth relationships as methodology (Mikraszewicz and Richmond 2019; Nightingale and Richmond 2021; Tobias and Richmond 2014), and it both drew from and expanded on a growing base of Nishnaabeg research and pedagogy (Bell 2013; Chartrand 2012; McGregor 2018b).

The first and most significant collaboration we embarked on was an Elder's project in the late 2000s. This project began as a series of sharing circles with Elders from various Nishnaabeg communities along the North shore of Lake Superior about their growing concerns over environmental changes happening in the territory—most notably mining, forestry, and wind development projects—and what these changes meant for Nishnaabeg wellness and connection to the land (Richmond 2018). Our adoption of the sharing circle methodology was important for many reasons. Sharing circles follow Nishnaabeg ceremonial protocol; they take as long as they need to, no one will be interrupted, and they open and close with prayer. This methodology offered plenty of room for memories to be shared, new ideas contributed, and respectful dialogue around all contributions provided throughout. Our circles sometimes went around more than once, as thoughts and ideas spurred memories among others, as well as alternative ideas and interpretations.

In our work, we opened deliberate space for conversation, story, and sharing of Nishnaabeg knowledge and experience. We initiated the project by asking: "What could or should research look like in Biigtigong, and how can it be useful?" Over various sessions, we brainstormed many ideas. One of the most exciting projects the Elders kept returning to was the idea of a film. They sat in a giant circle, laughing among themselves: "we want to be movie stars!" Looking back at that day, we are grateful for their persistence with this idea. At the time, a film seemed far outside the range of possibilities. But because we had not undertaken such an adventure before did not mean we could not do so in the future. With so many hearts and minds working on one vision, we drew on all possible relationships, skills, and knowledge to churn the idea into reality.

These early sharing circles set the trajectory for a longer-term project that was based on principles of listening and responding to Nishnaabeg leadership, thinking outside our capabilities, valuing Nishnaabeg ways of doing, and putting Nishnaabeg voices at the center of the work. Our days started and ended in prayer, we ate together, and we committed to doing work that would benefit the community. These discussions also highlighted the importance of placing Nishnaabeg youth into these studies and providing critical opportunities for generational knowledge acquisition. Elders were clear that Biigtigong youth must also participate in these studies to support their own skill building and confidence. The idea for the film blossomed into a collaborative project with youth and Elders from nearby Nishnaabeg community Batchewana First Nation of Ojibways and culminated in the production of *Gifts from the Elders* (www.giftsfromtheElders.ca), a 60-minute documentary film, produced by Nishnaabeg Film-maker James Fortier and released in 2013. The film follows five young Nishnaabeg who spend the summer months interviewing their Elders. While it is true that the Elders did indeed become movie stars, the true impact of the film was in its decolonizing methodology, whereby the community determined how it would engage in the research, for what purposes, and how the work would ultimately be shared (Richmond 2016). As we look back at those early days of the research journey, we are filled with mixed emotions: pride, strength, courage, and love, but also sadness, grief, and sorrow. Some of the Elders who supported this work have since joined the spirit world. That their words and images have been memorialized on film demonstrate the absolute lasting power of film, but also its ability to inspire and celebrate our own stories, history, and desires for the future in ways that can be shared broadly with other audiences. While the film seemed like an outrageous undertaking when the idea was first offered in 2008, in fact it set into motion a wave of transformative research that has continually empowered Biigtigong Nishnaabeg to use research as a tool to serve their own goals. These goals have been upheld through research with other scholars on matters relating to Biigtigong's relationship with the lands and resources of its wider territory, including a hydroelectric project (Krupa 2012; Krupa, Galbraith, and Burch 2015), and moose population monitoring (Popp, Priadka, and Kozmik 2019; Popp et al. 2020; Priadka et al. 2022). The work of documenting occupation and land use has been a key feature of the community's on-going land claim as well, including historical, genealogical, land use, and occupancy studies (Biigtigong Nishnaabeg 2022).

The research described in this particular chapter engages importantly from the work of allied scholar, Dr. Elana Nightingale, who came to work with Biigtigong for her PhD research on the concept of environmental repossession. Community leadership in Biigtigong had expressed a need to document ongoing strategies of environmental repossession in order to demonstrate why land reconnection is important and share lessons for other communities. With a background in economic development, Elana brought with her a range of community-based practices from other Indigenous contexts, notably from Inuit Nunangat, the Inuit regions of Northern Canada (Nightingale et al. 2017). Working alongside her academic supervisor, Chantelle Richmond, Elana was mentored at the community level by the Director of Sustainable Development, Juanita Starr, and the Manager of Culture and Heritage, Florinda Christianson, both of whom contributed to this chapter. Beginning in 2018, Elana and

Florinda worked closely to design and develop a research process that would both document and support land reclamation in Biigtigong by bringing together Elders and youth in significant places and collecting community history and knowledge about these lands. In particular, this process aimed to reclaim and encourage land use at Mountain Lake, an area along the western boundary of Biigtigong's territory, by hosting a week-long camp with Elders, knowledge keepers, community staff, and youth at this site in 2019. Working with the concept of environmental repossession, the broadest goal of this work was to demonstrate why being back in Biigtigong's territory is important for strengthening community members' connections to land, each other, and identity as Nishnaabeg.

To highlight what land reconnection means for Biigtigong, twenty story-based interviews were conducted between 2019 and 2022 with community members involved in these land reclamation efforts, including four Elders and knowledge keepers, six youth, and eight current or former staff of the department of Sustainable Development. These flexible interviews allowed community members to control the conversation and share the experiences, perceptions, and knowledge that are most important to their lived experience within the context of their family, community, and culture (Iseke 2013; Kovach 2009; Rieger et al. 2020). Interviews with Elders and knowledge keepers took place on the land, while interviews with staff members and students were done at the department's office. Due to COVID-19 and related lockdown measures, three interviews with staff members took place over the Zoom platform. All of the stories, history, and knowledge gathered through these conversations are owned by Biigtigong for their own use and shared here with permission. Pseudonyms have been assigned to participant contributions.

Biigtigong Experiences of Dispossession and Impact on Wellness

Biigtigong Nishnaabeg people are proud, hard-working people who are dedicated to pathways of healing from their experiences of colonialism and environmental dispossession. As outlined in the introduction to this book, environmental dispossession refers to the direct and indirect ways Indigenous peoples' and communities' ties to their land are severed or interrupted (Richmond and Ross 2008). These processes change the quality of Indigenous environments; for example, by fire, deforestation, or contamination events. They are also inclusive of political processes that remove Indigenous people's access to their lands—for example, in the case of forced migration events, the criminalization of Indigenous practices and/or ceremony, and the creation of Indian reserves. Among colonized peoples, loss of land is recognized as the most significant factor contributing to culture stress within Indigenous communities (Bartlett 2003; Berry 1990; Lewis et al. 2021). Culture stress can manifest physically and psychologically as homesickness, severe depression, and conditions brought upon by mourning for, and coping with, lost homelands and changing way of life (Gone 2013; Wexler 2014). The processes are damaging because they sever Indigenous peoples' natural capabilities to interact with, and be on, the lands in ways that support traditional foodways, ceremonial practices, governance, gathering, and many other land-based practices that foundationally underlie Indigenous ways of living and relating. These relational practices, done on the land and with other people, are key for wellness, belonging, and formation of strong cultural identity. The impacts of culture stress are immediate and pronounced, and they can also extend intergenerationally (Bombay, Matheson, and Anisman 2014) to include the sorts of health issues experienced by the people of Biigtigong Nishnaabeg: lower life expectancy, greater incidence of heart and metabolic diseases, and susceptibility to poor mental health.

Biigtigong's connection with its land base, culture, and way of life has been significantly disrupted through various processes directly related to setter colonialism. Nishnaabeg began to trade furs with white trappers in the late 1700s, leading to the establishment of a permanent camp at the Mouth of the Pic in 1792. The Hudson's Bay Company operated the post from 1821 to 1888. From the late 1800s to the mid-1950s, other significant changes were happening in the territory. Canada was declared a nation and various transportation routes and infrastructure were being developed to move settlers westward, including the Trans-Canada Highway and the Canadian National Railway. These transportation routes became vital for Marathon Paper Mill and Hemlo Gold, two prominent industries located in the heart of Biigtigong's territory, and which formed the economic background for the township of Marathon, located 20 kilometers northeast of Biigtigong Nishnaabeg. Until it closed its doors in 2015, the Marathon Mill was routinely identified as a toxic "hot spot" on Lake Superior. For years, the mill released various pollutants to the airs and waters, including a range of heavy metals, and various persistent organic pollutants. In the late 1980s, Biigtigong's drinking water supply was contaminated by a broken tailings line at the Golden Giant Mine (one of three mines developed to mine the Hemlo gold deposit). This event led the community to rely on bottled water for years until a new drinking water supply was created, but the effect of the contamination event led to a change in the ways the people of Biigtigong Nishnaabeg viewed the land, with reduced confidence in traditional foods and significant worry about the effect of the mines on the land, animals, and the waters that flow in and around them (Tobias and Richmond 2014).

Environmental dispossession can also occur through more indirect processes, such as federal policy. On a regulatory level, the most impactful change for the people of Biigtigong Nishnaabeg was the creation of the Indian Act (1876) and other legislation designed to support the goals of settler colonialism in the Canadian context. The Indian Act led to widespread land loss and cultural dispossession of Indigenous peoples through its assimilationist agenda; many of its regulations were developed to break Indigenous families apart, to reduce their land base, and by making it illegal for Indian people to practice their traditional governance systems, spirituality, and ways of living (Lavallee and Poole 2010). The most prolific impacts of dispossession among the people of Biigtigong Nishnaabeg relates to the marginalization of our Nishnaabeg knowledge systems, and the growing disconnect of our people from their traditional lands, territories, and cultural identities. For several hundred years, the nation state of Canada, the province of Ontario and various municipal, commercial, and industrial interests, including the town of Marathon, have acted in ways that have constrained and directly threatened Biigtigong Nishnaabeg's sacred relationship with the lands and waters of its traditional territory, which extend roughly 80,000 square kilometers across its traditional territory (Figure 5.1). Although our community refused to participate in the 1850 Robinson Superior Treaty Council, in 1905, the government restricted our First Nation to 800 acres of land, which is primarily swampland and represents only about 1% of our traditional territory. The Anishinaabe word for "reserve land" is *skungigun*, which translates to "leftovers."

Another significant piece of the Indian Act was its direct assault on Indian women who married non-Indian men. Such women lost their Indian status and were thereafter not permitted to live on reserve, or to benefit from any educational, economic, social, or other cultural programs or initiatives funded to Pic River 50 through the Indian Act for its registered Indians membership. The depth of exclusion, violence, and racism endured by affected women, and their subsequent children, has been described (Gehl 2000; Jamieson 1978). Of course, there were other means by which Biigtigong members could be disenfranchised;

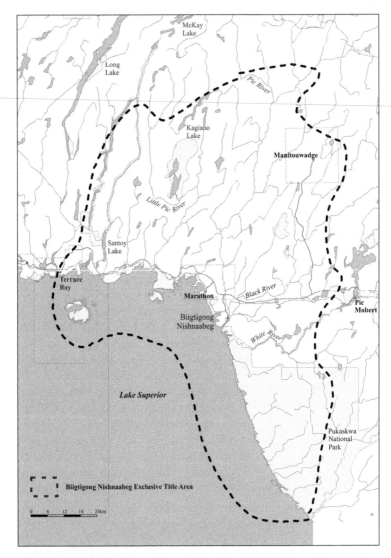

Figure 5.1 Land claim area

Illustrated by Brittany Moses, Environmental Coordinator, Biigtigong Nishnaabeg Ojibways of the Pic River First Nation, Heron Bay—Ontario, and used with permission. Please obtain permission from Biigtigong Nishnaabeg Sustainable Development Department if you wish to use this map in a non-internal setting.

for example, by serving in the Canadian armed forces, gaining a university education, or for leaving reserves for long periods. In 1985, a key amendment to the Indian Act was made. Bill C-31 was passed into law in April 1985 to bring the Indian Act into line with gender equality under the Canadian Charter of Rights and Freedoms. Modifications to various sections of the Indian Act were proposed, including changes to Indian status and band membership, with three major goals: to address gender discrimination of the Indian Act, to restore Indian status to those who had been forcibly disenfranchised due to previous discriminatory provisions, and to allow bands to control their own band membership as a step toward self-government. Across Canada 127,000 women and children subsequently had their Indian status restored following this amendment.

Biigtigong's Healing Movement

Starting in the late 1970s and growing through the twenty-first century, a massive wave of cultural regeneration and healing has taken place in Native communities across Turtle Island (Castellano and Archibald 2007; Lawrence and Anderson 2005) including among Biigtigong Nishnaabeg. This movement coincided with widespread recognition of the incredible harm and trauma experienced by Native people as a result of settler colonialism and the varied ways government, churches, and industry have enacted it, but then also of the painful ways these processes have been internalized by our own people, and reproduced through addiction, violence, and abuses of many forms. This wave coincided with key national moments in Indigenous-Canadian relations, including the Oka Crisis (1990), the initiation of the Royal Commission on Aboriginal Peoples (1996), and the reversal of several Indigenous rights violations that had been upheld and regulated by the Indian Act. Related to the revision of the Indian Act, for example, Bill C-31 reinstated the legal status of Indian women (and their children) who had lost their Indian status as a result of marriages with non-Indian men.

These moments were key in solidifying First Nations peoples' ambitions for community healing and recovery. This regeneration led to the revival of many cultural practices, including traditional healing, ceremony, and language revitalization among Native people living in communities on reserve lands, and in towns and cities across Canada. It was also at this time that many communities, including Biigtigong, set legal motions in place to secure their Aboriginal rights and title. Biigtigong is strong in its desire to maintain and grow its relationship with the land, and to continue to live a way of life that respects Nishnaabeg values.

In its pathway to healing, Biigtigong has prioritized its land claim process. For greater than thirty years, Biigtigong Nishnaabeg have been in a comprehensive land claim process with Canada to restore our Aboriginal rights and title over the lands of our traditional territory. To support and defend our Aboriginal rights and title within our ancestral territory, several generations of community leaders and their staff have worked with a legal team to coordinate a great body of knowledge and information to support this claim, including the community's history, genealogy, land use, occupancy, and rights within our ancestral territory. This has been a lengthy, frustrating, and very expensive process, but still the Nation persists and will not give up until the matter is settled. To Biigtigong Nishnaabeg, the return of land is understood as key to our identity as Anishinaabe people.

Alongside the land claim process, Biigtigong leadership have encouraged community members to be active and present users on our traditional territory: on trap lines, hunting, fishing, harvesting berries and medicines, and restoring key transportation routes, including hiking trails and waterways. At the community level, political leaders have invested heavily in several projects designed to support community healing, demonstrate cultural responsibilities, and strengthen Anishinaabe knowledge. These include the creation of new school curriculum, several land-based wellness programs, an Anishinabemoen language project, and major investments in gathering activities across the territory, including the installation of permanent structures:

> We're connecting with the people that are here now—young or old—and connecting with the land that our ancestors used to walk on. It is such an honor to be able to walk the same land that our ancestors did. For what our people have been through, we could have been moved or we could have been killed off or you know something like that, but we're still walking on the same land that our ancestors did and—to think that we're still here and we're resilient and we're still fighting through all the stuff that the government throws at us—and not even the government, just people who think lowly of us. And just being able to connect on the land and the territory, it's amazing to see what we're fighting for.
>
> (Youth 4)

Collectively, these activities matter greatly for Biigtigong's healing journey because they re-establish wider community connection with places in our territory, they offer opportunities to reclaim Nishnaabeg knowledge and cultural practices, they encourage belonging, and they protect our sacred places.

Reclaiming Our Original Gathering Place at the Mouth of the Pic

In spite of restrictions placed on the movement of Nishnaabeg people, Biigtigong never stopped travelling to and gathering at the Mouth of the Pic. At the place where the river meets the lake, there is a wide sandy beach that extends roughly 2 kilometers north. The beach backs onto soft and hilly sand dunes where families would gather to picnic, swim, and camp:

> At the mouth of the Pic, at the sand beach—that used to be a family area. You could see people all the way from the point of the river all the way to the end of the rocks. That's where people were. It's not only the Nishnaabeg, but people from town side, Heron Bay North. We were all down there enjoying one another, having fun with each other. We had those fires, share meals with each other, those things. But mostly, we were at the middle of the beach. That's where our Nabigon, Moses, Fisher, our clan used to picnic—used to sleep overnight, picnic, sleep over a day later. See, on a sand beach, you don't need any place, any sleep quarters, the sand is soft enough, just tents. They had the whole family sleeping in there. And I miss some of these things here that I'm talking about. I really miss that.
>
> (Elder 1)

The Mouth is a place of family memories and summer laughter. The community comes to the Mouth to celebrate special events and to enjoy it as a place of tranquility. The dunes and logs make for a natural playground. Here children are taught stories of the land, and are encouraged to make new stories with the land:

> My mom grew up in a small house on a hill overlooking the Biigtig. In summer, the family would pack a picnic and spend the day at the mouth of the Pic. Many families gathered on the beach, enjoying food and making fires to warm themselves. As a child, I camped in this place with my parents, sisters and cousins. We fished here, came to pow wow, received our first traditional names in this place. Many

years later, I bring my own children to this place. We swim in these same waters. We play in the Dunes. We float on the masses of logs that scatter the beach. We span generations, yet this land remains locked in time. It is a gift to know this place and to return to it season by season, year after year. We celebrate its permanence, and we honour the sense of belonging it provides.

(Interviewee 1)

The lands that make up the Mouth of the Pic are not only historically important to the community, but they are also part of an exceptionally fragile ecosystem that the community has worked together to protect as the original caretakers of these lands. Freshwater coastal dunes are globally rare ecosystems that form over thousands of years. The dunes are home to many rare plants and animals, and their fragility makes them of high conservation concern. Protecting the fragility of this ecosystem, combined with the community's desire to support continued access to this place led to the development of a boardwalk across the sand dunes, including two lookouts that contain patio spaces and seating. Especially for the most vulnerable community members, or those requiring access to mobility supports, the boardwalk has made it so that a wider body of the community can be on these lands:

I just always think of like my nephew and my future children and my future grandchildren and I think of the protection and preservation of our territory. The feeling that I get when I walk onto the mouth of the Pic and I look out and I have all those memories of just being a child and swimming. And everybody used to just all go down to the mouth and it used to be so busy down there in the summertime and it was just so amazing. I want those future generations to have the opportunity to experience what we felt and we experienced down at the mouth.

(Staff 2)

When Biigtigong initiated its own process of reclaiming, the knowledge holders determined that the reintroduction of Nishnaabeg ceremonies would be essential for healing. The Elders determined that bringing the community together in ceremony would nourish the spirits of the Nishnaabeg. Being on the land together would make the people whole again by connecting them to who they are spiritually, and reintroducing the ceremonies needed through differing cycles of life to maintain wellness. From the mid-1980s onward, Biigtigong reintroduced several of its ceremonies, including the pow wow. Many of these ceremonies involved the construction of lodges, some built at the Mouth of the Pic, and many built on reserve in protected areas near people's homes:

> It's quite amazing just what's out there and what we're reclaiming as part of who we are. It just makes sense that we would become more involved and become more aware of our surroundings because growing up, this [reserve] is what we had and we never had much of traditional practices, cultural practices … until the mid-'80s when they decided to re-introduce the practices, bring back ceremonies as a means of healing community. Because—as a culture—you have an identity to something and when you're missing that part of who you are, I think you get lost as a people.
>
> (Staff 4)

In 1985, Biigtigong hosted its first annual pow wow at the Mouth of the Pic. The reintroduction of the pow wow was a huge celebration for the community, but also immensely challenging as the reclamation of this practice required the gathering of significant social and cultural intelligence from our Anishinaabe relatives in Ontario, Manitoba, and Minnesota. The sheer amount of work, planning, and cultural resources needed to make the event a success is a massive undertaking. This remains even after thirty-seven years of the pow wow being reinstated.

Located just above the Mouth, the pow wow grounds extend the length of a few kilometers, with camp grounds and family sites scattered around the arbour where the pow wow takes place. The arbour is a circular covered structure where the drums sit, in the center of a much larger circular arena where the dancing occurs. The arbour sits atop a hill that rises about half a kilometer from the place where the Biigtig Ziibi empties into the lake. Biigtigong's annual pow wow is one of the busiest times of the year. In the days leading up to the annual pow wow, which always takes place on the second weekend in July, dancers, cooks, artisans, knowledge holders, and community members from across the region arrive at the Mouth and ready themselves for a weekend of visiting and dancing. Pow wow weekend is an exciting time for all Biigtigong members, as it is a time when many who no longer live in the territory return home to visit family and friends:

> My connection to this place does not fade because I live away. In some regards it grows. I have a strong sense of belonging here, and a depth of pride and gratitude. Even when I am simply talking about

this place, or when I show photos to others, I can feel the spirit of this place welling up in me. It has shaped me, continues to shape me. I wanted that for my kids. They were both born away. We knew we needed to make the connection early for them. That's why we buried their placentas in this land. I need them to know this place like I do, to love it like I do. I want them to know this is their place. They have rights to this place. But they also need to care for it. To come here to show their love and appreciation. To be strong and proud Nishnaabeg children.

(Interviewee 1)

The pow wow brings together old childhood friends and family, Elders and their grandchildren and great-grandchildren. It is a celebration of Nishnaabeg people and traditions, and of our enduring connection to the Mouth of the Pic, and our desires to always be in this place.

Moose Camp

Another significant reclamation practice that Biigtigong Nishnaabeg have embraced is the revitalization of the moose hunt. For centuries, family moose camps were common among Nishnaabeg, but they became significantly less common in the middle part of the 1900s as government policies limited travel and attempted to banish traditional harvesting activities, including hunting, across the territory. While some men continued to hunt, these activities went largely "underground" and their efforts were done quietly and in small groups (Pettipas 1994). If and when the Indian Agent questioned children about what foods they were eating, they did not talk about moose meat or any other wild food or fish. Although fewer families were participating in the moose hunt, the knowledge, practices, and desires to engage in moose hunting and to consume traditional foods has not lessened.

In the early 2000s, Elders and leaders of Biigtigong came together and decided that if families did not have the time or knowledge or skills to hunt and harvest moose, then the community as a whole would have to do it together. For one week in October, the community gathers on the land to hunt, harvest, socialize, and learn together. The schools take their curriculum outdoors, the band operations pause, and families are invited to head into the bush. All community members are welcomed to participate in ways that make sense to them; by sharing their wisdom and memories, through offering information about moose movement, hunting tips and abilities, in preparation for meals, the setting up of collective harvesting areas, caring for children, and many more, including visiting.

Planning for moose camp begins in late summer. Activities are developed and scheduled, tents are cleaned out and set up, meals are organized, and key knowledge holders and hunters are invited. The inaugural moose camp took place in 2008, and its participants were grade 7 and 8 students of Pic River Elementary. The following year, moose camp was opened to all of Biigtigong's staff and community members. The 2009 location was selected purposefully to serve as a strategic occupation of an alienation attempt by the township of Marathon, who were at the time, searching to relocate its landfill. The location of moose camp did not change for the first three years, as Biigtigong actively demonstrated the siting of Marathon's landfill. Since 2011, the location of moose camp has changed year to year; its location is determined annually based on recommendations from hunters and a desire to show children the beauty and bounty of our vast territory. Gathering each year across different places, moose camp brings young people and children into the traditional territory and provides an expanded view of what Biigtigong's land base and responsibilities look like. This gathering provides an opportunity for community members to connect on lands they may have never been to, and to see and witness the varying social, cultural, and ceremonial aspects of moose hunt. But more foundationally, the moose hunt is meant to demonstrate the breadth of Biigtigong Nishnaabeg's territory, which extends far beyond the reserve land:

On one of our very first Moose Camps, all the kids came there. So, as an Elder, they asked me to talk about it a little bit. So, I talked. But I made sure that I was telling the kids—they were small, schoolkids—and I told them, "Don't forget," I says, "this is your land." The land that the department gave us—which is not even one square mile down here—it's 800 acres, I think it was. The IA gave that to us—the federal government—we're bigger than that. We've got a big land claim going. And there's one woman, she had her young little baby, and I was telling her—the mother, "Make sure you tell your child that this is their land. Nobody else's land, no matter what the province says or whatever. Keep that in your head. So, it's there. It's strong."

(Elder B)

The people of Biigtigong Nishnaabeg have always lived in close relationship with the moose on these lands; its very existence has supported the survival and wellness of the community. For Nishnaabeg, moose are more than a source of food. While the lean meat provides important nutrients and sustenance, the whole of the animal is understood as a gift for Nishnaabeg ingenuity. The moose's hide can be transformed into many everyday items, including clothing, waterproof moccasins, and drums for ceremony. The large and small bones can be used as tools and knives. Even the brain can be used to tan and protect the skins.

The knowledge and skill needed to track and call the animal, to kill it respectfully, to clean it, to bring it out of the bush, and to subsequently prepare it for various important uses requires a collaborative effort that could not be accomplished by one person alone. Fathers, sons, uncles, and grandfathers work together to track and hunt the large animal, skin it, debone it, and bring it back to the family camp. Mothers, daughters, aunts, and grandmothers will transform the moose into its many gifts, working together to cook and smoke the meat, clean, and soften the hide, and prepare clothing and other items. Younger family members share their energy and physical strength while the Elders share their experience, knowledge, and stories.

In exchange for these sacred and life-sustaining gifts, Nishnaabeg are responsible for preserving the lands in their territory, hunting only what is needed, treating each animal that gives its life with respect, and sharing the meat with others. The relationship between moose and Nishnaabeg has been passed on through generations as Elders, parents, and families teach children from a young age how to uphold their responsibilities to the moose, how to hunt it, how to use every part of the animal, and how to share the work and the resulting food:

> One of the first places I seen them out tanning a moose was while we were picking blueberries. That's the very first time I ever seen that. The women used to tan. You used to see my grandmother—They all did the tanning with my mom. I used to see them take their hide down, the raw hide, and take it down to the river and soak it until the hide gets soft. Then they used to bring it up, put it on a little stand, then they'd get that bone from the top of the leg and scrape the hide back and forth. Then they'd take it back to the river, soak it some more just to get the hide softened and until it's fully stretched. I asked them how'd they get that smell when they're tanning. You know the brain of the moose and the smell they have in the tan hide. You use the brain to get that smell.
>
> (Elder 1)

For children who have grown up with more exposure to electronic devices than they have to the land, the learning that takes place at moose camp goes far deeper than the skills needed to skin a moose. Hunting moose means putting into practice the teachings and responsibilities that the Nishnaabeg have always lived by: patience, humility, cooperation, and putting others before yourself. The quiet of the bush creates moments for young people to be with their Elders, to sit around a fire, drink tea, and listen to Nishnaabeg stories and teachings:

> I love Myra. I think Myra's the one who has the most [stories]. I think she's our oldest Elder now, so she has the most stories in her and I know I have stories from when I was working with her. She used to tell us all about the different things how we would go moose hunting and all the Elders would get pieces of the moose first and then the families who needed more would get it first and stuff like that. We're a sharing kind of people and that's all the different stories that she told us.
>
> (Youth 4)

At moose camp, the community is afforded the opportunity to live as one family, sharing with each other, learning from each other, and enjoying each other's company. Daily schedules look different, as does the work. Children move between campsites to join activities, eat, or visit. Away from the routines of daily life, the big family that is Biigtigong has the time and space to bond, reconnecting with each other and their land:

> You just have that just that community, like when we're out at moose camp it's just, "Okay, I'm gonna paint" and you have just tons of kids that are coming around you. There's no question like, "Why are you here?" It's just like, "No, pick up a paintbrush and we're gonna have fun" right? And it's just that connection, so that when those kids are old enough and they recognize that something needs to be protected, they know exactly what to do and they're willing to protect that because they have those connections instilled and built into them. And I think that connection and love for our territory just runs through our veins, and you can't protect something that you don't love.
>
> (Staff 2)

The sentiments of belonging and shared connection that Biigtigong community members associate with moose camp are treasured. Moose camp grows bigger year to year as more community members join, as families return home from the city, and visitors turn up from other communities. What began as the vision of community leaders has become a little city in the bush:

> When you go over there, just you and your crew, by the time you put those tents up and you come back the next day, it's like a little city, moose camp. There are so many trailers, I couldn't believe them. I couldn't believe how many trailers they have. At moose camp at Manitouwadge it was just chuck full of trailers. I've never seen them, they're getting bigger and bigger every year. More and more people are coming home to do them, too. It's nice.
>
> (Knowledge Holder 2)

For our Elders moose camp was never an annual event, it was simply life. In fall, hunting moose was common practice. Every day, Nishnaabeg enjoyed the gifts provided by the moose, and in turn they understood they held responsibilities to the moose and to the wider set of relations that maintain wellness of the territory.

Bringing Our Women Back Home

Nishnaabeg are a naturally creative, adaptable, and welcoming people. We have worked for generations to be active and present on our traditional lands. The efforts described in the previous pages showcase examples that detail how our people are reclaiming practices inherent to our ancestral knowledge by strengthening our relationships with key places and people in our territory. Our Elders have centrally directed many of the efforts we describe here, including a very lengthy and expensive land claim process that awaits decisions from the Crown. Alongside the legal process of environmental repossession, Biigtigong's leadership is staunch in their stance that we must continue to rebuild our Nishnaabeg knowledge, language, and ceremonies: "We are re-discovering who we are as a People so can govern ourselves in a way that reflects the traditions and knowledge we held before colonial ideas took over" (Interviewee 2). Biigtigong's strength as a nation cannot be defined exclusively to the Lands and people who live within our ancestral territory, however, and there needs to be significant reflection on how colonial ideas and policies have not only impacted our relationships with our territory, but also relationships among our people.

Our collective healing journey must acknowledge the depth of wounds we have suffered as a result of colonial laws and other forms of cultural dispossession. Indeed, these processes created significant social and political cleavages among Biigtigong members, the most important indicator being that greater than half of our membership lives off-reserve, and a significant portion of our off-reserve membership lives outside our traditional territory. Of course, many factors lead Indigenous peoples to migrate from the reserve, including educational, economic, and healthcare needs, but a significant root cause of this pattern can be explained by the Indian Act's goals of "disenfranchisement," described earlier in these pages, and also in Chapter 1. By extension of this process, Biigtigong's disenfranchised members were subsequently dispossessed of their rights to land, culture, kinship, language, and belonging. During the second part of the twentieth century, gendered pieces of the Indian Act unfairly targeted women, meaning many were essentially "kicked out" of the community. What makes this experience especially tragic is the way many communities enforced this regulation upon their own members, who were often friends or family:

> I was born and raised in Marathon, and never really connected with the people in this community [Biigtigong] until my 20s, but I always had a very close connection with the land. My Dad was raised by my Grandpa and his Auntie. They lived all over the place. When they were told they could come back to the reserve, they chose not to because this was not a healthy place.
>
> (Interviewee 3)

Many of our women and their children subsequently moved to towns and cities in areas proximal to our reserve site and territory: Coldwell, Marathon, Red Rock, and Thunder Bay among others. The struggle to fit into rural and urban community and social life was not easy:

> As a young person growing up in Marathon, I didn't feel comfortable talking about my Indigenous self with my white friends. I was shy and had a lot of anxiety. I visited family in Biigtigong and was always welcomed. I felt welcome. But something was missing. My confidence in that cultural part of me was missing. Yes, I come to pow wow and see the ribbon skirts, and the ceremonies, but that's not part of what I know or do. Maybe one day it will be.
>
> (Interviewee 2)

Coulthard (2014) and others argue that recognition of Indigeneity cannot be based on colonial politics, such as those related to the Indian Act, but rather must come through other cultural and community expressions and spaces of belonging, including self-recognition. The pathways by which disenfranchised women and families undertake this process of healing and self-recognition have occurred largely in places away from the reserve, and often with Indigenous people who are not family or community members:

> For me, things really changed when I went to college in Toronto, where I reconnected with a lot of Indigenous peoples from all over the place. Being around these personalities helped me to grow and learn. I went to land-based and social events. That experience helped me see some of the things I could not see when I was younger. Those experiences also helped me see that I needed to focus my efforts at home, in this territory.
>
> (Interviewee 2)

Growing up as an off-reserve Anishnaabekwe, Interviewee 2 describes how limited her knowledge was about her family history and their experiences of colonialism. The shame and hurt her grandmother harbored from her residential school experiences, for example, was layered with the hurt and resentment of being excluded from the community. Interviewee 2's family did not speak openly about these experiences. Years later, after participating in a KAIROS Blanket Exercise, she described how important that experience was for helping her to see and empathize with her grandmother's history, and how these traumas extended to her dad, and to her as well.

The pain and judgment associated with exclusion from the community is not easily forgotten, yet many community members who have lived away because of their parents' or grandparents' disenfranchisement experiences are now searching for ways to reconnect with the people, lands, and knowledge that sits in our territory. And they are also searching for healing. Similar to Interviewee 2's experience of finding her sense of purpose while studying in Toronto, Interviewee 3 states:

> My connection to the Land is so strong that it brought me back. I moved to Thunder Bay, but being there was a barrier for me because I could not be or practice my rights as a member of Biigtigong Nishnaabeg. I have a rights-based focus of identity. When I was hired in my role, my boss told me: "You have a very important job

to protect this land. It is the same role your great grandmother had."
That makes me so proud.

(Interviewee 3)

Coming back into the community requires a well of courage that must be met with acceptance, and a shared responsibility to rebuild the varying relationships that have been so badly damaged from disenfranchisement experiences. To come back to this place, after being shunned for so many years, showcases the genuine love that Nishnaabeg have for this place, and a depth of resilience that matters greatly for the continued healing and strength of our nation. Biigtigong is committed to supporting these reconciliation efforts and strives to be inclusive of its broad membership. Doing the work of rebuilding relationships is hard work that requires both creativity and good intentions. Restoring community relationships across physical and cultural distance requires us to adopt new ways of connecting with our broad membership. Especially after the onset of the COVID-19 pandemic, digital platforms have become centrally important gathering spaces to engage, connect, and share Nishnaabeg knowledge, culture, and language.

In 2015, Biigtigong ratified its *Chi-Nakinigewin*, which refers to its Great Law. As the nation proceeds toward self-determination, the Chi-Nakinigewin provides the foundation from which laws will be developed to assert jurisdiction in the community, and over the whole of the territory. Alongside the restoration of our original laws, Biigtigong has been working for years in the reconstruction of our *Aadsokaanan*, which refers to our Sacred Stories. These stories have been developed through decades of work with Biigtigong Elders, and they are founded on Nishnaabeg philosophy. To support the widest possible sharing of the stories recreated to date, eight sessions were held on the zoom platform in late winter 2022. The stories were narrated live, and ahead of their sharing, participants were mailed interactive packages containing Nishnaabeg artwork, puzzles, and text to guide families through the readings of the stories. This process of connecting community across the digital and creating opportunities for inclusive participation of varying abilities (including children, Elders, and others who could not physically attend) showcases the intention and care for bringing community into the work, but also the incredible effort and meaning of these stories for our shared history and collective future.

Another key example relates to the 2021 International Women's Day event, when Biigtigong held two days of virtual speakers and panels. These events drew audiences from the local and from faraway, and they opened a critical space for dialogue and sharing of perspectives about what it means to be an Anishinaabe Kwe from Biigtigong Nishnaabeg. This event celebrated the diversity of places, knowledges, and identities we contribute to, with appropriate recognition of the hurts and challenges garnered along the way. There was a shared respect and demonstrated humility that not all Nishnaabeg Kwe share the same path; we cannot all live in the territory or be with Nishnaabeg people but that does not limit our potential or strength of contribution as Biigtigong's Nishnaabeg Kwe. What connects us is the part we play in Biigtigong's community history. We all connect because of the people and place that contains our original stories, and the love our ancestors had for that place. Biigtigong is a stronger nation when all of its members are able to contribute meaningfully to our goals of being self-determining. Embracing the concept of *mino biimadiziwin* in this work means understanding that everyone in the community is related and has a role to play in our continued success.

Being Anishinaabe Together Again

Biigtigong Nishnaabeg is in a time of healing and resurgence. After generations of colonial rule, we aspire to live and manage the full territory of our ancestral lands in a self-governing way. For more than thirty years, we have been working within a legal framework to repossess our lands. We are hopeful that settlement of our land claim will acknowledge our legal independence from Canada, thereby enabling Biigtigong to fully self-determine how the territory is managed, used, and occupied. Building from the strength of generations of Biigtigong leaders, the settlement of our land claim is one of the significant ways we will continue to protect, strengthen, and assert our rights and title as Nishnaabeg people.

But as described throughout this chapter, Biigtigong continues to assert its rights to the land even in the absence of Canada's long-overdue acknowledgment. Alongside this legal process, our community has developed several key strategies to protect and strengthen our connection to the land. In the broadest sense, to do the work of environmental repossession means engaging in social, cultural, and political practices that support our ongoing occupation of this Land. We have drawn on a story-based approach to describe the places Biigtigong gathers upon and how and why these places matter to us today. This chapter describes some of our key gathering practices, what they mean to our people in both a historical and contemporary sense, and specifically how they strengthen social relationships and a sense of belonging.

Every gathering on the land in Biigtigong is an act of resilience and resurgence. We come together as family, community, and as a Nation to be on the land, and to rebuild relationships with all of creation. Despite ongoing processes of colonization and dispossession, we always find ways to continue our ways of being and knowing this place and one another. Contemporary gatherings at moose camp and the Mouth of the Pic may look different from the gatherings of our ancestors. But they are just as important for maintaining our social connections, cultural continuity, identity-building, and for belonging. Through these gatherings, Biigtigong strengthens its cultural foundation and collective sense of belonging and purpose, which are essential for asserting our rights to this territory.

Aside from land-based processes of repossession, this chapter points to the important role of supporting community healing with focused attention on how we care for and nurture our social relationships. *Mino bimaadiziwin* recognizes the interconnection of one's relationships; with self, family, community, land, ancestors, and the spiritual realm. Being Anishinaabe and living these principles is critical for our continued wellness. Especially in this time of healing, special attention and creative approaches may need to be adopted so that we can be inclusive of our widest membership, including families who live off-reserve and outside our territory.

While we focus on gathering in this chapter, we recognize that it is through all of these projects together that Biigtigong is building a strong, healthy, and sovereign community. Gathering strengthens Biigtigong's connection to, occupation of, and protection of the lands and resources of our territory. But our gatherings also heal and strengthen our relationships with one other, which are the foundation of our identities as Nishnaabeg people. When Biigtigong comes together, it is healing and restoring the rights and responsibilities of every community member and family to each other, to the ancestors, to future generations, and to all living things.

Acknowledgments

Elana Nightingale was a PhD student during the research for this book and she completed research within Biigtigong Nishnaabeg territory for her doctoral thesis. She also contributed significantly to the book in a project management role. **Florinda Christianson, Cassandra Cress,** and **Juanita Starr** work for tribal governance and development agencies of Biigtigong Nishnaabeg. They convened meetings with and contributed to the interviewing of key informants, and they commented on early drafts of this chapter.

CONCLUSION—THE LAND IS WHO WE ARE

In this collection, we have argued that Indigenous environmental repossession is a diverse set of practices that share a common intent to reclaim connection with places, practices, and environments of importance to Indigenous communities. While the simple definition of the concept accommodates direct action to repatriate material objects and resources, it extends increasingly to subtle actions, lifeways, and everyday routines that unsettle neo/colonial governance and control. Indeed, the examples used in this book confirm that large-scale, extravagant actions and understated, daily approaches to Indigenous change-making are in a mutually reinforcing relationship. Just as we have concluded that Indigenous motivations, interventions, and stubborn resilience are embedded within relational ontologies of care, we also maintain that direct action is relationally entangled with daily practices, mundane pastimes, and neighborhood interaction.

We worked with members of our communities—Kānaka, Māori, and Anishinaabe people—in Hawai'i, Aotearoa, and Canada to describe the origins, uptake, and meanings of Indigenous environmental repossession. Those strategies are being employed to occupy and protect land, in the expression of Indigenous rights, and simultaneously to support community wellness, belonging, and identity. As detailed in the introduction, there has been an exciting uptake and engagement of research around the concept of environmental repossession, but those contributions have focused almost entirely on descriptive, qualitative case studies in the Canadian context and largely with First Nation communities on matters related to health and wellbeing.

We offer this book to re-engage in scholarly conversations and applied research about place-based activism, including the various practices and strategies through which environmental repossession is performed. Through analysis of repossession across distinct geographies and political landscapes, we shine a light on the deeply relational, place-based cultural philosophies that underlie those efforts. Specifically, we engage in key cultural concepts of kapu aloha, kaitiakitanga, and mino bimaadiziwin and how they make sense of strategies of Indigenous occupation, rights-making, and land protection. As outlined in Chapter 1, we have been deeply motivated in the ways we carry out our work on and with the land, or in our communities, because of the relational ontologies we know and respect as Indigenous peoples. Despite our partial alienation from those knowledge systems—a result of our own experiences with colonialism and the varied ways we interpret and practice them—we draw from these ways of knowing as philosophical anchors for our chapters. We stand in solidarity with one another to resist ongoing attempts by our respective nation states and the large-scale industrial interests who attempt to dispossess us from our lands and the knowledge, practices, and socio-ecological relationships contained therein. Yet, despite the deep philosophical intersections in our lifeways and the land-based protections we similarly engage in, we are not culturally homogenous. It is the very places we come from, and the unique social, cultural, and political histories encountered in these places that shape our unique acts of repossession.

The impacts of colonialism and dispossession have fundamentally changed Indigenous lifeways and community connections with their original people and places. Even when living on or near one's traditional lands, Indigenous peoples face enduring threats of displacement and exclusion. Those threats come from the nation states in which we live or from corporate actors and, increasingly, they will also come in the form of climate change. Whether because of colonial policies, or a range of other experiences or choices, Indigenous peoples are becoming increasingly organized in cities or other places that are far away from their traditional lands. We employ the concept of environmental repossession to highlight the diversity of modern Indigenous relationships to place and the variable ways Indigenous peoples and communities are expressing their rights in those places.

The goals of this book were manifold. First, we wanted to examine the diverse nature, meaning, and uptake of land repossession practices across varying communities and through different cultures and ecologies. This has enabled us to frame for other Indigenous communities a range of strategies to contest problematic environmental processes and to sponsor transformative action. Second, we sought to expand upon what is known about Indigenous methods and practices of land repossession through case studies with Indigenous communities from faraway places. We have showcased diverse practices of resistance and resilience in the expectation that other communities can learn from the examples. Third, we endeavored to record the similarities and tensions in practices of environmental repossession. The multiplicity of strategies, outcomes, and counteractions we reviewed suggests that there can be no singular or universal approach to Indigenous environmental repossession. Thus, we offer our own stories and experiences as messages of hope and inspiration for Indigenous communities and scholars alike.

As this project ended, we took the opportunity to engage in discussion about what we had learned from our individual case studies, and about the wider themes we could see extending across them, particularly as they related to theoretical and applied concepts that are central to environmental repossession. We were interested in how kinship relationships among the human and non-human motivate community action and enable unique environmental ethics. Likewise, we wanted to know how those communities approach transformative action and how they enact change. We recognized that Indigenous peoples confront existing and new challenges, so we intended to explore practices of adaptation and intergenerational learning. Last, we were eager to understand how Indigenous communities generate their own rights and how they perform in a self-determined manner. We use the remainder of this final chapter as a space to share our collective insights about what we learned, and what was similar or different in our case study areas. Perhaps recognizing the ongoing impact of COVID-19 and lockdowns—both of which were significant complications for the writing of this book—we used Zoom to interview one another about those topics. Highlights from our conversation are used below to share the unique and common learnings of the project.

Centering Kinship Relationships and Care in Environmental Repossession

Kinship relationships were a persistent theme threading across the three cases, particularly how they evoke care and support repossession. In each of the three cases, caring relationships—among and between humans and families, with the non-human, and with the spiritual—are the foundation upon which repossession efforts emerge and expand. These caring relationships grow from the social responsibilities and cultural knowledge of each community, and they are used to engage community for a range of purposes, including land protection and occupation. In the case of Taniwha Club, much of the social connection and leadership efforts that guide the club draw from networks of the families that are involved. As Brad noted, the role of family and extended family is essential to the success of the club, and particularly the ways children are brought into the work:

> **Brad**: The Club is never kids acting alone nor parents acting alone; it's always both of them working together and the parents are always there holding the hands of the kids, or they staff a shovel when they're planting. One digs a hole, the other plants something in it … I haven't stressed the importance of family enough … as families have held that club together, and most of the really positive things that have happened out of it have happened because of family, not in spite of it. There are types of support there; there are some progressive ideals associated with family that I just didn't credit [sufficiently].

Taniwha Club's membership extends broadly among Māori families who live in south Auckland, where many interact socially in such other ways as children's organized sports. Systems of care within Taniwha Club have been central to one of its original, albeit partially abandoned, missions: food sharing. As Brad recalls, this was a foundational element of the club that grew through the pandemic and beyond:

> **Brad**: I don't know whether perceptions of care created Taniwha Club or whether Taniwha Club created a perception of the need to care for people. They were always entangled, and the pandemic only made that more so. The focus on volcanic landscapes subsided a bit there for a while, because people recognized the need to take the organizational structures that formed around Taniwha Club and put them to another purpose … Kids' sport took over my life … but that was because many kids from Taniwha Club played basketball and softball. Eight softball clubs … formed a great big food co-op. One down in the most volcanically rich, fertile areas [of Auckland] had access to market gardeners who had a lot of food. Another one had a parent who … was a Chief Executive of a freight firm … It all just fell into line and the system for getting food from [the south] to other clubs in central Auckland sprang out of nowhere. Those central clubs became food banks for people in need. That's the sort of thing that

happened, but it's a real chicken and egg story so I don't want to say that Taniwha Club inspired the care. I think it's more the other way around.

Regarding Kānaka interactions on the Mauna, and in the development of the Kūkulu exhibit, notions of care embrace people, places, and the spirit of the entities that reside there. Renee comments on how Aunty Pua performs relationship-making with all community members, including non-human actors:

> **Renee**: Listening to the way Aunty Pua puts together any
> project she works on, especially those that have a spiritual
> component, she's very careful to make sure she has input
> from community members. In the interview, she spoke about
> how she goes into the communities and speaks with them,
> but it's not just how you're going to put together or curate
> an exhibit … It's also about engaging with those ancestral
> entities that she is familiar with, or that she has familiarized
> herself with and that we, as Kānaka, recognize as having been
> a part of the land already for generations. Some people call
> those entities by name—for example, Pohakuloa is another
> site on the Mauna where there's a big military installation.
> I've heard many people … refer to not just the land there,
> but the *entity* that resides in that space as Pohakuloa. Aunty
> Pua maintains social relationships with those kinds of
> entities also. Following protocols, she "opens" herself to
> the possibility of gaining information or learning or being
> directed and taught and led to certain types of practices or
> certain types of chants. She's maintaining a social relationship
> and interacting at a level that more and more of us need to
> at least be open to. I think that, by including and allowing
> ourselves to have that intimacy and to embrace that kind of
> energetics like our ancestors did, it just makes our connection
> much more vibrant. I don't know if it makes it more
> connected, but I think it adds a different vibrancy if we also
> can add those spiritual or ancestral alignments as part of our
> social relationships.

Ancestral alignments feature in every aspect of Kūkulu's activities, within the necessary ways community members conduct themselves when on the Mauna, and in activities relating to the Mauna. For example, they are important when sign waving in the streets of Hilo, at academic conferences, or when delivering testimony in the courtroom. The vibrancy that Renee refers to is a spiritual recognition that people and places are deeply connected. This way of knowing and relating to the Mauna powerfully shapes how people behave and the ways they interact socially, most notably in the ceremonial protocol that features how and why people continue to stand for the Mauna. That Kānaka are in a kincentric relationship with the Mauna underlies the continuation of the occupation on Mauna Kea, and the need for the Kūkulu exhibit.

In the Biigtigong chapter, gatherings are used to highlight the important ways that being on the land together form a space for Nishnaabeg to build and renew social relationships. These land-based gatherings create strategic spaces for Nishnaabeg to interact with key places in the territory, and they offer opportunities to demonstrate their responsibilities as caretakers of the land. While on the land, Nishnaabeg do the activities they have always done—they hunt and share food, they share stories and knowledge, and they laugh and enjoy one another's company. So much of this may seem everyday for the young ones who have grown up knowing moose camp and pow wow as a consistent and expected part of Nishnaabeg life. However, those efforts are central to a resurgence that has been in the making for some forty years, and which draws entirely from community desires to come back into its own way of knowing and being on the land. Our ceremonial protocol and recognition that healing comes from our connection with the land is central to those efforts:

> **Chantelle**: For us, every community event, every gathering, every time we come together. There are always words from an Elder and an opening song. It always closes in that way as well. Every gathering is built around that. That is a ceremonial protocol.

Our three narratives are distinct—with some emphasizing the role of family; others, the importance of spiritual dimensions; and also, the apparently trivial but, we suggest, vital impact of merely *being* in place. In that diversity, however, is a clear and singular message: the work of repossession carries with it and entrains many other social practices, functions, and strategic initiatives. In particular, within the medley of daily tasks and direct confrontations, *care*—broadly defined—is a core element that unites all practices of Indigenous environmental repossession. We have responsibilities and obligations to human and non-human kin, and that cuts across divergent circumstances and interests.

Linking Direct Action to Everyday Practices
of Environmental Repossession

Chapter 2 offers a variety of Indigenous-led strategies of repossession. As this book was fundamentally concerned with examining the various social, cultural, and political processes by which Indigenous communities do the work of repossession, here we look at the two key strategies of repossession employed in the case studies: direct action and the everyday. While it is useful to categorize those strategies in that way, we acknowledge that there are important elements that link the two, and that the practices and knowledge embedded in the everyday are in fact critical for direct action:

Brad: We started this project around the same time as DAPL was becoming prominent and Trans Mountain, Keystone XL, and all those other projects. They included direct action, blockades, occupations, and camps ... and maybe at that time we fitted in with that ... I don't believe we could have anticipated how much our three projects would be dominated by much more subtle, less aggressive actions like art exhibits or kids planting gardens or gatherings. *What role should direct action have in repossession?*

Renee: Here in Hawai'i, we're still doing direct action. We're still there. There are still people watching the Mauna. There was a presence up there when I drove to Kona this summer and so I think that [direct action] is still happening on the Mauna. But I also think we need to acknowledge that there are different scales of Indigenous repossession. There's an impact in the social scale as well as the direct action scale ... We still have the less aggressive—the art exhibits, the Mauna Wear Wednesdays ... There's a real subtlety to this strategy; it's not a direct, in-your-face action on the Mauna, but it is promoting camaraderie and community.

Chantelle: In our case, gathering and returning to these places has been much more subtle, but also very strategic as we ensure our continued occupation of the territory. So it's not direct action; its more doing what we do. Of course, as we gather on our territory, there are some cottagers who are not happy that we are there. White cottagers bought land on Mountain Lake, and they're upset and surprised that native people are now coming in to occupy the space. In 2019, our community made a conscious effort to get back to Mountain

Lake by building cottages there, and we have held gatherings there. So far there haven't been any standoffs. Our chief … has been very firm *that we are occupying* this place, but at the same time, we're going to build and maintain good relationships with the cottagers. Because that is our way of doing.

Brad: The kids at Taniwha Club … have a real love-hate relationship with decolonialism and decolonial practices. They discuss those concepts a lot but they'll come up with little gems like, "If you want to spend your life trying to pull down colonial structures, yeah, you're going to be disappointed" and "Maybe anything we can do to strengthen ourselves is going to be, long term, more useful for us than what we get out of trying to take down things that are built through others' power and strength … " That is relevant to the everyday side of it too.

Precisely because Indigenous actors are *expected* to be belligerent or violent, it is critical for Indigenous communities to counter those negative stereotypes with diversified portfolios of resistance and resilience. Consequently, it is important to recognize the appropriate balance between protest and kindness, and how they are entwined within successful strategies of repossession:

Chantelle: Standing up for our rights or doing these actions and exhibiting our relationships and rights to places takes many forms and it occurs through many functions … We do this by working through our knowledges and practicing our rights to be in these places. But none of that has to be newsworthy or grandiose. In the case of Biigtigong, we are working very hard to see resolution of our land claim, and a lot of time and resources have been invested in it. But at the same time, we continue with these other forms of gatherings. These are essential because we really want to see the continuation of ourselves as people in our knowledge, and the things that keep us healthy and well, and they're not extraordinary. They're just everyday things.

Renee recognized similar interrelationships between grand and casual strategies for making a cause known, and for attracting supporters to it:

Renee: There [were many] non-occupation … activities that happened in our case study. We … brought students in and that was not a direct action, occupation thing, but just having the exhibit available and for student groups to come into the exhibit. That allowed them to connect at a level that they themselves have never had … the opportunity to. It gave the parents … and the teachers that came with them opportunities to connect with the Mauna, with the movement, and get information that they would not have been able to have access to. So, I think the everyday activities were the ones that moved the needle the most in our community, because in 2015 when the Kia'i stood on the Mauna there were tens to hundreds of people, but as a result of the Kia'i social media contacts, they had way more than that in subsequent direct action activities. For others, reaching out and just having conversations, casual everyday conversations, sometimes with other members of the community in the grocery store. Then, when Kūkulu came up, there was a place to have those kinds of conversations while being among those mementos, those artworks that were contributed to the exhibition. I think that those everyday connections had far more weight than what has been given attention to. We need to have those subtle, not so prominently displayed acts of repossession that continue to sustain us in creative ways.

Throughout this book, we have been careful to provide coverage of both spectacular and mundane actions of Indigenous communities. It was important for us to acknowledge the international and cross-cultural focus provided by high-profile occupations at Mauna a Wakea and Ihumātao. In retrospect, however, one of the most important findings from our work is how disregarded the impact of daily renewal and everyday activism has been within academic and other forms of scholarship. While future research should unpack further the dimensions and intent of such micro-actions, we also suggest, however, that additional analysis should be directed to how "big" and "small" agencies across scales interact to provide momentum for transformative change. We conclude that Indigenous leaders have been acutely perceptive in diversifying their resistance strategies in multiple fora and at multiple levels to ensure a greater likelihood of success.

Affirming Indigeneity through Daily Renewal

The everyday aspects of Indigenous environmental repossession are effective political strategies, but they are also affective in a way that affirms individuals and communities. Colonial displacement in the past may in some ways justify aggressive reactions in the present, but *healing* requires more intimate, reflective, and vulnerable responses. This is particularly the case for those who have an incomplete understanding of their group cultures because of historical trauma or spatial displacements that they did not cause. In its more subtle forms, repossession may counter the associated shame or embarrassment in life-changing ways:

> **Chantelle**: What we attempt to do [in Biigtigong] is unpack our assumptions about what Indigenous relationships to land look like, and all of the meaning it supposedly holds. One of the big findings from our study related to … discomfort, and maybe reluctance, especially among people who grew up off-reserve, to be comfortable expressing their culture or spirituality. They're trying to find their places, right, and had come back to the territory. They'll say, "well I'm not really a cultural person," yet they just spent twenty minutes telling me about how their parents have set up a camp in the heart of our traditional territory. It worries me that our own people might think they ought to be or act in a certain way or else face cultural exclusion. For example, that if we're not learning languages in our homes, or if we haven't grown up doing ceremony then there is this notion that we don't have our cultures as Indigenous people.

Our discussions of the everyday practices of repossession link in important ways with everyday resurgence and its meaning for self-determined continuity (Corntassel et al. 2018; Corntassel and Hardbarger 2019). Healing is an emergent property that reveals itself one little action at a time, wherever we may be and however necessary so that Indigenous peoples can sense belonging and community. As Brad suggests, however, finding a way into these spaces and being comfortable with them is a learning process that can require reflexivity and openness to changing how things are done:

> **Brad**: There was talk of *desirable* practices. Again, [participants] wouldn't name it repossession, but they did discuss … getting

your land back or taking on big court action or staking a claim … One of the quite profound conclusions that the kids made, though … was, "You've got to get beyond [possessive thinking …] for your own health and for your community's health. You've got to learn." That there is not much good in trying to get things back if you don't stop the acquisitive mentality of owning or re-owning. And then—equally profound—the conclusion was that maybe you *have to go through* that phase of being an aggressive teenager to become a well-conditioned adult to get beyond that sort of outlook. So, for me, the most important thing in Taniwha Club was that moment where the older [children] decided that we should change the leadership structure and they should take it on. And more so, what they wanted to do with that, which was to go legit[imate]. Yeah, that "go legit" thing and how it was something that the adult advisors could never have come up with themselves is special.

Paralleling those learnings about the process of repossession, Chantelle contemplates the relationship between various conceptions of Indigenous authenticity and repossession:

Chantelle: My worst fear is that we paint images of community-driven action—protection and occupation— that might seem unrealistic or scary for other communities, or for other scholars who want to do this. I really want people to know that the simple, the everyday, *is really good* … Because if we're talking about the people who are the up-and-comers, or if we're thinking about community activists, we need to say, "You're doing amazing work"—whether it's standing and holding a picket line or sitting in classrooms and I just … want people to know that all of these jobs are very valuable.

While we have reverence for the wisdom, intelligence, and practices of our forebears, we also know we cannot return to old ways. Nonetheless, we may embrace that which has been retained, along with the gifts of knowing that remain relevant today. Indeed, while many do know and can connect with their original instructions, many more have incomplete knowledge and capacities and, for them, finding means to reconnect is significant. Environmental repossession may sometimes require direct action, but in other instances repossession must also rebuild serenely the strength of our cultural knowledge, skills, and capacities.

Indigenous Pedagogies and Leadership in Repossession

Another consistent connection across the chapters relates to the uptake of intergenerational learning and mentorship opportunities within Taniwha Club, the Kūkulu exhibit, and Biigtigong's gatherings. Within the three cases, the power and social learning capacities of Indigenous pedagogies are important trends, but that also occurs in big/colorful *and* small/intimate ways. It is realized through ceremony and other cultural performances, but also through everyday practices:

> **Renee**: It was daunting for me to be on the Mauna, to be connected with those elements, and to be surrounded by all the entities, because while you're up on the Mauna you're maintaining a presence and, for me, it's always a watchful kind of a presence, one where you're always alert, constantly alert. One person cannot do this alone. This is a *kākou* (all of us, together) kind of thing and it was intentional. That was the purpose of the sunrise ceremony in 2013: to open up the practice of proper protocol to the next generation so they could step up and take their turn … under the watchful mentorship of the Elders, of course.

On the Mauna and in the Kūkulu exhibit, social learning was strategic and specific. It was not just about learning chants and dances for protocol. It was also about preparing the next generation for roles in leadership. For example, on the Mauna during the 2019 occupation, there were tents set up specifically for training people in non-violent confrontations. The younger generation of Kānaka was being groomed into positions of leadership as they witnessed the actions of the older generation consistently and tirelessly demonstrate their knowledge, experience, courage, and fortitude.

Similarly strategic conceptions of intergenerational transfer were also revealed in the other case studies. Brad discusses his surprise at the direction of knowledge sharing and learning in Taniwha Club, and the important agency of young people in their own modes of learning:

> **Brad**: When I look back, what am I surprised about is the *direction* of the learning. The Old Trees like myself learned

more from the youth than they learned from us. Typically, that whole intergenerational learning thing [in academic literature] doesn't deserve that label because it's all so one-directional. It's all about Elders transferring their wisdom. [Regarding] Taniwha Club … any intergenerational learning has often been the other way around—from kids that are much more adaptive than we were, kids that could see the problems causing all the other problems better than we could, and kids that had the much more creative responses to those problems … particularly how they responded to the whole Covid thing. When I look back, that's possibly one of the more significant things about the whole project that perhaps I've underestimated. They did such a wonderful job of looking after people they met through Taniwha Club during the lockdowns.

Despite common assumptions, Indigenous approaches to learning do not flow in a solely hierarchical way, from Elders downwards, but likewise leadership is not static. Relatedly, Chantelle discusses the nature of leadership in Biigtigong's repossession efforts, and its natural evolution over time:

Chantelle: The repossession work in our community is driven by a core group who have been involved and engaged for a very long time. When I was just a child, these people were involved in political movements that were land based, and about protecting our land. They were working to create really good support structures in the community—for people to get back onto the land, in many different ways. Our community has been doing this for a very long time, and there are key leaders. We are in the process of reclaiming our traditional governance structure. Part of that entails re-learning our original stories and creating our own Nishnaabeg framework through which we can be self-determining people. The amazing thing, however, is that over time, many new people come into the work too. What's very exciting to me is to see young people take on leadership roles. One of the youths who was part of the research back in 2010 is now Director of Lands and Sustainability for the community, and she is a contributor to chapter five.

Personal growth of that nature reflects the unique experiences associated with Indigenous environmental repossession. In addition, though, we suggest that the realism, basis in practical activities and materialist aspects of doing repossession are also influential. By putting their hands in the dirt, for example, participants in Taniwha club could sense and know the land and make their own meanings of the gardening efforts. In Kūkulu, the exhibit's purpose was to facilitate access to key objects and symbols from the Mauna so to enliven the experience for people who wanted to learn more about the movement. In Biigtigong, families gather in distinct places in their territory where they can see, smell, touch, and be with the very resources and materials they have come together to protect. These material practices move learning away from the imaginary or the symbolic into real-life, where learners can experience and come to know and do cultural practices for themselves.

Indigenous leadership structures are routinely condemned as obsolete and elitist (Rata 2011a; 2011b), and the same critics also castigate Indigenist pedagogical strategies as separatist and ineffective (Rata 2012). In our case studies, however, we have witnessed creative, radical, and entertaining forms of learning that attest to the dynamism, adaptiveness, and thoughtfulness of Indigenous leaders. We recognize that there are many overlaps between our case studies and the *Land as Pedagogy* doctrine that we have at times critiqued in our analysis. We have such profuse admiration and professional respect for the sometimes amateur but always dedicated educators who dominate our case studies, however, that we envision ways forward that will realize many of the objectives for land-based pedagogies in bold and transformative ways. While the original texts on environmental repossession emphasized the capacity for knowledge transfer in landed practices, we now foresee that the pedagogical momentum of repossession work is broader. It sustains knowledge-practice-belief complexes, it provides opportunities not merely to learn but also to apply any learning, and it renders entire lifeways knowable for subsequent generations. In addition to relatively simple transmission of knowledge, the practices of repossession form the very connections to place which are essential for Indigenous relational ontologies to thrive. Therefore, we contend that repossession work is fundamental for Indigenous continuity, community wellness, and intergenerational capacity building.

A final but important point about leadership relates to the very roles we have taken in researching practices of environmental repossession within the context of our own families and communities. We initiated the projects in this book in a deeply collaborative manner with our communities, and their presence in the analysis, co-writing, and subsequent discussion has been a critical part of our process of *doing*.

Completing research with one's own community may introduce the potential for bias—manipulation even—but it also bypasses many of the ethical dilemmas in such approaches as community-based participatory research. In our respective cases, constant return to community for verification and support enabled each of us to be viewed as leaders in this work, rather than mere researchers, and we are confident that the benefits of this work far outweigh any challenges. Accordingly, we anticipate that it is easier to convert research into action when Indigenous scholars work within their own family, community, clan, or tribal networks.

Environmental Repossession as an Expression of Indigenous Rights

Environmental repossession refers to the varied land-based practices Indigenous peoples engage in to express their rights and responsibilities to their families and communities. Whether from political, legal, cultural, or various other pressures, Indigenous peoples endlessly work to defend against marginalization, even in respect of their own lands. In Chapters 3 and 5, we reported how Kānaka and Nishnaabeg draw on bold expressions of repossession to assert their rights within their homelands. While Kūkulu centers on sharing the cultural and spiritual significance of the Mauna and the careful ways these messages were created and shared through an art exhibit, the gatherings in Biigtigong's territory emphasize the important ways it continues to occupy land in the traditional territory—simply by doing activities that Nishnaabeg have always done.

The blending of rights-making practices with attention to the spiritual status of key places is another signifier of repossession work in our case studies. *#Landback* is not and has never been solely about repatriation of land but includes commitments to abolition of private property to make space for the re-sanctifying of landed relations (Keisch and Scott 2023; Landback 2023). Likewise, in our case studies we witnessed subtle, innovative, and non-essentialized handling of the sacred and the ceremonial as a motivational stimuli and a guide for claims making. This includes, but is not limited to, a sophisticated reconnecting of such rights-making activities as land claims with a reinstatement of our original instructions as a covenant for modern living. While the strategies of repossession in our case studies may seem different because of their specifically local uptake, they all center ceremonial protocols with the gathering of people, and the depth of spiritual connections to sites of cultural importance:

> **Renee**: Each of the projects embrace those ancestral alignments, those spiritual kinds of values that connect and add a layer of connection to the projects. And the activities that are being worked upon on the land, whether it is ancestral land or lands up for grabs ready for plantings, it was done in a manner that included those elements. It's bringing to life and energizing ancestral alignment and bringing it into a modern and creative way that allowed for that creativity to continue … I think that all of our projects had that spiritual alignment, and that's just an observation that I see throughout all of our projects.

As confirmed in the case of Taniwha Club, however, when Indigenous peoples migrate from their homelands and traditional territories, for whatever reason they carry with them their needs for cultural, social, and other expressions related to their Indigeneity:

> **Brad**: At the stonefields, I think they probably feel quite comfortable with that sort of interpretation, apart from the spiritual part of it. It's hard to explain, but with most of them not being from that land, but from faraway places, with their parents migrating into that space, they feel that they don't have *a right* to be spiritual about that place. Yeah, if you took the word "spiritual" and replaced it with "historical" they'd be intensely proud. What they're doing with gardening reflects a whole tradition of gardening at that site that they didn't know much about until quite recently.

The stories and messages shared in Chapter 4 demonstrate a matter of increasing importance, whereby Indigenous peoples are occupying spaces with which they may have no ancestral connection. In those new spaces, their rights as Indigenous peoples may not be recognized, acknowledged, or honored, thus making it necessary to lay claim or take actions that center their rights as Indigenous peoples. In the case of Taniwha club, those claims were also "staked" through community gardening. Brad discusses how he came into the work of rights-making as a Māori academic from far away:

Brad: When I shifted to Auckland for my very first year of
teaching, I had some real characters in my third-year class
… two Tongans and a Samoan [who] were … the only
Polynesian faces in a class of 100, so the four of us got along
quite well. They would take me on about certain topics …
"You're always providing case studies from rural places or
about national parks … Why don't you … do something
more related to this place." I didn't initially get … the
challenge [but] they had a role they thought I could play.
They were associated with a group [which …] was protesting
a gas-fired power station, which is something you don't
often get in New Zealand, but this one is located right next
to a massive state housing subdivision, mostly occupied by
Polynesian peoples and in the thick of social deprivation.

The big issue for them is what you do if you've got no
rights, and that's what they were fighting. They had all sorts
of good reasons for not wanting to live by one of the only
urban gas-fired power stations in New Zealand. But the only
rights that could be accessed were for so-called "Tangata
Whenua"—people of the land. Māori associated with Otara
weren't considered legitimate because their parents came
from other parts of the North Island. So, what do you do?
They found all sorts of creative ways to gain rights outside
of formal or legal processes—and always very creative: Hip
Hop to deliver a message, or later gardens to stake a claim.
By just planting and highlighting the discrepancy between
a gas-fired power station next to a garden that sprang out of
nowhere to draw attention to the disparities there. Eventually,
that morphed into the idea to do more of the gardening [at]
the stonefields … but it was all the same thing … If formal
rights-making processes won't *give* you any rights, you need
creative means to *make* them, simply because none of the
conventional means were available to that group.

Through the everyday *and* the extravagant practices of repossession
in our case studies, Indigenous peoples are re-writing the manual for
Indigenous activism and legal redress. They engage in a variety of rights-
making processes, demonstrating their resilience to displacement and
dispossession and protecting their wellbeing. Increasingly, Indigenous
scholars are concerned that formal rights-making does more damage

to Indigenous interests than it provides solutions (Borrows and Coyle 2017; Coulthard 2014). In our case studies, however, we have witnessed how creative Indigenous leadership can playfully substitute formal or *de jure* with informal or *de facto* rights. Indigenous communities secure their interests through subtle manipulation of public concerns, thought-provoking moments of transcultural contemplation, and through their resilience to neo/colonial practice.

When the idea for this project emerged some five years ago, one of our key goals was to document our own stories and experiences so that we could share them with other communities. The strategies of environmental repossession we describe in these pages have been successful because they were developed from *our own* culturally and politically distinct origins and ways of knowing. In this journey, we have learned much about the intentions and practices our community members use to engage in the work, and we have also witnessed the intensity of love, pride, and hopefulness that underlies those efforts. We urge other communities to similarly embrace their own unique ways of knowing and doing as the basis for their environmental repossession efforts, and to take comfort in knowing that there is no universal way to do this work. Rather, doing environmental repossession may be a messy process involving a range of practices that extend across scales and include both big actions and the everyday. As we have detailed here, being present in the work of Indigenous environmental protection may also look different day to day, and across the many places it occurs. It will take time and courage. As we have concluded here in our own cases, Indigenous communities seeking to engage in this work should take confidence knowing that their own cultural practices and knowledge offer the most promising solution to the environmental challenges they face. Indigenous peoples can draw on practices of environmental repossession to celebrate and proudly enact their *rights to be Indigenous* in *all of the places* we find ourselves, including on the land.

GLOSSARY OF INDIGENOUS PHRASES

Hawai'i Terms

ahu altar
'āina land; literally, that which feeds
Akua divine natural entities and processes who are our kinfolk
Ali'i chiefs
alo face to face
aloha the sharing of breath, *ha*, face to face, *alo*
aloha 'āina love of land as both a concept and practice
ha breath
hae Hawai'i Hawai'i flag
hale Hawai'i house
Hale Kū Kia'i Mauna the name of the original hale constructed in 2015 during the Mauna Kea occupation
hale-o-pili Hawai'i house of native grass thatching
Hāloa a second human child of Ho'ohōkūkalani and Wākea
Hāloanakalaukapalili an unformed fetus and first child of Ho'ohōkūkalani and Wākea
haumana student
Haumea divine natural entity considered to be a progenitor of all life on earth
hoaaloha friend
Ho'ohōkūkalani divine natural entity considered to be the generator of stars in the heavens
hula Hawai'i dance
'ili'ili small smooth stones
ipu gourd instrument
kahea call
ka'i a chant during which dancers enter onstage before their hula performance
kākou all of us, together
kala'au sticks as a musical instrument
kalo taro
Kānaka Maoli Native Hawaiians
Kanaka Native Hawaiian, singular form
kani ka pū blow the conch shell
Kapu Aloha a code of conduct informed by Kānaka ontologies and epistemologies that aligns with Kānaka cultural practices and notions of the sacred and delivered through non-violent direct action
keiki Hawai'i child
kia'i guardian, protector

kiaʻi mauna mountain protectors
kilo observation, examination, and forecasting, as well as a person who is an
　　expert in those skills
kinolau body form
kūkulu pillar
kuleana responsibility
kumu hula Hula teacher
kumulipo a 2,000-line chant of origin and ordered evolution
Kupuna Hawaiʻi elders
lāhui nation
lei floral garland
lono divine natural entity associated with socio-geophysiological concepts
　　such as fertility, peace, and recreation, as well as the wet season and its
　　accompanying atmospheric and terrestrial disturbances
lua Hawaiʻi form of hand-to-hand combat
makaʻāinana general population
manaʻo thought
Mauna a Wākea the highest point of the Hawaiʻi island, often shortened to
　　Mauna Kea
mele Hawaiʻi song
mele koʻihonua Hawaiʻi cosmogonic genealogies
mele hānau birth chant
Moku o Keawa an affectionate term for Hawaiʻi island
moʻolelo Hawaiʻi historical narrative account
ʻohana family
oli Hawaiʻi chant
pahu Hawaiʻi drum
Papa shortened name of Papahānaumoku
Papahānaumoku divine natural entity considered to be earth mother who
　　births islands and a manifestation of Haumea
piko navel, umbilical cord, summit
pohaku rock
pono balanced, reciprocal relationship, goodness, uprightness, morality,
　　virtuous, in perfect order
pū conch shell
pule Hawaiʻi prayer
Puʻu Huluhulu a hill situated in the saddle between Mauna Kea and
　　Mauna Loa
wā epoch
wahine woman
wai fresh water
Wākea divine natural entity considered to be sky father
Wao Akua realm of divine entities and energetics
Wao Kānaka realm where humans lived and cultivated

Nga kupu Māori

awa river
hapori community
hapū sub-tribe
harakeke flax
hui meeting
iwi people, tribe
kai food
kainga village
kaitiaki guardian
kaitiakitanga guardianship; the practice of being one who watches over
kapa haka Māori performing arts
kaumātua Elder
kaupapa purpose
kuia grandmother
kupapa traitor
mahi work
mana whenua those with land-based or customary authority
mara kai food gardens
marae consecrated land often associated with a carved or meeting house
mātāwaka in-migrant
maunga mountain
mutunga conclusion, ending
pa fortified village
Pākehā somebody of non-Māori origin
patiki flounder
pepeha statement of identity
rangatiratanga chieftainship
rohe ancestral or tribal area
rohe pōtae homelands
rūnanga council, often a tribal governance unit
tamariki child, children
taniwha mythological being or monster, often with a guardianship role
tangata whenua people of the land
tapu holy, sacred
tauiwi unexpected, foreign
te reo Māori the Māori language
tika correct, proper
tohunga expert, priest
tūrangawaewae literally a place to rest one's feet; a place conveying identity
wananga university; place of advanced study
whakapapa genealogy
whānau family

wharenui large house, often associated with a carved or meeting house
whenua land

Anishinaabe Terms

Aadsokaanan original stories, sacred stories
aki land
Anishinaabe original people
Anishinaambemoen Ojbway language
Biigtig place of the muddy waters
Biigtig ziibi Pic River
chi-Nakinigewin Great law
gimiigiwemin we are sharing gifts
inawendiwin an Anishinaabe concept of interconnection
kwe woman
mino bimaadisiwin to live a good life
Nishnaabeg Anishinaabe (plural)
ziibi river

REFERENCES

Abram, D. (2012), *The Spell of the Sensuous: Perception and Language in a More-Than-Human World*, New York: Vintage.

ABWN 8102 W5279/156 AUC 128 (1852), "Fairburn's Block—Claims On," Archived files of the Department of Lands, Wellington Branch: Archives New Zealand.

ABWN 8102 W5279/156 AUC 129 (1854), "Wairoa Block—Fairburns Claim," Archived files of the Department of Lands, Wellington Branch: Archives New Zealand.

AIA (2021), "Auckland International Airport—Master Plan Amendment," Auckland: Auckland International Airport.

Alfred, T. (2014), "The Akwesasne Cultural Restoration Program: A Mohawk Approach to Land-Based Education," *Decolonization: Indigeneity, Education & Society*, 3 (3): 134–44.

Aloua, R.-R. T. L. (2014), *Community-Based Research in Hawai'i: From the Perspective of a Hawaiian Graduate Student Abroad*. http://www.sfu.ca/ ipinch/outputs/blog/community-based-research-hawai-i-perspective-hawaiian-graduate-student-abroad/

Ambtman-Smith, V. and Richmond, C. (2020), "Reimagining Indigenous Spaces of Healing: Institutional Environmental Repossession," *Turtle Island Journal of Indigenous Health*, 1 (1): 27–36.

Anderson, A., Binney, J., and Harris, A. (2014), *Tangata Whenua: An Illustrated History*, Wellington: Bridget Williams Books.

Anon (2001), "Otuataua Stonefields Historic Reserve," *New Zealand Geographic*, 50: 14–21.

Apostolopoulou, E. and Kotsila, P. (2022), "Community Gardening in Hellinikon as a Resistance Struggle against Neoliberal Urbanism: Spatial Autogestion and the Right to the City in Post-Crisis Athens, Greece," *Urban Geography*, 43 (2): 293–319.

Archibald, J. A. (2008), *Indigenous Storywork: Educating the Heart, Mind, Body, and Spirit*, Vancouver: UBC Press.

Armaline, W. T., Glasberg, D. S., and Purkayastha, B. (2017), "De Jure vs De Facto Rights: A Response to 'Human Rights: What the United States Might Learn from the Rest of the World and, Yes, from American Sociology,'" *Sociological Forum*, 32 (1): 220–4.

Armstrong, C. G. and Brown, C. (2019), "Frontiers Are Frontlines: Ethnobiological Science against Ongoing Colonialism," *Journal of Ethnobiology*, 39 (1): 14–31.

Arsenault, R., Diver, S., McGregor, D., Witham, A., and Bourassa, C. (2018), "Shifting the Framework of Canadian Water Governance through

Indigenous Research Methods: Acknowledging the Past with an Eye on the Future," *Water*, 10 (1): 49–58.

Arvin, M. (2019), "Mauna Kea Protests Aren't New. They're Part of a Long Fight against Colonialism," *TruthOut*. https://truthout.org/articles/mauna-kea-protests-are-part-of-a-long-fight-against-colonialism

Atleo, C. and Boron, J. (2022), "Land Is Life: Indigenous Relationships to Territory and Navigating Settler Colonial Property Regimes in Canada," *Land*, 11 (5): 609.1-09.12.

Auckland Council (2016), "Plan Variation Application by Fletcher Residential Proposed Plan Variation 9," Auckland: Auckland Council.

Auckland Council (2022), *Te Puna Ā-Whare Me Ngā Wāhi Ā-Whare Motuhake*, Retrieved November 10, 2022, from https://www.aucklandcouncil.govt.nz/grants-community-support-housing/Pages/housing-supply-special-housing-areas.aspx

Auckland Regional Council (2012), "Wiri-Mangere Archaeology Report," Auckland: Auckland City Council.

Auckland War Memorial Museum (1864), "Hochstetter—Geological Field Notes," File PH-NEG-B3405, Auckland: Auckland War Memorial Museum.

Audette-Longo, P. H. (2018), "'Fighting the Same Old Battle.' Obscured Oil Sands Entanglements in Press Coverage of Indigenous Resistance in the Winter of 1983," *Canadian Journal of Communication*, 43 (1): 127–46.

Barker, A. J. and Pickerill, J. (2012), "Radicalizing Relationships to and through Shared Geographies: Why Anarchists Need to Understand Indigenous Connections to Land and Place," *Antipode*, 44 (5): 1705–25.

Barker, A. J. and Pickerill, J. (2020), "Doings with the Land and Sea: Decolonising Geographies, Indigeneity, and Enacting Place-Agency," *Progress in Human Geography*, 44 (4): 640–62.

Barnes, H. M., Harmsworth, G., Tipa, G., Henwood, W., and McCreanor, T. (2021), "Indigenous-Led Environmental Research in Aotearoa New Zealand: Beyond a Transdisciplinary Model for Best Practice, Empowerment and Action," *AlterNative—An International Journal of Indigenous Peoples*, 17 (2): 306–16.

Bartlett, J. G. (2003), "Involuntary Cultural Change, Stress Phenomenon and Aboriginal Health Status," *Canadian Journal of Public Health*, 94 (3): 165–7.

Bawaka Country, Burarrwanga, L., Ganambarr, R., Ganambarr-Stubbs, M., Ganambarr, B., Maymuru, D., Lloyd, K., Daley, L., Suchet-Pearson, S., Wright, S., Tofa, M., and Hammersley, L. (2023), "Bala Ga' Lili: Communicating, Relating and Co-Creating Balance through Relationships of Reciprocity," *Social and Cultural Geography*, 24 (7): 1203–23. https://doi.org/10.1080/14649365.2022.2052166.

Bawaka Country, Wright, S., Suchet-Pearson, S., Lloyd, K., Burarrwanga, L., Ganambarr, R., Ganambarr-Stubbs, M., Ganambarr, B., Maymuru, D., and Sweeney, J. (2016), "Co-Becoming Bawaka: Towards a Relational Understanding of Place/Space," *Progress in Human Geography*, 40 (4): 455–75.

Bell, N. (2013), "Anishinaabe Bimaadiziwin: Living Spiritually with Respect, Relationship, Reciprocity, and Responsibility," in A. Kulnieks, D. Roronhiakewen Longboat, and K. Young (eds), *Contemporary Studies in Environmental and Indigenous Pedagogies*, 89–107, Rotterdam: Sense Publishers.

Bell, N. (2016), "Mino-Bimaadiziwin: Education for the Good Life," in F. Deer and T. Falkenberg (eds), *Indigenous Perspectives on Education for Well-Being in Canada*, 7–20, Winnipeg: ESWB Press.

Bennett, M. M. (2020), "Scale-Jumping in the Arctic Council: Indigenous Permanent Participants and Asian Observer States," in C. Yuan Woon and K. Dodds (eds), *"Observing" the Arctic: Asia in the Arctic Council and beyond*, 54–81, Cheltenham: Elgar.

Berry, J. W. (1990), "Acculturation and Adaptation: Health Consequences of Culture Contact among Circumpolar Peoples," *Arctic Medical Research*, 49 (3): 142–50.

Betasamosake Simpson, L. (2016), "Indigenous Resurgence and Co-Resistance," *Critical Ethnic Studies*, 2 (2): 19–33.

Bickler, S. and Clough, R. (2016), "Proposed Northern Runway and Southern Runway Options, Auckland International Airport, Mangere: Archaeological Constraints Assessment," Report prepared for Auckland International Airport Limited, Auckland: Clough and Associates.

Big-Canoe, K. (2011), "Indigenous Knowledge, Social Relationships and Health: Community-Based Participatory Research with Anishinabe Youth at Pic River First Nation," Thesis Submitted for a Master of Arts, London: Western University.

Big-Canoe, K. and Richmond, C. A. (2014), "Anishinabe Youth Perceptions about Community Health: Toward Environmental Repossession," *Health and Place*, 26: 127–35.

Big Island Video News (2014), *Full Coverage of Thirty Meter Telescope Disruption*. https://www.bigislandvideonews.com/2014/10/09/video-full-coverage-thirty-meter-telescope-road-block/

Biigtigong Nishnaabeg (2022), *Land Claim*, Retrieved October 31, 2022, from https://www.picriver.com/about-us/land-claim/

Blackmore, L. (2022), "Cultivating Ongoingness through Site-Specific Arts Research and Public Engagement," *Journal of Latin American Cultural Studies*, 31 (1): 159–76.

Blomley, N. (1996), "'Shut the Province Down': First Nations Blockades in British Columbia, 1984–1995," *BC Studies*, 111: 5–35.

Bombay, A., Matheson, K., and Anisman, H. (2014), "The Intergenerational Effects of Indian Residential Schools: Implications for the Concept of Historical Trauma," *Transcultural Psychiatry*, 51 (3): 320–38.

Borrows, J. (2016), "Outsider Education: Indigenous Law and Land-Based Learning," *Windsor Yearbook on Access to Justice*, 33: 1.

Borrows, J. (2017), "Challenging Historical Frameworks: Aboriginal Rights, the Trickster, and Originalism," *Canadian Historical Review*, 98 (1): 114–35.

Borrows, J. and Coyle, M. (2017), *The Right Relationship: Reimagining the Implementation of Historical Treaties*, Toronto: University of Toronto Press.

Bosworth, K. and Chua, C. (2022), "The Countersovereignty of Critical Infrastructure Security: Settler-State Anxiety versus the Pipeline Blockade," *Antipode*, Early Release, 1–23. https://doi.org/10.1111/anti.12794.

Bradshaw, E. A. (2015), "Blockadia Rising: Rowdy Greens, Direct Action and the Keystone Xl Pipeline," *Critical Criminology*, 23 (4): 433–48.

Braun, S. F. (2020), "Culture, Resource, Management, and Anthropology: Pipelines and the Wakan at the Standing Rock Sioux Reservation," *Plains Anthropologist*, 65 (253): 7–24.

Bryan, D. and Viteri, C. (2022), "Re-Storying Participatory Action Research: A Narrative Approach to Challenging Epistemic Violence in Community Development," in R. Stoecker and A. Falcon (eds), *Handbook on Participatory Action Research and Community Development*, 417–35, Cheltenham: Elgar.

Burrell, M., Grosse, C., and Mark, B. (2022), "Resistance to Petro-Hegemony: A Three Terrains of Power Analysis of the Line 3 Tar Sands Pipeline in Minnesota," *Energy Research and Social Science*, 91 (article 102724): 1–11.

Canning, P. C. (2018), "I Could Turn You to Stone: Indigenous Blockades in an Age of Climate Change," *International Indigenous Policy Journal*, 9 (3): 1–24.

Case, E. (2019), "I Ka Piko, to the Summit: Resistance from the Mountain to the Sea," *The Journal of Pacific History*, 54 (2): 166–81.

Castellano, M. B. and Archibald, L. (2007), *Healing Historic Trauma: A Report from the Aboriginal Healing Foundation*, London: Western University.

Castillo Jara, E. and Bruns, A. (2022), "Contested Notions of Energy Justice and Energy Futures in Struggles over Tar Sands Development in British Columbia, Canada," *Futures*, 138 (article 102291): 1–13.

Castleden, H., Morgan, V. S., and Lamb, C. (2012), "'I Spent the First Year Drinking Tea': Exploring Canadian University Researchers' Perspectives on Community-Based Participatory Research Involving Indigenous Peoples," *The Canadian Geographer*, 56 (2): 160–79.

Chapman, J. M. and Schott, S. (2020), "Knowledge Coevolution: Generating New Understanding through Bridging and Strengthening Distinct Knowledge Systems and Empowering Local Knowledge Holders," *Sustainability Science*, 15 (1): 931–43.

Chartrand, R. (2012), "Anishinaabe Pedagogy," *Canadian Journal of Native Education*, 35 (1): 144–62.

Chazan, M. and Baldwin, M. (2021), "Learning to Be Refused: Exploring Refusal, Consent and Care in Storytelling Research," *Postcolonial Studies*, 24 (1): 104–21.

Christiansen, J. (2021), "The Water Protectors at Standing Rock: Survivance Strategies for Gendered Relinking," *Women's Studies in Communication*, 44 (3): 278–300.

Clark, S. E., Magrane, E., Baumgartner, T., Bennett, S. E. K., Bogan, M., Edwards, T., Dimmitt, M. A., Green, H., Hedgcock, C., Johnson, B. M., Johnson, M. R., Velo, K., and Wilder, B. T. (2020), "6&6: A Transdisciplinary Approach to Art–Science Collaboration," *Bioscience*, 70 (9): 821–9.

Cole, D. R. (2019), "The Designation of a Deleuzian Philosophy for Environmental Education and Its Consequences," *Australian Journal of Environmental Education*, 35 (3): 173–82.

Coombes, B. (2013), "Urban Maori and Environmental Justice—The Case of Lake Otara," in E. J. Peters and C. Anderson (eds), *Indigenous in the City: Contemporary Identities and Cultural Innovation*, 334–53, Vancouver: UBC Press.

Coombes, B. (2018a), "Evading the Neo/Colonial State without Running to the Hills: Nearly-Illegal Food Harvesting in Aotearoa," in J. Corntassel, T. Alfred, N. Goodyear-Ka'opua, N. Silva, H. Aikau, and D. Mucina (eds), *Everyday Acts of Resurgence: People, Places, Practices*, 98–102, Olympia: Daykeeper Press.

Coombes, B. (2018b), "Kaupapa Maori Research as Participatory Enquiry: Where's the Action?," in T. Hoskins and A. Jones (eds), *Critical Conversations in Kaupapa Maori*, 29–48, Wellington: Huia Publishers.

Coombes, B. (2021), "Personifying Indigenous Rights in Nature? Treaty Settlement and Comanagement in Te Urewera," in R.-H. Andersson, B. Cothran, and S. J. Kekki (eds), *Bridging Cultural Concepts of Nature: Indigenous Places and Protected Spaces of Nature*, 29–60, Helsinki: Collegium—University of Helsinki.

Coombes, B., Gombay, N., Johnson, J. T., and Shaw, W. S. (2011), "The Challenges of and from Indigenous Geographies," in V. J. Del Casino, M. E. Thomas, P. Cloke, and R. Panelli (eds), *The Companion to Social Geography*, 472–89, London: Wiley-Blackwell.

Coombes, B., Johnson, J. T., and Howitt, R. (2012), "Indigenous Geographies I: Mere Resource Conflicts? The Complexities in Indigenous Land and Environmental Claims," *Progress in Human Geography*, 36 (6): 810–21.

Coombes, B., Johnson, J. T., and Howitt, R. (2013), "Indigenous Geographies II: The Aspirational Spaces in Postcolonial Politics—Reconciliation, Belonging and Social Provision," *Progress in Human Geography*, 37 (5): 691–700.

Corntassel, J. (2012), "Re-Envisioning Resurgence: Indigenous Pathways to Decolonization and Sustainable Self-Determination," *Decolonization: Indigeneity, Education and Society*, 1 (1): 86–101.

Corntassel, J., Alfred, T., Goodyear-Ka'opua, N., Silva, N., Aikau, H., and Mucina, D. (2018), *Everyday Acts of Resurgence: People, Places, Practices*, Olympia: Daykeeper Press.

Corntassel, J. and Hardbarger, T. (2019), "Educate to Perpetuate: Land-Based Pedagogies and Community Resurgence," *International Review of Education*, 65 (1): 87–116.

Coulthard, G. (2014), *Red Skin, White Masks: Rejecting the Colonial Politics of Recognition*, Minneapolis: University of Minnesota Press.

Cunsolo Willox, A., Harper, S. L., Ford, J. D., Landman, K., Houle, K., and Edge, V. L. (2012), "'From This Place and of This Place.' Climate Change, Sense of Place, and Health in Nunatsiavut, Canada," *Social Science & Medicine*, 75 (3): 538–47.

Czyzewski, K. (2011), "Colonialism as a Broader Social Determinant of Health," *International Indigenous Policy Journal*, 2 (1): 1–16.

Daigle, M. (2016), "Awawanenitakik: The Spatial Politics of Recognition and Relational Geographies of Indigenous Self-Determination," *The Canadian Geographer*, 60 (2): 259–69.

Daigle, M. (2019), "Tracing the Terrain of Indigenous Food Sovereignties," *Journal of Peasant Studies*, 46 (2): 297–315.

Daigle, M. and Ramírez, M. M. (2019), "Decolonial Geographies," in N. Theodore, T. Jazeel, A. Kent, and K. McKittrick (eds), *Keywords in Radical Geography: Antipode at 50*, 78–84, London: Wiley-Blackwell.

De La Cadena, M. (2010), "Indigenous Cosmopolitics in the Andes: Conceptual Reflections beyond 'Politics,'" *Cultural Anthropology*, 25 (2): 334–70.

De Leeuw, S., Cameron, E. S., and Greenwood, M. L. (2012), "Participatory and Community-Based Research, Indigenous Geographies, and the Spaces of Friendship: A Critical Engagement," *Canadian Geographer*, 56 (2): 180–94.

De Leeuw, S. and Hunt, S. (2018), "Unsettling Decolonizing Geographies," *Geography Compass*, 12 (7): 1–14.

Debassige, B. (2010), "Re-Conceptualizing Anishinaabe Mino-Bimaadiziwin (the Good Life) as Research Methodology: A Spirit-Centered Way in Anishinaabe Research," *Canadian Journal of Native Education*, 33 (1): 11.

Deloria, P. J., Lomawaima, K. T., Brayboy, B. M. J., Trahant, M. N., Ghiglione, L., Medin, D., and Blackhawk, N. (2018), "Unfolding Futures: Indigenous Ways of Knowing for the Twenty-First Century," *Daedalus*, 147 (2): 6–16.

Diver, S., Eitzel, M. V., Fricke, S., and Hillman, L. (2022), "Networked Sovereignty: Polycentric Water Governance and Indigenous Self-Determination in the Klamath Basin," *Water Alternatives*, 15 (2): 523–50.

Dodson, G. and Miru, M. (2021), "Ngā Waihotanga Iho: Self-Determination through Indigenous Environmental Education in New Zealand," *Australian Journal of Environmental Education*, 37 (3): 254–65.

Dowling, R., Lloyd, K., and Suchet-Pearson, S. (2018), "Qualitative Methods III: Experimenting, Picturing, Sensing," *Progress in Human Geography*, 42 (5): 779–88.

Dudgeon, P. and Bray, A. (2019), "Indigenous Relationality: Women, Kinship and the Law," *Genealogy*, 3 (2): 23.

Estes, N. (2019), *Our History Is the Future. Standing Rock versus the Dakota Access Pipeline, and the Long Tradition of Indigenous Resistance*, New York: Verso.

Farrell, J., Burow, P. B., McConnell, K., Bayham, J., Whyte, K., and Koss, G. (2021), "Effects of Land Dispossession and Forced Migration on Indigenous Peoples in North America," *Science*, 374 (6567): 1–8.

Feinberg, P. P. (2021), "Re-Storying Place: The Pedagogical Force of Walking in the Work of Indigenous Artist-Activists Émilie Monnet and Cam," *International Journal of Education through Art*, 17 (1): 163–85.

Fletcher, M. L. (2017), "Anishinaabe Law and the Round House," *Albany Government Law Review*, 10: 88–111.

Fox, N. J. and Alldred, P. (2021), "Doing New Materialist Data Analysis: A Spinozo-Deleuzian Ethological Toolkit," *International Journal of Social Research Methodology*, 24: 1–14.

Gagné, N. (2016), "The Waxing and Waning of the Politics of Authenticity: The Situation of Urban-Based Maori through the Lens of Municipal Politics," *City and Society*, 28 (1): 48–73.

Gehl, L. (2000), "'The Queen and I.' Discrimination against Women in the 'Indian Act' Continues," *Canadian Woman Studies*, 20 (2): 64–9

Gergan, M. D. and McCreary, T. (2022), "Disrupting Infrastructures of Colonial Hydro-Modernity: Lepcha and Dakelh Struggles against Temporal and Territorial Displacements," *Annals of the American Association of Geographers*, 112 (3): 789–98.

Gibb, R. (2015), "Archaeological Assessment of Self Farm/Crater Hill, Papatoetoe, Auckland," Report Prepared for Self Family Trust, Auckland: Geometria Limited.

Ginn, C. S., Ginn, C. W. C., Barnabe, C., Gervais, L., Gentes, J., Dumont/ Vaness Bergum, D., Rees, N., and Camponi, A. (2022), "'Connection with the Creator So Our Spirits Can Stay Alive.' A Community-Based Participatory Study with the Métis Nation of Alberta (MNA)—Region 3," *Qualitative Inquiry*, 28 (10): 1007–18.

Global Witness (2022), *Stand with Defenders*, last visited November 11, 2022. https://www.globalwitness.org/en/campaigns/environmental-activists/

Gobby, J., Temper, L., Burke, M., and von Ellenrieder, N. (2022), "Resistance as Governance: Transformative Strategies Forged on the Frontlines of Extractivism in Canada," *Extractive Industries and Society*, 9 (article 100919): 1–11.

Gone, J. P. (2013), "Redressing First Nations Historical Trauma: Theorizing Mechanisms for Indigenous Culture as Mental Health Treatment," *Transcultural Psychiatry*, 50 (5): 683–706.

Goodyear-Ka'opua, N. (2013), *The Seeds We Planted: Portraits of a Native Hawaiian Charter School*, Minneapolis: University of Minnesota Press.

Goodyear-Ka'opua, N. (2017), "Protectors of the Future, Not Protestors of the Past: Indigenous Pacific Activism and Mauna a Wākea," *South Atlantic Quarterly*, 116 (1): 184–94.

Goodyear-Ka'opua, N. (2018), "Dreaming Is an Everyday Act of Resurgence," in J. Corntassel, T. Alfred, N. Goodyear–Ka'opua, N. Silva, H. Aikau, and D. Mucina (eds), *Everyday Acts of Resurgence: People, Places, Practices*, 82–8, Olympia: Daykeeper Press.

Goudreau, G., Weber-Pillwax, C., Cote-Meek, S., Madill, H., and Wilson, S. (2008), "Hand Drumming: Health-Promoting Experiences of Aboriginal

Women from a Northern Ontario Urban Community," *International Journal of Indigenous Health*, 4 (1): 72–83.

Greenwood, M. and Lindsay, N. M. (2019), "A Commentary on Land, Health, and Indigenous Knowledge(s)," *Global Health Promotion*, 26 (3): 82–6.

Grey, R. S., Muru-Lanning, C., Jones, N., Muru-Lanning, M., and Dawes, T. (2020), "Once Were Gardeners: Māra and Planting Protest at Ihumātao," *MAI Journal*, 9 (3): 219–25.

Grote, K. M. and Johnson, J. T. (2021), "Pipelines, Protectors, and Settler Colonialism: Media Representations of the Dakota Access Pipeline Protest," *Settler Colonial Studies*, 11: 1–25.

Guntarik, O. and Harwood, A. (2022), "Native Migrant Narratives in an Age of Alchemy and Activism," *AlterNative*, 18 (2): 257–68.

Hamilton Faris, J. (2022), "Ocean Weaves: Reconfigurations of Climate Justice in Oceania," *Feminist Review*, 130 (1): 5–25.

Hancock, F., Lee-Morgan, J., Newton, P., and McCreanor, T. (2020), "The Case of Ihumātao: Interrogating Competing Corporate and Indigenous Visions of the Future," *New Zealand Sociology*, 35 (2): 15–46.

Hancock, F. and Newton, P. (2022), "Becoming Whānau: Māori and Pākehā Working Together on the Indigenous-Led Campaign, #Protectihumātao," *Ethnicities*, 22 (5): 642–62. https://doi.org/10.1177/14687968211062655.

Harcourt, N., Awatere, S., Hyslop, J., Taura, Y., Wilcox, M., Taylor, L., Rau, J., and Timoti, P. (2022), "Kia Manawaroa Kia Puawai: Enduring Māori Livelihoods," *Sustainability Science*, 17 (2): 391–402.

Hardman, M., Chipungu, L., Magidimisha, H., Larkham, P. J., Scott, A. J., and Armitage, R. P. (2018), "Guerrilla Gardening and Green Activism: Rethinking the Informal Urban Growing Movement," *Landscape and Urban Planning*, 170: 6–14.

Harper, S. L., Edge, V. L., Ford, J., Willox, A. C., Wood, M., IHACC Research Team, RICG, and McEwen, S. A. (2015), "Climate-Sensitive Health Priorities in Nunatsiavut, Canada," *BMC Public Health*, 15 (1): 605.

Hatala, A. R., Morton, D., Njeze, C., Bird-Naytowhow, K., and Pearl, T. (2019), "Re-Imagining Miyo-Wicehtowin: Human-Nature Relations, Land-Making, and Wellness among Indigenous Youth in a Canadian Urban Context," *Social Science & Medicine*, 230: 122–30.

Hawaiian Cultural Center of Hāmākua (2018), https://locals.hawaiiverse.com/listing/hawaiian-cultural-center-of-hamakua/

Hemsworth, K., Greer, K., Paulin, M., Sutherland, K., and McLeod Shabogesic, J. (2022), "Maada'oonidiwag Gete-Dibaajimowen ('Sharing Old Stories'): Reflections on a Place-Based Reparatory Research Partnership in Nbisiing Anishinaabeg Territory," *GeoJournal*, 87: 267–80.

Hitt, C. (2019), "The Sacred History of Maunakea", *Honululu*. https://www.honolulumagazine.com/the-sacred-history-of-maunakea/

Hohenthal, J. and Veintie, T. (2022), "Fostering Indigenous Young People's Socio-Environmental Consciousness through Place-Based Learning in Ecuadorian Amazonia," *Globalizations*, ArticlesFirst, 1–21. https://doi.org/10.1080/14747731.2022.2038831.

Hunt, J., Riley, B., O'Neill, L., and Maynard, G. (2021), "Transition to Renewable Energy and Indigenous People in Northern Australia: Enhancing or Inhibiting Capabilities?," *Journal of Human Development and Capabilities*, 22 (2): 360–78.

Hunt, S. (2014), "Ontologies of Indigeneity: The Politics of Embodying a Concept," *Cultural Geographies*, 21 (1): 27–32.

Hunt, S. and Holmes, C. (2015), "Everyday Decolonization: Living a Decolonizing Queer Politics," *Journal of Lesbian Studies*, 19 (2): 154–72.

Hurlbert, M. A. and Datta, R. (2022), "When the Environment Is Destroyed, You're Destroyed: Achieving Indigenous Led Pipeline Justice," *Energy Research and Social Science*, 91 (article 102711): 1–11.

Hurley, T. (2015), "Mauna Kea Telescope Petition Delivered with 53,000 Signatures," *Honolulu Star Advertiser*. https://www.staradvertiser. com/2015/04/20/breaking-news/mauna-kea-telescope-petition-delivered-with-53000-signatures/

Husbands, P. and Riddell, K. (1993), "The Alienation of South Auckland Lands," Wellington: Waitangi Tribunal.

Iared, V. G. and Hofstatter, L. J. V. (2022), "Our Sars-Cov-2 Teacher: Teachings of the Pandemic about Our Relations with the More-Than-Human World," *Journal of Environmental Education*, 53 (2): 117–25.

Ince, A. and Barrera de la Torre, G. (2016), "For Post-Statist Geographies," *Political Geography*, 55: 10–19.

Iseke, J. (2013), "Indigenous Storytelling as Research," *International Review of Qualitative Research*, 6 (4): 559–77.

Jamieson, K. (1978), "Indian Women and the Law in Canada: Citizens Minus," Ottawa: Advisory Council on the Status of Women.

Johnson, J. T. and Larsen, S. C. (2013), *A Deeper Sense of Place: Stories and Journeys of Indigenous-Academic Collaboration*, Corvallis: Oregon State University Press.

Johnson, M. (2021), "Indigenizing Self-Determination at the United Nations: Reparative Progress in the Declaration on the Rights of Indigenous Peoples," *Journal of the History of International Law*, 23 (1): 206–28.

Johnston, B. (1976), *Ojibway Heritage*, Lincoln: University of Nebraska Press.

KAHEA (2016), Mauna Kea Timeline. http://kahea.org/issues/sacred-summits/timeline-of-events

Kaʻiwakīloumoku (2022), *The Last Will and Testament of Bernice Pauahi Bishop*. https://kaiwakiloumoku.ksbe.edu/article/heritage-center-the-last-will-and-testament-of-bernice-pauahi-bishop

Kauanui, J. K. (2016), "'A Structure, Not an Event': Settler Colonialism and Enduring Indigeneity," *Lateral*, 5 (1): 1–9.

Kawharu, M. (2000), "Kaitiakitanga: A Maori Anthropological Perspective of the Maori Socio-Environmental Ethic of Resource Management," *The Journal of the Polynesian Society*, 109 (4): 349–70.

Keelan, K., Wilkinson, T., Pitama, S., and Lacey, C. (2022), "Exploring Elderly Māori Experiences of Aged Residential Care Using a Kaupapa Māori

Research Paradigm: Methodological Considerations," *AlterNative*, 18 (1): 67–74.

Keisch, D. and Scott, T. (2023), "'We Are the Land'—Reflections on KXL Resistance at Rootz Camp," *Rethinking Marxism*, 35 (1): 38–62.

Kiddle, R. (2021), "Aotearoa Towns and Cities Have Always Been Indigenous," in C. Hill (ed), *Kia Whakanuia Te Whenua: People, Place, Landscape*, 141–8, Auckland: Mary Egan.

Kimmerer, R. (2013), *Braiding Sweetgrass: Indigenous Wisdom, Scientific Knowledge and the Teachings of Plants*, Minnesota: Milkweed Editions.

King, L., Gubele, R., and Anderson, J. R. (2015), *Survivance, Sovereignty, and Story: Teaching American Indian Rhetorics*, Boulder: Utah State University Press.

Kino-nda-niimi Collective (2014), *The Winter We Danced: Voices from the Past, the Future, and the Idle No More Movement*, Winnipeg: ARP Books.

Kluttz, J., Walker, J., and Walter, P. (2020), "Unsettling Allyship, Unlearning and Learning towards Decolonising Solidarity," *Studies in the Education of Adults*, 52 (1): 49–66.

Kluttz, J., Walker, J., and Walter, P. (2021), "Learning towards Decolonising Relationships at Standing Rock," *Studies in the Education of Adults*, 53 (1): 101–19.

Kouros, T. (2022), "Reaping the Fruits of Informal Urbanism: An Ethnography of Tactical Gardening in Limassol, Cyprus," *Built Environment*, 48 (2): 188–205.

Kovach, M. (2009), *Indigenous Methodologies: Characteristics, Conversations and Contexts*, Toronto: University of Toronto Press.

Kovach, M. (2010), "Conversation Method in Indigenous Research," *First Peoples Child & Family Review*, 5 (1): 40–8.

Kreps, C. (2015), "Appropriate Museology and the 'New Museum Ethics.' Honoring Diversity," *Nordisk Muesologi*, 2: 4–16.

Kreps, C. F. (2008), "Appropriate Museology in Theory and Practice," *Museum Management and Curatorship*, 23: 23–41.

Kröger, M. and Lalander, R. (2016), "Ethno-Territorial Rights and the Resource Extraction Boom in Latin America: Do Constitutions Matter?," *Third World Quarterly*, 37 (4): 682–702.

Krupa, J. (2012), "Blazing a New Path Forward: A Case Study on the Renewable Energy Initiatives of the Pic River First Nation," *Environmental Development*, 3: 109–22.

Krupa, J., Galbraith, L., and Burch, S. (2015), "Participatory and Multi-Level Governance: Applications to Aboriginal Renewable Energy Projects," *Local Environment*, 20 (1): 81–101.

Krusz, E., Davey, T., Wigginton, B., and Hall, N. (2020), "What Contributions, If Any, Can Non-Indigenous Researchers Offer toward Decolonizing Health Research?," *Qualitative Health Research*, 30 (2): 205–16.

LaDuke, W. (1999), *All Our Relations: Native Struggles for Land and Life*, Boston: South End Press.

Landback (2023), "Manifesto," Accessed September 25, 2023, from https://landback.org/manifesto.

Lassiter, L. (2005), "Collaborative Ethnography and Public Anthropology," *Current Anthropology*, 46 (1): 83–106.

Latulippe, N. and Klenk, N. (2020), "Making Room and Moving Over: Knowledge Co-Production, Indigenous Knowledge Sovereignty and the Politics of Global Environmental Change Decision-Making," *Current Opinion in Environmental Sustainability*, 42: 7–14.

Lavallee, L. F. and Poole, J. M. (2010), "Beyond Recovery: Colonization, Health and Healing for Indigenous People in Canada," *International Journal of Mental Health and Addiction*, 8 (2): 271–81.

Lawlor, I. (2009), "An Assessment of Heritage Resources Located within the Proposed Otuataua Stonefields Historic Reserve Visitor Centre Development 'Footprint', and Measures to Avoid, Remedy and Mitigate Effects," Report for Manukau City Council, Makaurau Marae and OSHR Visitor Centre Design Team, Manukau: Manukau City Council.

Lawrence, B. (2004), *"Real" Indians and Others: Mixed-Blood Urban Native Peoples and Indigenous Nationhood*, Lincoln: University of Nebraska Press.

Lawrence, B. and Anderson, K. (2005), "Introduction to 'Indigenous Women: The State of Our Nations,'" *Atlantis: Critical Studies in Gender, Culture & Social Justice*, 29 (2): 1–8.

Leah, R. J. (2016), "Earth Love: Finding Our Way Back Home," *Canadian Woman Studies*, 31 (1–2): 15–18.

Lewis, D., Castleden, H., Apostle, R., Francis, S., and Francis-Strickland, K. (2021), "Linking Land Displacement and Environmental Dispossession to Mi'kmaw Health and Well-Being: Culturally Relevant Place-Based Interpretive Frameworks Matter," *The Canadian Geographer*, 65 (1): 66–81.

Lightfoot, S. (2016), *Global Indigenous Politics: A Subtle Revolution*, Oxfordshire: Routledge.

Lightfoot, S. R. (2021), "Decolonizing Self-Determination: Haudenosaunee Passports and Negotiated Sovereignty," *European Journal of International Relations*, 27 (4): 971–94.

Lloyd, K., Wright, S., Suchet-Pearson, S., Burarrwanga, L., and Country, B. (2012), "Reframing Development through Collaboration: Towards a Relational Ontology of Connection in Bawaka, North East Arnhem Land," *Third World Quarterly*, 33 (6): 1075–94.

Longman, N., Riddle, E., Wilson, A., and Desai, S. (2020), "'Land Back' Is More than the Sum of Its Parts," *Briarpatch*, 49: 2.

Louis, R. P. with Kahele, M. (2017), *Kanaka Hawai'i Cartography: Hula, Navigation, and Oratory*, Lincoln: Oregon State University Press.

Lynch, J. and Mannion, G. (2021), "Place-Responsive Pedagogies in the Anthropocene: Attuning with the More-Than-Human," *Environmental Education Research*, 27 (6): 864–78.

Mackintosh, L. (2021), *Shifting Grounds: Deep Histories of Tamaki Makaurau Auckland*, Auckland: Bridget Williams Books.

Maly, K. and Maly, O. (2005), "Mauna Kea—Ka Piko Kaulana O Ka 'Aina. Mauna Kea—The Famous Summit of the Land: A Collection of Native Traditions, Historical Accounts, and Oral History Interviews for: Mauna Kea, the Lands of Ka 'Ohe, Humu 'Ula and the 'Aina Mauna on the Island of Hawai'i," Prepared for the Office of Mauna Kea Management, Hilo: Kumu Pono Associates LLC.

Mangioni, T. L. (2021), "Confronting Australian Apathy: Latai Taumoepeau and the Politics of Performance in Pacific Climate Stewardship," *Contemporary Pacific*, 33 (1): 32–62.

Marizzi, C. and Bartar, P. (2021), "Art in Science and Science in Art—Reflections through the Lense of Citizen Science," *Proceedings of Austrian Citizen Science Conference 2020—PoS (ACSC2020)*, 393 (Article 22): 1–5.

Mays, K. T. (2019), "Decolonial Hip Hop: Indigenous Hip Hop and the Disruption of Settler Colonialism," *Cultural Studies*, 33 (3): 460–79.

McCarty, T. L., Romero, M. E., and Zepeda, O. (2006), "Reclaiming the Gift: Indigenous Youth Counter-Narratives on Native Language Loss and Revitalization," *American Indian Quarterly*, 30 (1/2): 28–48.

McCoy, P. C., Nees, R., Weisler, M. I., and Zhao, J.-X. (2012), "230 Thorium Dating of Toolstone Procurement Strategies, Production Scale and Ritual Practices at the Mauna Kea Adze Quarry Complex, Hawai," *The Journal of the Polynesian Society*, 121 (4): 407–20.

McCreary, T. (2020), "Between the Commodity and the Gift: The Coastal Gaslink Pipeline and the Contested Temporalities of Canadian and Witsuwit'en Law," *Journal of Human Rights and the Environment*, 11 (3): 122–45.

McGregor, D. (2004), "Coming Full Circle: Indigenous Knowledge, Environment, and Our Future," *American Indian Quarterly*, 28 (3/4): 385–410.

McGregor, D. (2018a), "From 'Decolonized' to Reconciliation Research in Canada: Drawing from Indigenous Research Paradigms," *International Journal of Critical Geography*, 17: 810–31.

McGregor, D. (2018b), "Toward an Anishinaabe Research Paradigm: Theory and Practice," in D. McGregor, R. Johnson, and J. P. Restoule (eds), *Indigenous Research: Theories, Practices, and Relationships*, 243–56, Toronto: Canadian Scholars Press.

McGregor, D., Littlechild, D., and Sritharan, M. (2022), "The Role of Traditional Environmental Knowledge in Planetary Well-Being," in K. Ruckstuhl, I. Velásquez Nimatuj, J.-A. McNeish, and N. Postero (eds), *The Routledge Handbook of Indigenous Development*, 203–11, London: Routledge.

McGregor, D., Whitaker, S., and Sritharan, M. (2020), "Indigenous Environmental Justice and Sustainability," *Current Opinion in Environmental Sustainability*, 43: 35–40.

McGregor, D. P. and Aluli, N. E. (2014), "Wao Kele O Puna and the Pele Defense Fund," in Noelani Goodyear-Ka'opua, I. Hussey, and E. K. Wright (eds), *A Nation Rising*, 180–98, Durham: Duke University Press.

McGuire, P. D. (2013), "Anishinaabe Giikeedaasiwin—Indigenous Knowledge: An Exploration of Resilience," PhD Thesis, Saskatoon: University of Saskatchewan.

McIntosh, T. and Workman, K. (2017), "Māori and Prison," in A. Deckert and R. Sarre (eds), *The Palgrave Handbook of Australian and New Zealand Criminology, Crime and Justice*, 725–35, New York: Palgrave Macmillan.

McIver, S. (1995), "Aboriginal Women's Rights as 'Existing Rights'," *Canadian Woman Studies*, 15 (2): 34–8.

McLeay, C. (2020), "Housing Accords and Special Housing Areas Act 2013 and the Erosion of Democracy," *New Zealand Geographer*, 76 (2): 127–34.

Mergler, D. and Da Silva, J. (2018), "The Legacy of Mercury Exposure in Grassy Narrows First Nation," Proceedings of the ISEE Conference, International Society of Exposure Science and the International Society for Environmental Epidemiology. Ottawa, August 26–28, 2018.

Metge, J. (2021), *A New Maori Migration: Rural and Urban Relations in Northern New Zealand*, London: Routledge.

Mika, J. P., Dell, K., Elers, C., Dutta, M., and Tong, Q. (2022), "Indigenous Environmental Defenders in Aotearoa New Zealand: Ihumātao and Ōroua River," *AlterNative*, 18 (2): 277–89.

Mikadze, V. (2020), "Landscape Urbanism and Informal Space-Making: Insights from a Guerrilla Gardening Case in Montreal, Canada," *Journal of Urban Design*, 25 (6): 794–811.

Mikraszewicz, K. and Richmond, C. (2019), "Paddling the Biigtig: Mino Biimadisiwin Practiced through Canoeing," *Social Science & Medicine*, 240: 112548.

Millie, A. (2022), "Guerrilla Gardening as Normalised Law-Breaking: Challenges to Land Ownership and Aesthetic Order," *Crime, Media, Culture*, 19 (2): 191–208. https://doi.org/10.1177/17416590221088792.

Moewaka Barnes, H., Harmsworth, G., Tipa, G., Henwood, W., and McCreanor, T. (2021), "Indigenous-Led Environmental Research in Aotearoa New Zealand: Beyond a Transdisciplinary Model for Best Practice, Empowerment and Action," *AlterNative*, 17 (2): 306–16.

Moewaka Barnes, H., Henwood, W., Murray, J., Waiti, P., Pomare-Peita, M., Bercic, S., Chee, R., Mitchell, M., and McCreanor, T. (2019), "Noho Taiao: Reclaiming Māori Science with Young People," *Global Health Promotion*, 26 (3): 35–43.

Morse, M., Blenkinsop, S., and Jickling, B. (2021), "Wilding Educational Policy: Hope for the Future," *Policy Futures in Education*, 19 (3): 262–8.

Morton, D., Bird-Naytowhow, K., Pearl, T., and Hatala, A. R. (2020), "'Just Because They Aren't Human Doesn't Mean They Aren't Alive': The Methodological Potential of Photovoice to Examine Human-Nature Relations as a Source of Resilience and Health among Urban Indigenous Youth," *Health and Place*, 61: 102268.

Murdoch, G. (2013), "Maori Ancestral Relationships with Mangere-Otahuhu," Auckland: Auckland City Council.

Murphy, L. (2016), "The Politics of Land Supply and Affordable Housing: Auckland's Housing Accord and Special Housing Areas," *Urban Studies*, 53 (12): 2530–47.

Nagy, R. (2022), "Transformative Justice in a Settler Colonial Transition: Implementing the UN Declaration on the Rights of Indigenous Peoples in Canada," *International Journal of Human Rights*, 26 (2): 191–216.

Ndlovu, M. L. (2020), "Dancing with Mountains," *Education as Change*, 24: 1–20.

New Zealand Government (2014), "Housing and Special Areas Bill," *Cabinet Minutes*, 13: 36–12/14.

Newell, D. (2016), *Tangled Webs of History: Indians and the Law in Canada's Pacific Coast Fisheries (Heritage)*, Toronto: University of Toronto Press.

Nightingale, E., Czyzewski, K., Tester, F., and Aaruaq, N. (2017), "The Effects of Resource Extraction on Inuit Women and Their Families: Evidence from Canada," *Gender & Development*, 25 (3): 367–85.

Nightingale, E. and Richmond, C. A. (2021), "Reclaiming Mountain Lake: Applying Environmental Repossession in Biigtigong Nishnaabeg Territory, Canada," *Social Science & Medicine*, 272: 113706.

Nightingale, E. and Richmond, C. A. (2022), "Building Structures of Environmental Repossession to Reclaim Land, Self-Determination and Indigenous Wellness," *Health and Place*, 73: 102725.

Nupepa Kuokoa (1866), "No Kalani 'Kauikeaouli Kamehameha III'," *Ka Nupepa Kuokoa*, V (12): 4, March 24, 1866.

O'Malley, V. (2016), *The Great War for New Zealand: Waikato 1800–2000*, Wellington: Bridget Williams Books.

Pâquet, L. (2020), "'Putting the Cult in Cultivate': A Rhetoric of Guerrilla Gardening in Green Valentine," *Green Letters*, 24 (2): 185–98.

Paquette, E. (2020), "Reconciliation and Cultural Genocide: A Critique of Liberal Multicultural Strategies of Innocence," *Hypatia*, 35 (1): 143–60.

Park, A. S. J. (2020), "Settler Colonialism, Decolonization and Radicalizing Transitional Justice," *International Journal of Transitional Justice*, 14 (2): 260–79.

Pasternak, S. (2017), *Grounded Authority: The Algonquins of Barriere Lake against the State*, Minneapolis: University of Minnesota Press.

Paul, F. M. (2010), "Bill C-31: The Experience of Indian Women Who 'Married Out'," Master of Arts Thesis, Department of Sociology, Frederickton: University of New Brunswick.

PBS NewsHour (2016), *The Sacred and the Scientific Clash on Hawaii's Mauna Kea*. https://www.pbs.org/newshour/show/sacred-scientific-clash-hawaiis-mauna-kea#transcript

Peach, L., Richmond, C. A., and Brunette-Debassige, C. (2020), "'You Can't Just Take a Piece of Land from the University and Build a Garden on It.' Exploring Indigenizing Space and Place in a Settler Canadian University Context," *Geoforum*, 114: 117–27.

Peralto, L. N (2014), "Portrait. Mauna a Wākea: Hānau ka Mauna, the Piko of Our Ea," in N. Goodyear-Kaōpua, I. Hussey, and E. K. Wright (eds), *A Nation Rising*, 232–44, Durham: Duke University Press.

Pettipas, K. (1994), *Severing the Ties That Bind: Government Repression of Indigenous Religious Ceremonies on the Prairies*, Winnipeg: University of Manitoba Press.

Philibert, A., Fillion, M., and Mergler, D. (2020), "Mercury Exposure and Premature Mortality in the Grassy Narrows First Nation Community: A Retrospective Longitudinal Study," *The Lancet Planetary Health*, 4 (4): 141–8.

Pieratos, N., Manning, S., and Tilsen, N. (2021), "Land Back: A Meta Narrative to Help Indigenous People Show Up as Movement Leaders," *Leadership*, 17 (1): 47–61.

Popp, J. N., Priadka, P., and Kozmik, C. (2019), "The Rise of Moose Co-Management and Integration of Indigenous Knowledge," *Human Dimensions of Wildlife*, 24 (2): 159–67.

Popp, J. N., Priadka, P., Young, M., Koch, K., and Morgan, J. (2020), "Indigenous Guardianship and Moose Monitoring: Weaving Indigenous and Western Ways of Knowing," *Human–Wildlife Interactions*, 14 (2): 17.

Priadka, P., Moses, B., Kozmik, C., Kell, S., and Popp, J. (2022), "Impacts of Harvested Species Declines on Indigenous Peoples' Food Sovereignty, Well-Being and Ways of Life: A Case Study of Anishinaabe Perspectives and Moose," *Ecology and Society*, 27 (1): 30.

Proulx, G. and Crane, N. J. (2020), "'To See Things in an Objective Light': The Dakota Access Pipeline and the Ongoing Construction of Settler Colonial Landscapes," *Journal of Cultural Geography*, 37 (1): 46–66.

Pukui, M. K. and Elbert, S. H. (1986), *Hawaiian Dictionary: Hawaiian-English English-Hawaiian Revised and Enlarged Edition*, Honolulu: University of Hawaiʻi Press.

Quarries Inspectorate R20483490 (1936–1988), "Annual Reports of the Mines and Quarries Inspectorate," Archived Files of the Department of Mines, Auckland Branch: Archives New Zealand.

Rao, N., Narain, N., and Sabir, G. (2022), "Cameras in the Hands of Indigenous Youth: Participation, Films, and Nutrition in India," *Current Developments in Nutrition*, 6 (8): 1–13.

Rata, E. (2011a), "Discursive Strategies of the Maori Tribal Elite," *Critique of Anthropology*, 31 (4): 359–80.

Rata, E. (2011b), "Encircling the Commons: Neotribal Capitalism in New Zealand since 2000," *Anthropological Theory*, 11 (3): 327–53.

Rata, E. (2012), "Theoretical Claims and Empirical Evidence in Maori Education Discourse," *Educational Philosophy and Theory*, 44 (10): 1060–72.

Reed, G., Brunet, N. D., Longboat, S., and Natcher, D. C. (2021), "Indigenous Guardians as an Emerging Approach to Indigenous Environmental Governance," *Conservation Biology*, 35 (1): 179–89.

Reihana, K. R., Wehi, P. M., Harcourt, N., Booth, P., Murray, J. M., and Pomare-Pieta, M. (2021), "Indigenisation of Conservation Education in New Zealand," *Pacific Conservation Biology*, 27 (4): 493–504.

Reitmeier, V. (2022), "Digital Geographies of Indigenous Health: Exploring Indigenous Mental Health Content from Turtle Island during Covid-19," Master of Arts Thesis, London: Western University.

Reo, N. J. (2019), "Inawendiwin and Relational Accountability in Anishnaabeg Studies: The Crux of the Biscuit," *Journal of Ethnobiology*, 39 (1): 65–75.

Richmond, C. (2018), "The Relatedness of People, Land, and Health: Stories from Anishinabe Elders," in M. Greenwood, S. de Leeuw and N.M. Lindsay (eds), *Determinants of Indigenous Peoples' Health: Beyond the Social*, Second Edition, 167–85, Toronto: Canadian Scholars.

Richmond, C., Coombes, B., and Pualani Louis, R. (2022), "Making Space for Indigenous Intelligence, Sovereignty and Relevance in Geographic Research," in M. Rosenberg, S. Coen, and S. Lovell (eds), *The Routledge Handbook of Methodologies in Human Geography*, 83–93, London: Routledge.

Richmond, C., Kerr, R. B., Neufeld, H., Steckley, M., Wilson, K., and Dokis, B. (2021), "Supporting Food Security for Indigenous Families through the Restoration of Indigenous Foodways," *The Canadian Geographer*, 65 (1): 97–109.

Richmond, C. A. (2016), "Applying Decolonizing Methodologies in Environment-Health Research: A Community-Based Film Project with Anishinabe Communities," in N. E. Fenton and J. Baxter (eds), *Practicing Qualitative Methods in Health Geographies*, 173–86, London: Routledge.

Richmond, C. A. and Big-Canoe, K. (2018), "The Geographies of Indigenous Health," in V. Crooks, G. Andrews, and J. Pearce (eds), *Routledge Handbook of Health Geography*, 179–88, Abingdon: Routledge.

Richmond, C. A. and Ross, N. A. (2008), "Social Support, Material Circumstance and Health Behaviour: Influences on Health in First Nation and Inuit Communities of Canada," *Social Science & Medicine*, 67 (9): 1423–33.

Richmond, C. A. M. and Ross, N. A. (2009), "The Determinants of First Nation and Inuit Health: A Critical Population Health Approach," *Health and Place*, 15 (2): 403–11.

Rickard, V., Veart, D., and Bulmer, S. (1983), "A Review of Archaeological Stone Structures of South Auckland," Auckland: New Zealand Historic Places Trust.

Rieger, K. L., Gazan, S., Bennett, M., Buss, M., Chudyk, A. M., Cook, L., Copenace, S., Garson, C., Hack, T. F., and Hornan, B. (2020), "Elevating the Uses of Storytelling Approaches within Indigenous Health Research: A Critical and Participatory Scoping Review Protocol Involving Indigenous People and Settlers," *Systematic Reviews*, 9 (1): 1–9.

Robertson, S. and Ljubicic, G. (2019), "Nunamii'luni Quvianaqtuq (It Is a Happy Moment to Be on the Land): Feelings, Freedom and the Spatial Political Ontology of Well-Being in Gjoa Haven and Tikiranajuk, Nunavut," *Environment and Planning D: Society & Space*, 37 (3): 542–60.

Royal Commission of Aboriginal Peoples (1996), "Indian Act: Indian Women," in Royal Commission on Aboriginal Peoples', *Looking Forward Looking Back*, Ottawa: Royal Commission on Aboriginal Peoples.

Salmón, E. (2000), "Kincentric Ecology: Indigenous Perceptions of the Human–Nature Relationship," *Ecological Applications*, 10 (5): 1327–32.

Schneider, L. (2022), "'Land Back' beyond Repatriation: Restoring Indigenous Land Relationships," in S. Bernardin (ed), *The Routledge Companion to Gender and the American West*, 452–64, New York: Routledge.

Scott, J. C. (2009), *The Art of Not Being Governed: An Anarchist History of Upland Southeast Asia*, New Haven: Yale University Press.

Secretary of Lands (1928), "Land Confiscated under the New Zealand Settlements Act 1863," *Appendices to the Journals of the House of Representatives*, G-7: 1–39.

Self Family Trust v AC (2018), "Self Family Trust v Auckland Council," Decision 2018 EnvC 49, Auckland: Environment Court.

Simpson, L. B. (2014), "Land as Pedagogy: Nishnaabeg Intelligence and Rebellious Transformation," *Decolonization: Indigeneity, Education & Society*, 3 (3): 1–25.

Simpson, L. B. (2016), "Indigenous Resurgence and Co-Resistance," *Critical Ethnic Studies*, 2 (2): 19–34.

Simpson, L. B. (2017), *As We Have Always Done: Indigenous Freedom through Radical Resistance*, Minneapolis: University of Minnesota Press.

Simpson, M. and Le Billon, P. (2021), "Reconciling Violence: Policing the Politics of Recognition," *Geoforum*, 119: 111–21.

Snider, S. (2021), "#Nobodyisdisposable: Visual Politics and Performance in Collective Activist Movements," *Fat Studies*, LatestArticles, 1–14.

Spiegel, S. J. (2021), "Climate Injustice, Criminalisation of Land Protection and Anti-Colonial Solidarity: Courtroom Ethnography in an Age of Fossil Fuel Violence," *Political Geography*, 84 (article 102298): 1–14.

Stephens, C. (2015), "The Indigenous Experience of Urbanization," in Minority Rights Watch, *State of the World's Minorities and Indigenous Peoples 2015*, 54–61, London: Minority Rights Watch.

Strang, V. (2014), "The Taniwha and the Crown: Defending Water Rights in Aotearoa/New Zealand," *WIREs: Water*, 1 (1): 121–31.

TallBear, K. (2011), "Why Interspecies Thinking Needs Indigenous Standpoints," *Cultural Anthropology*, 24: 1–8.

Taniwha Club (2014–2022a), Debrief Discussions on Planting Day, Records of Taniwha Club and Incorporated Society, Auckland.

Taniwha Club (2014–2022b), Minutes of Trustees Meetings, Records of Taniwha Club and Incorporated Society, Auckland.

Taniwha Club (2014–2022c), Minutes of Public Meetings, Records of Taniwha Club and Incorporated Society, Auckland.

Taniwha Club (2014–2022d), Minutes of Parental Focus Groups, Records of Taniwha Club and Incorporated Society, Auckland.

Taniwha Club (2014–2022e), Minutes of Tamariki Council, Records of Taniwha Club and Incorporated Society, Auckland.

Te Karu, L., Harwood, M., Bryant, L., Kenealy, T., and Arroll, B. (2021), "Compounding Inequity: A Qualitative Study of Gout Management in an Urban Marae Clinic in Auckland," *Journal of Primary Health Care*, 13 (1): 27–35.

Te Waka Hi Ika v ToWFC (1998), "Te Waka Hi Ika O Te Arawa and Ors. v Treaty of Waitangi Fisheries Commission," Auckland Registry—CP 395/93, Auckland: High Court of New Zealand.

Te Whata (2021), *Te Whata.Io—Iwi Affiliations and Inter-Census Change*, Wellington: Statistics NZ.

Te Whiti Love, M. (2003), "Resource Management, Local Government and the Treaty of Waitangi," in J. Hayward (ed), *Local Government and the Treaty of Waitangi*, 21–37, Melbourne: Oxford University Press.

Temper, L. (2019), "Blocking Pipelines, Unsettling Environmental Justice: From Rights of Nature to Responsibility to Territory," *Local Environment*, 24 (2): 94–112.

Tenbruggencate, J. (1971), "32 Arrested in Peaceful Kalama Eviction," *The Honolulu Advertiser*, May 15, 1971, 37.

Tobias, J. and Richmond, C. (2014), "'That Land Means Everything to Us as Anishinaabe … ' Environmental Dispossession and Resilience on the North Shore of Lake Superior," *Health & Place*, 29: 26–33.

Tobias, J. K. and Richmond, C. (2016), "Gimiigiwemin: Putting Knowledge Translation into Practice with Anishinaabe Communities," *International Journal of Indigenous Health*, 11 (1): 228–43.

Trask, H.-K. (1987), "Birth of the Modern Hawaiian Movement: Kalama Valley, O'ahu," *Hawaiian Journal of History*, 21: 126–52.

Trujano, C. Y. A. (2008), *Indigenous Routes: A Framework for Understanding Indigenous Migration*, London: Hammersmith Press.

Truth and Reconciliation Commission (2015), *Canada's Residential Schools: The Final Report of the Truth and Reconciliation Commission of Canada*, Montreal: McGill-Queen's Press-MQUP.

Tuck, E. and Yang, K. W. (2012), "Decolonization Is Not a Metaphor," *Decolonization: Indigeneity, Education & Society*, 1 (1): 1–40.

Tweedie, W. (1864), *The New-Zealand Government and the Māori War of 1863–64, with Especial Reference to the Confiscation of Native Lands and the Colonial Ministry's Defence of Their War Policy*, London: Aborigines' Protection Society.

Tynan, L. (2021), "What Is Relationality? Indigenous Knowledges, Practices and Responsibilities with Kin," *Cultural Geographies*, 28 (4): 597–610.

Waitangi Tribunal (1998), "Te Whanau o Waipareira Report," Wellington: Waitangi Tribunal.

Wander, M. (2021), "Making New History: Contemporary Art and the Temporal Orientations of Climate Change in Oceania," *Journal of New Zealand and Pacific Studies*, 9 (2): 155–78.

Wexler, L. (2009), "The Importance of Identity, History, and Culture in the Wellbeing of Indigenous Youth," *The Journal of the History of Childhood and Youth*, 2 (2): 267–76.

Wexler, L. (2014), "Looking across Three Generations of Alaska Natives to Explore How Culture Fosters Indigenous Resilience," *Transcultural Psychiatry*, 51 (1): 73–92.

Whetung, M. and Wakefield, S. (2019), "Colonial Conventions: Institutionalized Research Relationships and Decolonizing Research Ethics," in L. Tuhiwai Smith, E. Tuck, and K. W. Yang (eds), *Indigenous and Decolonizing Studies in Education: Mapping the Long View*, 146–58, New York: Routledge.

Whyte, K. P. (2018), "Settler Colonialism, Ecology and Environmental Justice," *Environment and Society: Advances in Research*, 9: 125–44.

Whyte, K. P. and Cuomo, C. J. (2016), "Ethics of Caring in Environmental Ethics," in S. Gardiner and A. Thompson (eds), *The Oxford Handbook of Environmental Ethics*, 234–47, New York: Oxford University Press.

Wiebe, S. M. (2016), "Guardians of the Environment in Canada's Chemical Valley," *Citizenship Studies*, 20 (1): 18–33.

Wildcat, M., McDonald, M., Irlbacher-Fox, S., and Coulthard, G. (2014), "Learning from the Land: Indigenous Land Based Pedagogy and Decolonization," *Decolonization: Indigeneity, Education & Society*, 3 (3): I–XV.

Willis, F. (2021), "A Reconciled Nation? Mabo and the Reimagining of Australia's National History," *Journal of Australian Studies*, 45 (4): 455–70.

Wilson, N. J. and Inkster, J. (2018), "Respecting Water: Indigenous Water Governance, Ontologies, and the Politics of Kinship on the Ground," *Environment and Planning E: Nature and Space*, 1 (4): 516–38.

Winter, K. B. and Lucas, M. (2017), "Spatial Modeling of Social-Ecological Management Zones of the Ali'i Era on the Island of Kaua'i with Implications for Large-Scale Biocultural Conservation and Forest Restoration Efforts in Hawai'i," *Pacific Science*, 71 (4): 457–77.

Wright, S., Suchet-Pearson, S., Lloyd, K., Burarrwanga, L., Ganambarr, R., Ganambarr-Stubbs, M., Ganambarr, B., Maymuru, D., and Graham, M. (2018), "Everything Is Love: Mobilising Knowledges, Identities, and Places as Bawaka," in N. Gombay and M. Palomino-Schalscha (eds), *Indigenous Places and Colonial Spaces*, 51–71, London: Routledge.

AUTHOR BIOGRAPHIES

Brad Coombes teaches Geography and Environmental Management at the School of Environment, the University of Auckland, New Zealand. He affiliates with Kati Mamoe and Ngati Kahungunu and he regularly contributes to the claims settlement process under the Treaty of Waitangi acts.

Chantelle Richmond (Biigtigong Nishnaabeg) is Professor in the Department of Geography & Environment at Western University in London, Ontario (Canada), where she holds the Canada Research Chair in Indigenous Health and the Environment. Her research is based on a community-centered model of research that explores the intersection of Indigenous people's health and knowledge systems within the context of global environmental change.

Renee Pualani Louis is Kanaka 'Ōiwi from the Island of Hawai'i and a scholar of Indigenous cartographies, Indigenous geographies, and Indigenous research methodologies. She is passionate about exploring the varied dimensions of Hawai'i cartographic expressions, increasing awareness of Indigenous perspectives of science, and promoting Indigenous research sovereignty.

INDEX